ROUTLEDGE LIBRARY EDITIONS:
GERMAN POLITICS

Volume 8

POLITICAL CULTURE IN
FRANCE AND GERMANY

POLITICAL CULTURE IN FRANCE AND GERMANY

Edited by
JOHN GAFFNEY AND EVA KOLINSKY

Routledge
Taylor & Francis Group

LONDON AND NEW YORK

First published in 1991

This edition first published in 2015
by Routledge
2 Park Square, Milton Park, Abingdon, Oxon, OX14 4RN

and by Routledge
711 Third Avenue, New York, NY 10017

Routledge is an imprint of the Taylor & Francis Group, an informa business

British Library Cataloguing in Publication Data
A catalogue record for this book is available from the British Library

ISBN: 978-1-138-83837-6 (Set)
eISBN: 978-1-315-72630-4 (Set)
ISBN: 978-1-138-83839-0 (Volume 8)
eISBN: 978-1-315-73437-8 (Volume 8)
Pb ISBN: 978-1-138-83843-7 (Volume 8)

Publisher's Note
The publisher has gone to great lengths to ensure the quality of this reprint but
points out that some imperfections in the original copies may be apparent.

Disclaimer
The publisher has made every effort to trace copyright holders and would
welcome correspondence from those they have been unable to trace.

Political Culture in France and Germany

Edited by
John Gaffney and Eva Kolinsky

ROUTLEDGE

London and New York

First published by Routledge 1991
11 New Fetter Lane, London EC4P 4EE

Simultaneously published in the USA and Canada
by Routledge
a division of Routledge, Chapman and Hall, Inc.
29 West 35th Street, New York, NY 10001

Printed and bound in Great Britain by Mackays of Chatham PLC, Kent

British Library Cataloguing in Publication Data

Political culture in France and Germany : a
  contemporary perspective.
  1. Europe. Politics, history. Cultural aspects
  I. Gaffney, John, *1950–* II. Kolinsky, Eva
  320.94
  ISBN 0–415–02321–1

Library of Congress Cataloging-in-Publication Data

Political culture in France and Germany : a contemporary
  perspective / edited by John Gaffney and Eva Kolinsky.
      p. cm.
  Includes bibliographical references.
  ISBN 0–415–02321–1
  1. Political culture—France. 2. France—Politics and
government—1958– 3. Political culture—Germany (West) 4. Germany
(West)—Politics and government I. Gaffney, John, 1950–
II. Kolinsky, Eva.
JN2594.2.P64 1990
306.2'0944—dc20   90–8417
                                                          CIP

Contents

Abbreviations

ASF	Arbeitsgemeinschaft Sozialdemokratischer Frauen
CDU	Christlich-Demokratische Union
CGT	Confédération générale du travail
CSU	Christlich-Soziale Union
DGB	Deutscher Gewerkschaftsbund
DNVP	Deutschnationale Volkspartei
DVP	Deutsche Volkspartei
EEC	European Economic Community
FDP	Freie Demokratische Partei
FN	Front National
KPD	Kommunistische Partei
NDP	National Demokratische Partei
NSDAP	Nationalsozialistische Deutsche Arbeiterpartei
OAS	Organisation de l'armée secrète
PCF	Parti communiste français
PS	Parti socialiste
RPF	Rassemblement du peuple français
RPR	Rassemblement pour la république
SA	Sturmabteilung
SMIC	Salaire minimum interprofessionnel de croissance
SPD	Sozialdemokratische Partei
UDF	Union pour la démocratie française

Tables

Introduction

Eva Kolinsky and John Gaffney

The modern political histories of France and Germany bear the benchmarks of apparently conflicting and distinctly different political cultures. Traditional contrasts between society and community, between political polarisation and consensus, between confrontation with and subservience to the state all imply that, in France, social and political conflict has been central to the political process while in Germany system allegiance has held prime of place.

In the contemporary setting of both political cultures, the traditional demarcation lines of conflictual or consensual politics are becoming blurred as social mobility and economic changes have modified cleavages and blunted partisan positions. Indeed, from a comparative perspective a certain inversion seems to have taken place. In France, the political *cohabitation* between right and left and its legacy point to a new relevance of consensus, and to new patterns of collective participation which do not tally well with the traditional view that conflictual individualism constitutes the moving force and the social basis of politics. In West Germany, the opposite appears to be happening. New modes of participation, electoral realignments, and the emergence of issue-based politics at both parliamentary and extra-parliamentary level have reduced the centrality of the formal political process and the dominant place of consensus in the political culture. Paradoxically, therefore, the two polities, the one moving away from individualism, the other towards it, are in certain key respects coming closer together. This does not mean that inherited or acquired social, political and cultural traits are levelling into a melée-culture of advanced industrial politics with a supranational or European flavour. Drawing on national legacies and cultural specificities, the link between citizen and polity remains distinctive in each country as the contemporary political cultures are recast towards a relative system consensus in France, and a relative conflict and individualism in West Germany.

FRENCH PERSPECTIVES ON POLITICAL CULTURE

The development of the study of political culture in representative democracies has been greatly influenced, even determined for decades, by Almond and Verba's seminal work *The Civic Culture*

(1963). France, however, was omitted from their five nation comparison as a country too exposed to regime confusion to offer a focus on the attitudes which might underpin the institutional structure and stability of democratic political systems (Almond and Verba, 1980). At the time of Almond and Verba's research in the 1950s, France was undergoing a major political crisis involving the collapse of one regime, the Fourth Republic (1946-58) and the establishment of the Fifth. We can observe in passing that the analysis of such a democratically discordant voice would, nevertheless, have offered some fascinating insights. The study — and the omission — were based on two related and influential assumptions. The first was that relative system stability was necessary for the assessment of degrees of allegiance to the democratic process. This is, arguably, an uncontentious point, of methodological rather than of any wider significance. The second, however, has wider implications for the way in which democratic allegiance should itself be conceptualised, in that it took as relatively unproblematic the notion of allegiance to (or acceptance or approval of) some kind of political, social and possibly ideological *status quo*. Such a view raises not only questions of a political or value-judgemental nature but also those concerning the social and political dynamics of a given democracy, how these are to be measured, and the analytical framework within which analysis is set.

In the case of France, we can make two related points here. First, over and above the much discussed problem of the undeclared normative implications in Almond and Verba's work concerning the rectitude of system stability *per se* (irrespective of France's exclusion from *The Civic Culture*, the approach has been as influential in France as elsewhere), we can say that there is a danger that such an approach reifies the notion of political 'system' itself which is perhaps far more fluid than is commonly assumed. The second point is linked to this. The Fifth Republican regime, since 1958, has survived and, in terms of allegiance to it, become 'accepted' rationally by a large majority of the population (and of course its arrival was, or rather the rise to power of its founder was, tumultuously received in 1958). It is also arguable that the regime today is in certain respects cherished by a large majority of the population (a crude though illustrative measure of this is the continually strong electoral participation in presidential elections). The Fifth Republic has, nevertheless, been in a state of constant institutional, political and cultural evolution: 1958, 1960, 1961, 1962, 1965, 1969, 1974, 1981, 1986 and 1988 all witnessed major reorientations *within* the parameters of the regime's overall stability or survival (1968, when the regime was seriously threatened, is the obvious exception, though was by no means unambiguous evidence of the regime's instability). It is, however, the nature of allegiance to the regime in the context of what has been, since 1958, a rapidly evolving society and polity which is of the utmost interest to the observer. How things *are* is essential to an understanding of politics. How, through a myriad of political, institutional, and cultural exchanges they *change* is of equal importance, but is much less easily measurable. One of the enigmas, therefore, of post-1958 France is that the Fifth Republic has developed around it a relatively strong consensus, and yet, politically, culturally, and institutionally, has been in a state of breathtaking evolution. Given the changing influence, powers, and 'weight' of the various political institutions (to name only those at the 'top': the presidency, the government, the bureaucracy, the media, the political parties, the Constitutional Council, the Council of State, and the trade unions) one is drawn to speculate on quite *when* would have been the opportune moment for a study such as that of *The Civic Culture*.

This is not to say that the sensitive use of the questionnaire, of opinion polls and of attitudinal survey analysis in the context of normative allegiance or acceptance of a given political process are not valuable, but that wider questions should also be asked about how a polity functions or changes or is 'reproduced' culturally, how allegiance is generated, how language functions as a vehicle for the discursive deployment of the myths underpinning a polity, how individuals or groups effect reorientations in political perceptions, how 'culture' (in its more restricted aesthetic sense) reflects and informs politics, and so on. Quantitative analyses do measure and assess certain factors, and valuable conclusions can be drawn from them. They do not measure, however, — indeed they are, to a certain degree, designed to preclude measurement of — the secondary, tertiary and unconscious responses of individuals or groups of individuals in a given community. And in the case of the Fifth Republic and its establishment and subsequent *enracinement*, it is incontestable that these 'other' responses have been involved to a significant degree. Allegiance to the *person* of de Gaulle, not only in 1958, but also in 1961 (when the regime was threatened by a military coup), in 1962 (when he amended the constitution in order that, henceforward, the President of the Republic be elected by direct universal adult suffrage), in the 1962 legislative elections which followed the dissolution of parliament as a result of the dispute over the validity of the constitutional amendment, and in 1965 when he was re-elected President under the new system, are all evidence of this 'personality' factor and its highly complex relationship to the political culture. And allegiance to a person and, by extension, the role of individuals in political change (or even 'system stability') raise a myriad of questions concerning these secondary, tertiary and unconscious responses within the polity, and their role and effect upon the institutions inside that polity. This brings us to the question of what we mean here by political culture.

Our approach proceeds from the conviction that many

3

approaches hitherto have been insensitive to or neglectful of some of
the wider questions concerning how regime, regime allegiance,
regime acceptance and, ultimately, regime stability are to be
assessed. Both the Fifth Republic's establishment and its continuing
existence have been partly dependent upon attitudes and responses
which do not lend themselves to quantitative analysis. Taking only
the question of presidentialism, and only one aspect of that — de
Gaulle's perceived relationship to a myth of France — it is clear that
any appraisal of the relationship of the French to the myth and to de
Gaulle or his legend, the relationship of subsequent contenders for
power to him, and the extent to which an economic crisis, or social or
cultural change, and the continuing traditions of republicanism or
nationalism and their relation to the highly-personalised contest for
the supreme political office, call for interpretative understanding of
a particular kind in any assessment of the role of the Presidency of
the Republic within the political system.

In terms of political culture, it is uncontentious to assume that
the polity informs civil society. Such is, of course, its ostensible
function. At its most basic, the existence or abolition of capital
punishment, for example, has effects upon civil society and attitudes
within it; the maintenance of a high exchange rate has effects upon
business and investment; abortion legislation affects womens' lives;
currency restrictions affect holiday plans; in a word, laws are
'applied' and have effects upon society. It is also uncontentious to
assume that these effects in their turn affect the formal political
institutions themselves: pressure groups, interest groups and political
parties, for example, respond to the polity's affects upon civil society
and organise accordingly to exert influence upon it. What is less clear
is the manner in which civil society informs the polity both within
and outside formal politics: how non-political 'personalities' affect
French political attitudes, how myths inform political discourse, how
discourse in its turn affects the organisational cycles of politics, how
culture (in its artistic sense) reproduces a vision of the world and, of
course, the divisions within it, and how political movements are
linked to and influenced by factors other than straight 'political'
(consciously articulated interest group) choices. We shall return to
these points below. Let us first examine the question of political
culture in the West German context.

GERMAN PERSPECTIVES ON POLITICAL CULTURE

In 1987, the German Political Studies Association devoted a special
issue of its membership journal to a theme which had hitherto
remained in the background: political culture. In close to 40
contributions, it explored questions of national identity, generational
socialisation, new politics, electoral preferences, elite mobility,

political rituals in the two Germanies, and in their historical predecessors (Berg-Schlosser and Schissler, 1987). At first glance the special issue was merely the product of five years' discussion and research by a study group which held regular meetings in the congenial atmosphere of the Akademie für politische Bildung on the shores of Lake Starnberg near Munich. In a more serious vein, the focus on political culture marked a demonstrative break with a history of distrust in the theme and its academic respectability. Until the late 1970s and the Greiffenhagens' essayistic glance at contemporary politics, attitudes and values, political culture had been, at best, only an implicit theme of West German political research (Greiffenhagen and Greiffenhagen, 1979). Less than a decade later it had gained star quality, and even seemed to hold the promise of rejuvenating the study of West German politics itself: 'Political Culture may one day turn out to be an "aphrodisiac" for an administratively slackened political science' (Iwand, 1985). On a more casual level, reference to political culture has entered everyday political discourse with parties accusing each other of political culture deficiencies, newspapers stressing their resolve to preserve and protect the political culture, and the inevitable pun that musical entertainment during an election rally was a true sign of political culture.

When the term first appeared in the early 1960s, it faced a number of obstacles before being absorbed into German political communication and the academic study of German politics. The very ligature of 'politics' and 'culture' joined two words and two fields of activity which had traditionally occupied opposite ends on the spectrum of human endeavour: did not politics concern themselves with the issues of the day, adopt a pragmatic, even opportunistic, approach and were they not, as a German proverb suggests, likely to corrupt the mind? Did not culture, by contrast, rise above the fray, articulate lasting values, and reveal beauty and ideals behind everyday mediocrity and confusion? As an import from the United States, and untroubled by continental — and especially German — notions of the elevated status of culture, the neologism 'political culture' sent a shudder of disbelief and critical revulsion across the academic community when it first crossed the Atlantic as a concept to analyse the linkage between citizens and polity.

There were other reservations too. One of the cornerstones of political culture research has been the assumption that socio-economic and political environments shape the values and preferences of the people who experience them and that people's orientations do not necessarily match the political order of the day. For Germany, the study of political culture focused in particular on the question of how the experience of the National Socialist political environment had conditioned post-war attitudes to the democratic system and to political participation in the Federal Republic. The

5

very fact that the concept of political culture purported to locate the roots of contemporary political behaviour in traditions, conventions and, in the German case, legacies of anti-democratic politics, conflicted with the zero-hour spirit of political reconstruction. At a time when the West German state focused exclusively on the present as if the past had not left any traces in its institutions, practices or civil administration, and when many West Germans were busy forgetting their own personal part in running the National Socialist system of government, control and persecution, any suggestion that such zero-hour politics were figments of wishful thinking, and involved repressing the past instead of facing up to it, met with hostility. Probing into the continued relevance of the National Socialist past was not only rejected as an awkward heritage for a new democracy, but, in a curious fashion, the manner in which East German ideology utilised National Socialism underpinned the West German resolve to build a 'fatherless' future. And since East Germany and its official ideology chose to equate Western capitalism, and the Federal Republic in particular, with fascism, and refused to acknowledge the progressive political changes and democratic developments which had taken place, any reference to the National Socialist past tended to activate the anti-communist sentiments on which the Federal Republic of the 1950s and 1960s built its precarious national identity.

Nevertheless, an accumulating body of post-war research bore the message that traces of non-democratic or anti-democratic politics had remained in place beneath a surface of model democratic politics. West Germans seemed obedient rather than democratic: they would vote as required, they knew the rules by which their political system operated, they were better informed than citizens of other countries about tiers of government and names of political leaders, but had little affection for that democracy. They complied, it seemed, as long as democracy delivered the goods of stability, economic prosperity, and personal affluence. In probing beneath the façade of normalisation, political culture research laid itself open to accusations of muck-raking by a generation whose members had themselves been shaped by the anti-democratic environments of the past and which were now keen to declare themselves children and products of the post-war era.

Reservations about the concept of political culture were not only expressions of political unease. The German academic tradition has been characterised by a strong emphasis on methodology and the scientific reliability of approaches and findings in all fields of research, including the social sciences. The multifaceted themes which inform the study of political culture constitute an elusive target for quantitative and quantifiable analysis. How can methodological accuracy and precision accommodate processes of social and economic change, the perception of political institutions, the articulation of attitudes and values, as well as differences between age cohort, social groups or classes, regions, social milieus, to name but a few settings? The difficulty of clarifying the boundaries of the subject sufficiently to apply quantitative methods and scientific measurements prompted Kaase, himself an expert in the empirical analysis of changes in attitudes, political participation and electoral preferences, to compare the task of analysing the political culture to an attempt 'to nail a pudding against the wall' (Kaase, 1983). Referring to Kaase's culinary metaphor, but with some confidence that his elusive target bore more visible signs of its ingredients than a pudding and was specific in structure, Berg-Schlosser compared political culture to a 'multilayered cake with numerous tasty ingredients, a variety of lighter and darker sections' (Berg-Schlosser, 1987). If Kaase nails his pudding against the wall to display it to public scrutiny, Berg-Schlosser displays his gateau in a shop window for all to see, reflect upon and penetrate its secrets. Both, however, assume that, in the final analysis, political culture is a compound of ingredients which, mixed together, create one specific structure, one political culture in which all the component parts interrelate, and through which they receive their relevance. Yet Berg-Schlosser's emphasis on the complex internal structure of a political culture and his confidence that it can be understood also reach beyond the traditional concern with system stability and focus on the dynamics of political culture change itself.

The new confidence in the concept of political culture may be linked to generational change: most of the scholars who have written on political culture and even seized upon it in the hope that it might become an aphrodisiac of academic study belong to the post-war generations whose political and intellectual socialisation has been shaped by a democratic polity and an affluent economic and social environment. While the founder generation of political culture research — and its critics — were particularly concerned with the conditions and attitudes which ensured or endangered the stability of a political system, their successors have begun to probe the internal dynamics of the polity, the socio-economic environments, and the historical experiences which support and shape it. Political culture research, it appears, has undergone a reorientation and value change which parallels that of advanced industrial societies more generally. Inglehart's theory of value changes, for instance, maintains that people whose socialisation occurs in conditions of affluence can emphasise qualitative and subjective aspects of their environment because they need not concern themselves primarily with physical and material survival (Inglehart, 1977). In such a setting, political culture research need no longer fear the collapse of political democracy, and can focus on its diversities and personal environments. Initially, political culture research relied on empirical studies and attitude surveys in an attempt to gain reliable data for the linkage between socio-economic and political structures on the one hand, and human awareness or action on the other; by so doing, it expected to unravel and explain one overriding political culture. Contemporary interest in groups, regions, localities and other enclaves of mainstream society, however, is more than a hunt for undiscovered niches of academic scholarship: it assumes that, like the ingredients in Berg-Schlosser's layered cake, many different components converge to constitute the political culture. Contemporary political culture is a culture of change and diversity; if 'the system' could come into view it would have to be that of the process of change itself, a mobilisation of attitudes and orientations which renders even the metaphoric gateau too rigid a framework to catch the dynamic stability of contemporary democratic polities.

The linkage between political parties and their electorates is a good illustration of the new diversity of political culture which is the theme of this book. When Lipset and Rokkan analysed Western European party systems in the mid 1960s they noted that electoral preferences seemed to be determined by class and religious denomination, the same socio-economic cleavages that had shaped preferences 40 years earlier. Party systems, they found, were frozen, with electorates aligned to partisan camps (Lipset and Rokkan, 1967). Within a decade, new social movements and political parties had emerged and none of the major parties could rely fully on previously loyal electorates. Socio-economic modernisation, educational opportunities and occupational mobility combined to generate a new middle class and a new climate of party realignment as voters based their personal preferences on politically salient issues or on their own perceptions of party competence. Political parties today are faced with the challenge of winning and retaining potential voters who no longer look to a specific party as a matter of tradition. As party loyalties declined with the socio-economic and cultural environments which had bred them, political communication emerged as a major device to create the political support which seemed to exist naturally in the past. While West German political culture continues to be built around a strong consensus, it has become less predictable, more open to dissent and new avenues of participation, and also prone to a new radicalisation of extra-parliamentary actions.

THE STRUCTURE OF THE BOOK

The multidimensional changes of political articulation and participation have thrown the agenda of political culture research wide open to include the study of communication, of media, of custom and ritual, of organisational adjustments to attitude changes, of leadership styles, along with the established landmarks of system support and political participation such as voting patterns or turnout. Our concern in this book is to contribute to an understanding of how civil society both informs and operates within the formal institutions and practices of two democratic political environments, namely, France and West Germany. The site or point at which civil society and institutional structures cross or touch can highlight how the two dimensions interact and thus shape aspects of the contemporary political culture.

For France, Chapter One (John Gaffney) examines the reasons for the relative silence over the last 30 years, on the part of both academics and political actors, concerning the philosophy which ostensibly underpins the regime itself, namely, republicanism, and elaborates certain of the elements which constitute a new or continuing republican tradition.

For West Germany, Chapter Two (Eva Kolinsky) surveys the impact in the post-war era of social and economic environments, generational change, and the rise of issue politics on the balance between consensus and conflict in the political culture. Prosperity and the experience of choice in shaping personal lives and selecting avenues of participation mellowed the role of system allegiance and consensus. As affective support for democracy grew and political involvement began to reflect individual or generational rather than inherited preferences, the West German polity was faced with the challenge to accommodate conflict as a constituent element of democratic changes, a challenge it has yet to meet in full.

The extreme right in France, in unashamed national organisational form, has kept its political head well down since 1944 (and when on occasions it did step forward, as in the presidential elections of 1965 and 1981, it was always generally regarded, irrespective of any moral attitudes, as politically marginal). Chapter Three (James Shields) on the National Front in the 1980s demonstrates not only how the formal political institutions and processes (essentially, in this case, the victory of the Left in 1981) gave the extreme right political 'space' to establish itself, but also how some of the deeper cultural springs of such an inscription into the topography of formal politics were made possible, and facilitated the inscription of the 'hard' right into formal politics at the national level by the late 1980s.

Chapter Four (John Gaffney) on neo-Gaullism focuses upon the way in which the language of public occasions, that is, the ostensible currency of democratic politics (language) and its mode of exchange (public occasions) are used in the construction of a political personality which would be deployed at a later stage as part of a strategy for the conquest of the highest national office.

Much has been made in political and media studies of how national politicians become, of necessity — if they wish to gain or hold on to office — media personalities. What is less clear, however, is the manner in which media personalities themselves make the *pantouflage* in the other direction, and what the modalities and effects of such a phenomenon might be, upon both the formal institutions and upon the political attitudes and dispositions of the French more generally. Chapter Five (Pamela Moores), through a case study analysis of the political involvement of the film stars, Yves Montand and Simone Signoret, assesses this phenomenon.

Chapter Six (Susan Hayward) examines how a cultural artefact, the 'arty', as opposed to the popular, cinema reproduces not only the dominant ideas (which, as Marx argued, were those of the dominant class), but the inflexions and tendencies which exist within these as they develop and reproduce themselves as visions of the world within a given cultural mode.

Chapter Seven (Mark Roseman), using the example of the Ruhr, examines the decline of economic and political environments as explanatory factors in the shaping of preferences and in the determining political participation. The fading of a politically distinctive working-class culture in the Ruhr cannot be explained as social levelling since social dichotomies have, in fact, not disappeared. Rather, the style of everyday life and the networks of political communication which leave their mark on views and orientations changed in such a way as to close the visible gap between mainstream society and a specific socio-economic and cultural environment. The political culture change did not produce the classless worker but the integrated worker who looks to the polity rather than to his specific environment for orientations and opportunities.

The generational dimension has played a major part in recasting West German political culture. The children of post-war democracy, who have come to expect a choice of education, employment and political participation for themselves, are beginning to confront established institutions with these expectations and challenge them in a West German equivalent of *glasnost*. Chapter Eight (Eva Kolinsky) argues that women, who used to take a backseat in politics and whose role inside political parties seemed to be largely restricted to organising coffee mornings and instilling the relevant political ideals in the next generation, have begun to claim a share of political influence and leadership positions. As the party which has made the largest gains among the young, educated and ambitious women of the post-war generations, the Social Democratic Party faces the challenge of adapting its party organisation and practices to meet the new expectations of equality, and stemming the drift among younger women towards issue politics and the Greens.

Chapter Nine (Michael Townson) evaluates the role of language in eliciting party support at a time when loyalties have become open to change and the political environments which bred them in the past no longer condition the policy orientations of the young generations.

INTRODUCTION

The Christian Democratic Party (CDU) was the first party to concentrate systematically on the study of language with the aim of creating political allegiances via key terms which would be associated by the general public with Christian Democratic policy answers, and, in this way, would feed into the party vote. Since the CDU had lost the commanding position it had held until the mid 1960s among young voters and among women, turning to language (the essential component of all social exchange) was an attempt to create party loyalty in a politically mobile generation given to individual preferences and personal choice. The attempts of the CDU to associate key terms with its own policy tradition, was, in part, an attempt to fill the void left after the decline of traditional socio-economic environments through the generating of newly persuasive communicative environments in the contemporary political culture.

The underlying argument of this book is that political culture — the site where formal politics and certain expressions of civil society intersect — is a highly complex phenomenon requiring interpretative analysis. The chapters in this book are indications of this complex relationship but, by the same token, suggest that a multiplicity if not an infinity of sites for analysis are possible. The chapters which follow are an indication of that multiplicity of sites and a contribution to an understanding of them.

REFERENCES

Almond, G. and Verba, S. (1963) *The Civic Culture: Attitudes and Democracy in Five Nations*, Princeton University Press, Princeton.

Almond, G. and Verba, S. (eds) (1980) *The Civic Culture Revisited: An Analytical Study*, Little Brown & Co., Boston.

Berg-Schlosser, D. 'How to Analyse Political Culture'. Paper prepared for the meeting of the Research Committee on 'Crisis, Compromise, Collapse — Conditions of Democracy in Inter-War Europe', Berlin, 24-29 September 1987.

Berg-Schlosser, D. and Schissler, J. (1987) 'Politische Kultur in Deutschland. Bilanz und Perspektiven der Forschung', *Politische Vierteljahresschrift*, 18.

Greiffenhagen, M. and Greiffenhagen, S. (1979) *Ein schwieriges Vaterland. Zur politischen Kultur Deutschlands*, List, Munich.

Inglehart, R. (1977) *The Silent Revolution. Changing Values and Political Systems among Western Republics*, Princeton University Press, Princeton.

Iwand, W.M. (1985) *Paradigma politische Kultur*, Westdeutscher Verlag, Opladen.

Kaase, M. (1983) 'Sinn oder Unsinn des Konzeptes "Politische Kultur" für die vergleichende Politikforschung, oder auch: der Versuch, einen Pudding an

INTRODUCTION

die Wand zu nageln'. In: M. Kaase and H-D. Klingemann (eds), *Wahlen und politisches System. Analysen aus Anlaß der Bundestagswahl 1980*, Westdeutscher Verlag, Opladen.

Lipset, S.M. and Rokkan, S. (eds) (1967) *Party Systems and Voter Alignment. Cross-National Perspectives*, The Free Press, New York.

1

French Political Culture and Republicanism[1]

John Gaffney

As the Fifth Republic, created in 1958 in order to resolve the grave but relatively short-lived political crisis caused by the Algerian issue (1954-62), enters upon its fourth decade, it is appropriate to review this, by traditional republican standards, strange republic. Deep social and political divisions have characterised all French regimes since the Revolution of 1789. The Fifth Republic, with its ambiguous constitution, has, for two decades since the death of its founder, Charles de Gaulle, seen a developing consensus of opinion to the point where opponents of the regime, with the ambiguous exception of 'the events' of 1968, have been politically powerless. Since 1958, elections, referenda and national opinion polls have indicated repeatedly that a large majority of the French (doubtless for varying reasons and with differing degrees of allegiance) support the regime. The same elections, referenda and opinion polls, over the last 30 years, moreover, seem to indicate a significant and developing consensus of support for the main institutions and orientations of the Republic: the Presidency, the National Assembly, the Senate, French foreign policy, and the role of France within Europe; and an equal consensus upon a more diffuse set of issues concerning the economy, the procedures (conflictual and consensual) for resolving disputes between economic actors, law and order, the role of the state, national defence, women's rights, personal aspirations, life-styles, education, and civil rights. Moreover, the Fifth Republic is the first to have won acceptance by the Catholic population, historically hostile to republicanism.[2] Consensual attitudes on many issues have not only indicated support for the regime from within civil society, but have also been a significant causal element in major revisions in political ideologies as political parties and movements have responded to the evolving political culture.[3] As the economic crisis which began in the 1970s continues, the developing politico-cultural consensus has not embraced all issues. The combination of developing consensus and continuing economic crisis has indeed strengthened certain aspects of non-consensual political life, the rise in the 1980s of the Front National being the most spectacular demonstration of this.

Varying degrees of dissensus persist on issues such as immigration, the redistribution of wealth, employment, the relation between state and private education, the roles of and relationships between the several political 'actors' (the President and the government, the media, trade unions, and state-owned companies), the rights and responsibilities of employers, the state and the workforce, state centralisation, and state *dirigisme* in economic affairs. This dissensus sometimes involves only the political elites as they labour to distinguish themselves from their electoral opponents. The left marked itself off from the right in this way in the late 1970s; the traditional right did the same in the first half of the 1980s for identical reasons when the left was in power between 1981 and 1986.

This limited dissensus and political uncertainty throws into high relief the importance and meaning of 'consensus' and 'support for the regime', as well as the question of the strength of the regime's institutions. To what extent is regime support an active phenomenon? If, from opinion polls and surveys, it can be concluded that more than three-quarters of the population are generally in favour of the Fifth Republic, what are the springs and the limits of this sympathy? How are degrees of allegiance to be assessed? Is 'consensus' the reflected view of a population which passively or indifferently tolerates the regime, but which would not defend the Republic if a major crisis in the economy were to provoke a social and political crisis? How embedded in the political culture and 'hearts and minds' of the French is the Fifth Republic? Does 'the Republic' mean anything to a generation brought up on television, consumerism, the technological revolution, and the threat of unemployment?

As I have already suggested, all previous regimes since the Revolution of 1789 have been unstable. Whether one measures such instability in terms of their *durée* or of how suddenly they collapse, it is clear that France's regime instability is, by European standards, endemic. Since 1789, there have been ten major regime changes, half of which were the result of internal political or social crises (rather than military invasion). Even in the post-war period, there have been two new regimes, and observers have referred recently to the need for another major constitutional revision concerning the role and function of the Presidency, the hallmark of the Fifth Republic. Such observations raise the fundamental question of the inter-relation between French society and the traditionally fragile political structures which govern it.

A striking feature of France's post-Revolution regimes is that each has sought a legitimation and consequential stability after its establishment which would transcend the exceptional circumstances of its creation. All have wished to *s'enraciner* in the society and political culture of their time, whether or not they were established democratically (and 'democratic' acceptance at a time of acute national crisis is perhaps only a measure of acceptance at the time of the crisis itself). If, however, we acknowledge, along with those who have tried to assure themselves of it, that allegiance to a regime is a crucial, it is also the case that such allegiance is a very difficult phenomenon to identify and assess, let alone nurture. Let us, then, look briefly at the theoretical frameworks which have informed the assessment of political attitudes and allegiance in the modern period.

Perhaps the greatest influence upon the way European political behaviour has been perceived in the twentieth century has been the theories and writings related to the notion of 'Mass Society'.[4] The increasing urbanisation and industrialisation of nineteenth and twentieth century Europe coincided with the accession to democracy (the suffrage) by the quasi-totality of the adult male (and, later, female) population. What, in the nineteenth century, was seen as the possible replacement of 'popular culture' by 'mass culture' has been assumed in the twentieth century to be a fact. And of the three major theoretical perspectives in social analyses: the liberal, the Marxian and the mass society perspective, it is perhaps the last which has dominated thinking in twentieth century France. In practice, the mass society perspective has probably informed the other two interpretations to such an extent that they can often be viewed as sub-theories of the first. In the post-war period, with the advent of further modernisation, television, the extensive ownership of motor cars, access to holidays, travel, and consumerism generally, assumptions concerning the cultural 'homogenisation' of French citizens have attained the status of near self-evident truths.

Two main consequences have flowed from this. The first is that, in spite of the generalised exercise of the suffrage in France, the 'mass society' perspective has been underpinned by the view that political power or potential power has been withdrawn from the voting public and transferred elsewhere, even that the suffrage itself is one of the essential mechanisms of the withholding of power, because it maintains the electorate in blissful ignorance of its actual powerlessness (Alliot-Marie, 1983; Gaxie, 1978; Lefort, 1981). Moreover, the mass society perspective has never resolved the question of whether the generalised exercise of the suffrage is evidence of the limits of active political participation or is an indication of a deeper desire for more participation. The second consequence of an assumed cultural homogenisation is the assumption that the population has become depoliticised (Vedel, 1962; Duhamel, 1985): as new patterns of life-style and more consumerist expectations have emerged, traditional, professional, family and regional influences and class-orientated allegiances have been replaced — as in Europe generally — by an 'end of ideology' France as it falls under the increasing cultural influence of the US.

Although mass society theories were of European origin, the subsequent influence upon social science thinking of American mass society theories in the post-war period cannot be underestimated, and has contributed significantly to the way French political behaviour and attitudes have been perceived. Two essential, though differing, emphases have informed these approaches, the first heavily influenced by Marxism, the second by liberalism. The Frankfurt School's influence upon the notion of a 'culture industry' in modern 'mass' urban industrial societies which has robbed other internal 'popular' cultures and class perspectives of their political potential has had considerable influence upon the way in which European political behaviour has been perceived (Adorno *et al.*, 1950; Adorno and Horkheimer, 1973; Habermas, 1976; Kirchheimer, 1966; Marcuse, 1974; Jay, 1976). The liberal influence has encouraged the view that, with the developments of a cultural convergence, a new kind of European society, far closer to the American model, has emerged and with it a new kind of European who is less political, more materialist, modern and so on (Almond and Verba, 1963; Riesman, 1978). This view has in fact largely shaped the methodological approaches (opinion polls, surveys, questionnaires) — and perhaps findings — of much of the politico-sociological research in post-war France.

One cannot deny the validity of much that is contained in these approaches and interpretations. It is even self-evident that there has been in France a Paris-led cultural 'nationalisation' in the last 40 years, and a move away from traditional and local political, social, professional and class allegiances and the development of new outlooks, aspirations and life-styles. Nor is the very real influence of the US to be denied. However, the weakness of these theoretical and methodological approaches, irrespective of the shortcomings of the inevitably superficial opinion poll, questionnaire and quantitative analyses themselves, is that they tend to screen out from analysis the effect of history as a cultural influence upon political perceptions and behaviour (while, conversely, making a series of assumptions about what constituted political and class allegiance, social aspirations and so on in preceding periods). It is not proven that the wide-ranging socio-economic and technological changes which France has undergone in the post-war period have eradicated the influence of French history upon contemporary political perceptions. One of the consequences of the predominance of synchronic analytical approaches is that research has often measured contemporary French attitudes to democracy but rarely the historically informed notion of republicanism. It is an appraisal of the latter, *in conjunction with* a consideration of the great socio-economic and cultural transformations in post-war France, which is crucial to an understanding of the Fifth Republic and its relation to French society.

It is interesting to note that many analyses have indicated the significant changes in class position, class identification, social expectations, and so on, which have taken place in France since the Second World War, and how these have effected a reorientation in political beliefs and attitudes. Given established assumptions concerning the relation between social class and political behaviour, these analyses are essentially measurements of distance *from* a previous socio-political relation, and are sometimes simply the restatements of a truism (that, for example, a civil servant in Paris will have a different attitude to political and social life from that of his or her blue-collar father or church-going mother). What concerns us here, however, is the nature of the relationship between social being and political attitudes in the Fifth Republic in the context not only of widespread socio-economic change, but also of the Fifth Republic's relation to French republicanism within French culture. The following discussion proposes some of the elements essential to the establishing of a framework for the analysis of contemporary republican allegiance.

Braud has pointed out that the socio-professional category in France does not play the decisive role it 'should' in electoral sociology: that in France there has never been an inclusive workers' party, no exclusively rich persons' party, no intellectuals' party, for example (Braud, 1980; Michelat and Simon, 1977). There are traditional bastions (right-wing parties for the rich, left-wing for workers and intellectuals), but the deviations from these norms are enormous, and it is the relation of these normative variations to the millions of voters who, say, are not rich but who vote for the right, who are not workers but who vote for a party with a workerist political ideology that reveals the complexity (and mutability) of political allegiance. In terms of what we said above concerning the historical dimension of political orientation, Braud argues that religion in France seems to play a part, in fact could be argued as being the strongest factor, in voting behaviour. France, however, can no longer be called a Catholic country in the traditional sense of the word. Besides, as Braud notes, there is something very strange in the idea of the least secular of allegiances (religion), being, in the valley of tears, one of the most influential allegiances in that quintessentially secular area of activity (politics). Braud's research demonstrates, therefore, that political choice is no longer related in any strict sense (if ever it was) to class position, material interests, or the political attitudes that are assumed to derive from them.

In one of the major studies of voting behaviour in the late 1970s, Capedevielle makes a similar point to Braud: that there exists a non-correspondence between the 'social' and its expected effect upon political choice, especially when one examines voting behaviour (Capedevielle *et al.*, 1981). Nuancing earlier assumptions concerning 'depoliticisation', Capedevielle argues that a majority of the French 'thought' left while voting right (the instance he uses is the 1978 legislative elections, but the point is a general one), and that the changes of the last 40 years: urbanisation, *'salarisation'*, tertiarisation, women in work, the decline of religion, have given rise to a politically informing *libéralisme culturel* which involves such things as a relative social permissiveness, tolerance, and a belief in women's rights, within the groups exposed to such changes.

An assumed convergence of life-styles, aspirations and social outlook, an assumed growing political consensus, the developing urbanisation, salarisation and tertiarisation identified by Braud, Capedevielle and others, a *libéralisme culturel*, not identifiably rooted to profession or locality, but now assumed to be shared by a growing percentage, if not a majority, of the French, all raise the question of the politico-cultural identity of this new France, a question which modifies the belief in a cultural homogenisation into a more nuanced focus upon the huge 'middle' section of society (Beaud, 1984; Bidou, 1984; Grunberg, 1979; Lavau *et al.*, 1983; Mallet, 1969; Thélot, 1982). A growing conviction that this group is the motor of political orientation and the dominant constituency of the future has meant that research into it has constituted the main thrust of politico-cultural study in the last decade or so. Conversely, because of assumptions concerning the politico-cultural rootlessness of this middle group and the (mass society based) notion that it is *prey* to new cultural changes because it has no historically rooted class allegiance, theories concerning its manipulability have also been reinforced. The problems of identification and explanation which such a group raises, however, are considerable. And this for three related reasons: 1) the group is so diverse, arguably not constituting a group at all; 2) because of its only indirect relationship to the means of production, it was long considered as of minor importance historically (in spite of the fact that since 1830 it has been arguably the most politically significant social group in French history); 3) its conceptualisation has traditionally involved the inclusion of all those who do not fit into the two 'real' groups of producers or owners of the means of production. We could in fact categorise French research into the social status, political attitudes and identification of this group as being that of the search for the French middle classes (*classes moyennes*) (Lavau *et al.*, 1983).

An initial problem in assessing the politico-cultural significance of this large and politically determining group is the value of the framework in which such analysis is set. What does a French *employé(e)* have which relates him or her to a French *ingénieur* apart from the fact that neither are identifiably proletarian according to a nineteenth century categorisation created before they came into existence? In the nineteenth century, Radicals and the right were too preoccupied with the development of a national consensus around the Republic or the Nation to develop an ideology that deliberately represented the middle class. The Socialists in the twentieth century, moreover, were doctrinally prohibited from doing so. And the Church was preoccupied with either defending the positions of the established order or recruiting the allegiances of the emerging working classes to itself or to a pre-industrial and pre-republican social order. Ironically, the only significant *political* actor to have theorised in any way the middle class was the French Communist Party. And it is true that the Marxian definition and perspective has been the dominant one, with all which that connotes of a class lacking any coherent sense of its social role and political interests. The interest now directed at this huge group (in the middle of a technological revolution, where many previous assumptions are thrown into doubt) is relatively new. What are the ideological links between a supporter of Poujade, a Communist Party intellectual, a typing pool secretary, a Socialist Party member, a wages clerk, a school teacher, a floor manageress in Galeries Lafayette, a Parisian lawyer, a social worker, an advertising agent, a provincial sales representative, a physiotherapist and so on? This complexity has not halted attempts at definition, however. Indeed, the multiplicity of definitions is part of the problem. The most significant recent piece of collective research into the middle classes is Lavau's book published in 1983; and one of the first points made in this work is that the middle class enjoys just such a multiplicity of definitions, that is to say, an elusiveness of sociological and political categorisation (Lavau *et al.*, 1983).

Whether or not, however, the emphasis is misplaced or overstated, the developing cultural and politico-cultural significance of this or these groups of people is undeniable. In the 1954-75 period alone, *employés* increased by 86 per cent, *cadres moyens*, by 149 per cent, *ingénieurs*, by 238 per cent (Lavau *et al.*, 1983). Much of this growth, moreover, was in the public sector, where employees have a relationship to the state and to authority in general that is of a particular and, perhaps, because of its scale, a new kind. It was the members of this or these 'middle' groups who were instrumental in putting Mitterrand in the Elysée in 1981 (thus affecting a fundamental change within the operative political parameters of the Fifth Republic). For Bidou, it is less important to decide whether this new phenomenon of a change in life-styles and attitudes in the last 30 years has created a 'new' middle class, a new working class or just a new class. Of greater significance is the fact that it has created a new *culture*, and a *'brouillage de référentiels'*. Bidou points out that those at the crossroads of social mobility in France (whether in new jobs, different jobs, or in a new social class) constitute the largest single group and are, therefore, the agents of a new culture. Over 50 per cent of working people now work in service industries. Industrial workers now constitute only one-third of the work force, agricultural workers, like small business people, only a small percentage. And with this change, a different *local* culture has developed, replacing traditional extended family and class allegiances with new structures, in particular those which make up the local *vie associative*. Even ten years ago, for example, there were already 20,000 associations in France (parent-teacher associations, consumer associations, socially-minded Christian groups, voluntary groups, tenants' associations, for example); these have acted as a new focus for social (and, by extension, political) perceptions (Wright, 1978). In terms of political allegiance, one of the essential consequences in this change is that work and politics should no longer be seen as being strictly related. De Angelis and Gorz have argued that such a separation has also taken place within the working class itself (De Angelis, 1982; Gorz, 1980).

With varying emphases, many writers, including Beaud (1984), Debray (1980), Touraine (1969) and Sartre (1972) have argued that the cultural influence of the new middle classes has gone a stage further to the point where 'intellectuals' have disengaged as a group from their class and have become the autonomous, or relatively autonomous, representatives of society to itself, particularly through their occupation of all levels of the media. According to this view, the 'new mediators' are universalising the values of this new middle class, (Barel, 1984) or are filling a social vacuum (*vide social,* Beaud) and are dictating the way society now perceives itself economically, socially, culturally, and politically. There are those, however, who do not subscribe to the view that the middle class or disengaged intellectuals (essentially those in the media) are now filling the *vide social* and offering to society a particular way of considering itself, but who argue, more traditionally, that this class is 'represented' by those values it expresses in the media (Bourdieu, 1982; Gaxie, 1978). Where nearly all commentators do agree is on the question of the influence of the mediation itself: that the agencies of political communication are now the media, in particular, television; and that, taken together, marketing, opinion polling, the television, and the jingle-filled radio constitute and direct the cultural reference points of the new France. It is worth pointing out here that the literature on this area of the media generally and political communication particularly is massive. The size alone of the literature is an indication of the ascription to the media of enormous power and influence. The literature is also, in its sheer volume, very diverse. It nearly all, nevertheless, shares three basic findings and/or assumptions: 1) the determining cultural and political power and manipulative influence of the media, even its qualitative difference from hitherto existing forms of cultural and political influence; 2) the media's destructive quality, that is to say, its having destroyed the influence, even the relevance, of those hitherto existing forms; 3) the duality of the media's *démarche*, that is to say, on the one hand, its attractive, if not irresistible, quality, and on the other, its transmission of hidden culturally and politically consequential messages.[5]

Research over the last few years, therefore, leads to the inescapable conclusion that marketing and the media are significant influences within French society and political culture. It is worth pointing out, nevertheless, in the context of what we said earlier concerning the historical framework of French republicanism, that, however great the influence of these forces, the media has existed in French society for barely more than 20 years. We should also note the fact that research has also indicated that the medium is not necessarily the message, that television, for example, reinforces views, rather than changes them (Michelat, 1964; Bourdieu, 1973). Nevertheless, there is a perhaps fashionable temptation to upgrade television's influence and the manipulative effect of political marketing in much of the literature, based as it is upon the assessment of the effect of the new and the immediate. As Monica Charlot pointed out more than a decade ago:

> L'exploration de l'inconscient, le sondage d'opinion, la télévision, l'informatique se prêtent trop aisément à une mythologie démagogique, qui leur confère une toute-puissance quasi magique. La science viole l'homme, la machine l'écrase. On oublie vite leur origine humaine, leur neutralité éthique et leur limites (Charlot, 1970).

> The exploration of the unconscious, the opinion poll, television, information technology, lend themselves very easily to the notion of their all-persuasive, quasi-magical power. Science assaults mankind, the machine crushes it. Their human origin, their ethical neutrality, and their limits are too easily forgotten.

Before identifying some of the elements involved in an assessment of the republicanism of the Fifth Republican French, let us the suggest the value for such an assessment of the research we have identified. However one defines it, France has witnessed the recent development of a large class or group, arguably two-thirds of the population, which is no longer subject to many of the influences which informed political culture hitherto; there have been many profound changes as a result of this socio-economic shift, and the influence of the rest of Europe, and especially the US, is unmistakable; France has seen a revolution in work patterns, life-styles, social expectations and personal orientations and the break-up of traditional allegiances to the point where we might speak of depoliticisation (concerning those particular allegiances); and the media now occupies a central place in the shaping and orientation of attitudes. Let us add to these other influences: changes in family socialisation, the cultural effect of the cinema, the women's movement and other non- or trans-party social movements, increased foreign travel, a changed youth culture, the move away from full employment, and the notable increase of women in the job market and workforce. These are some of the elements which would have to be borne in mind for any full assessment of the nature of the relationship of contemporary French society to its polity.[6] Before elaborating upon some of these points, let us first address the fundamental question concerning the Fifth Republican polity, the nature of its 'republicanism'.

One of the paradoxes of the Fifth Republic is that, throughout its 30 year existence, discussion of republicanism itself on the part of political scientists has been minimal.[7] The great body of research and publications in the post-1962 period has been orientated towards describing the multiplicity of social and political institutions of contemporary France, or else narrating the history of the new Republic. And the rise of the *médiatique* society has prompted, as I have said, a huge media studies industry, the essential emphasis of which has been upon the mass society manipulation aspect of political allegiance (or the cultural creation of a lack of allegiance) to modern institutions. The lack of scholarship concerning the republican tradition within contemporary France leaves unanswered fundamental questions about the nature of contemporary political allegiance, and leaves unchallenged the assumption that (manipulated) political allegiance today is intrinsically different from an earlier republicanism (with its implicit concomitant assumption that republican allegiance was previously relatively unproblematic).[8] Between the beginning of the Fifth Republic and the mid-1980s, the only major discussion of French republicanism was Pierre Mendès France's *La république moderne* (Mendès France, 1962), published in 1962 (and we should note, in passing, that Mendès France contested the legitimacy of the Fifth Republic). The absence of discussion in this period is, from an intellectual standpoint, quite staggering. Politically, however, the near silence is understandable. 1962 coincided with a change in the institutional nature of the Fifth Republic which directed all political efforts towards a regime, the power base of which (the Presidency, from 1962, to be elected by direct universal adult suffrage) seemed to make concern with an assumed traditional republicanism secondary. Culturally, the change in 1962 brought in an apparently new (supra- or non-republican) form of political allegiance which (alongside the socio-cultural changes already mentioned) made 'republican' allegiance seem archaic. Both of these assessments, however, assumed republicanism to be a phenomenon more restricted than it perhaps is.

When the Fifth Republic was created in 1958, there were opponents to it whose opposition was based upon a republican critique of Caesarism or Bonapartism (Mitterrand, 1965). Many republicans, moreover: Gaullists, Socialists, Radicals, and the centre and centre-right parties and groupings of the Fourth Republic, while welcoming de Gaulle, assumed confidently that the Fifth Republic would 'conform' to an assumed republican model once de Gaulle had left office, or when he had overcome the crisis posed to France by the Algerian issue. The Socialists in particular, but others also, including the Gaullist architect of the constitution, Michel Debré, assumed that the new Fifth Republic would revert to a republican form with a strong (prime ministerial) executive. After 1962 and the constitutional change, however, French republicanism had inscribed into it an institutional structure which in its relation to the population was deemed by many as being potentially, if not in essence, anti-republican. Such a conclusion was based upon three notions: 1) that republicanism is based upon the rejection of arbitrary rule, particularly the rule of *un seul*; 2) that the precedents for 1958 were the two Bonapartist experiences which involved individuals who used the Republic 'from within' in order to establish other forms of political authority before destroying it; 3) that the crisis circumstances of de Gaulle's taking power in 1958 involved a controlled recourse to that tradition which was deemed necessary but expedient. The writers and politicians who commented on this situation during the 1960s directed their attention to the discussion of an institutional reform which would rectify this intrusion rather than to an understanding of how such an intrusion was able to survive within a constitutionally republican form (Chandernagor, 1967; Club Jean Moulin, 1965). Moreover, de Gaulle's style of leadership between 1958 and 1969, on the one hand, and the continuing fear of France drifting back into the political chaos of the 1950s, on the other, ensured that, in the first case, the new regime was perceived as near Bonapartist (while de Gaulle remained), and, in the second, that a 'return' to republicanism might see a return to *la pagaille* and disorder. Both of these influential analyses reduced further the desire to understand the dynamic of Fifth republicanism. The main sources of potential political opposition at the institutional level to the prevailing regime were the French Socialist and Communist Parties. The Socialists, however, after 1971, made a concerted attempt to conquer the state by means of a rally of opinion around a providential leader, the rather Gaullian, François Mitterrand, and were supported in this effort throughout the 1970s by the declining Communist Party. Such a situation placed a further taboo upon an analysis by the left of the new Republic in any meaningful way.

The Fifth Republic, then, — in as much as its republican identity has been addressed — has been generally assumed to be a republican regime with an apparently non-republican form within it, that is, a strong Presidency which inspires more support than other institutional forms, but which establishes a structure of authority which can operate within an overall republican institutional framework, and one to which the 'republican' adversaries of the Fifth Republic finally resorted as a tactical necessity rather than as a doctrinal reference point. One of the points made by Capedevielle, but a point that is perhaps understressed, is that in the Fifth Republic there has developed a difference between voting for a parliament, party or government and voting for a President (the most obvious examples of this being the substantial electoral support among traditional Communist voters for de Gaulle, and Mitterrand's opinion poll popularity as President in the context of a rightist parlimentary majority in the 1986-88 period and his decisive victory in the 1988 presidential elections), and that there has emerged in the Fifth Republic the phenomenon of the 'presidential' voter, that is, a section of the electorate which votes in presidential elections but not in legislative elections. And it is the nature of allegiance to this form of republicanism, or this political institution within republicanism, which is crucial to an assessment of contemporary French political culture.[9]

The essential questions concerning this form of allegiance are: whether it is an 'alien' form which an overall republicanism can 'tolerate' systemically; whether republicanism is now so weak culturally that it has been replaced by a modern form of elective monarchy which uses the empty shell of republicanism as an alibi, and therefore does not need to search for allegiance outside the allegiance to an elected President; or whether, in fact, the dominant institutional feature and politico-cultural focus of the Fifth Republic (the Presidency) is part of the republican tradition itself. The emphasis upon the Presidency in the Fifth Republic distinguishes it markedly from other Republics (the case of the election of Louis Bonaparte, given his family connections, being a case apart). Recent research (Nicolet, 1982) has indicated that the Presidency in the Third Republic was 'stronger' (particularly in foreign affairs) than has been traditionally assumed. It is the nature of the voting system, however (and the political power the President possesses, particularly when he commands a politically sympathetic majority in the National Assembly), which distinguishes the Presidency of the Fifth Republic from previous republics.

The first point to note here is that, contrary to the view that French history has been characterised either by the order/movement conflict (in which a personality is often portrayed as the catalyst of change or the agency of rectification of system dysfunction),[10] or by a conflict between republicanism and personal leadership (Bonapartism, monarchism, authoritarianism),[11] republicanism in practice has itself always 'tolerated', if not been dependent upon, strong leadership: Gambetta, Clemenceau, Poincaré, Daladier, de Gaulle, Mendès France, Mitterrand (not to mention Danton, Saint-Just and Robespierre), are all republican figures. Republicanism as a *discourse*, however, has been characterised by its search for or claim to an *impersonal* idea of political rule. It is here that the reasons for the silence concerning the Fifth Republic's republicanism lie: social theory has never theorised such a republicanism, and, as we have seen, political actors, too concerned with calling themselves republicans while aiming for presidential power, have always avoided confronting the problem in their public discourse. Many observers have argued that in contemporary French politics major contenders for power (and especially the successful ones) mobilise support around their persona rather than around a programme or an identifiably doctrinal tradition,[12] and that, therefore, there is little meaningful political discussion any more at the national level, and that this is an indication of how far French politics has drifted from the republican tradition.

The traditional hypothesis, therefore, is that French republicanism vies with a 'personalist' strain that is continually threatening it or else has replaced it. Our hypothesis, however, is that 'personalism' is an integral part of republican French political culture (a part which is heightened by the new forms of communication and a less doctrinally bound electorate). Observers have noted recently that increasing reference is being made to republicanism by all political personalities in the 1980s, and have argued that such reference is in part due to its contemporary lack of specificity or substance. In this way, political actors can portray themselves as all things to all people. The choice of such a symbol (the Republic), however, begs the question of the multiplicity of significance and connotations of 'republicanism' in French political culture. The term or the symbol's diversity is not proof of its emptiness as a cultural reference point. Indeed, the opposite is equally arguable.[13]

Why then do leaders use such a term? How is it that 'the Republic' as something to be appealed to survives, and informs, such a strong presidential orientation? The logical conclusion is that personal leaders are somehow able to offer a national 'vision' of republican France to a national electorate, and that this 'vision', though interpreted and presented by individuals (de Gaulle and Mitterrand, for example), and drawing upon 'sub-cultures' (French nationalism or socialism, for example) is summoned essentially from within a republican political culture, and that, in some sense, the Presidency 'represents' the nation as a personified Republic. Dupoirier has speculated that in this new sense de Gaulle is the 'founding father' of a new republicanism (Dupoirier, 1987). It is arguable, therefore, that the rise and dominant position of the mass media in the last 30 years, and the major changes within social class, have altered the relative strengths of the personalist and the elaborated impersonal doctrinal traditions *within* republicanism, but have in no way destroyed or replaced the phenomenon itself — in fact, in many ways, the evolutions of the last 30 years (more information, the reduction of control by local political *notables*, a complete political equality (all adults possessing the suffrage) have perhaps enhanced it, entrenching republicanism in the political culture of France more than ever before, within a context where the social and cultural conditions informing political choice have increased rather than decreased.

It is worth speculating that there has been a surreptitious, or perhaps unconscious, division of labour on this issue which has fostered the presumed vested interests of politicians and the media alike; the media focuses upon personalities, asserting that ideas are far less relevant, and the politician protests the contrary; the one stresses modernity and apoliticism, the other, a traditional claim to an impersonal legitimacy. The cultural question raised by these developments, however, concerns the nature of the relation of leadership to republicanism. It is true that leaders, whether or not 'republicans', have always appealed to a France *réelle* or *profonde*, or, more prosaically, to a silent majority, which goes beyond the institutional expression of an apparent republican status quo. Today, however, such claims, though as persistent as ever, never contest the Republic's legitimacy (this is equally true of the Front National in most of its public discourse in the late 1980s). What they do indicate is that personal claims to vision, though not necessarily anti-republican, reveal a continuing belief in a privileged and unmediated relationship between an individual leader and his/her followers. And it is the 'nationalisation' and institutionalisation of such a relationship which is different, and which has posed so many problems in interpretation in the recent period. It is worth noting, moreover, that it is, in part, the ambivalence within republicanism itself which allows such a phenomenon to occur. The guiding principle of the Republic is that the ultimate source of authority is the people. The manner in which such ultimate authority should be expressed *institutionally*, however, has never been resolved definitively.

It is incontestable that the Fifth Republic has seen an emphatic orientation of the national electorate towards allegiance to presidential candidates (and within political movements towards potential presidential candidates). Because of the mass media and the loosening of traditional allegiances, and because of transformations of and within social classes,[14] the orientation has doubtless been heightened further. Political participation in the republican system, however, has remained strong, and, significantly, 'informal' mass demonstrations in the 1980s have been highly 'political' events yet have never contested the legitimacy of the Republic itself.

It is arguable, therefore, that behind the image of a France that is either too 'modern', consumerist and apolitical to be attached to such a notion as 'the republican tradition', or too orientated, willingly or unwillingly, towards the razzmatazz of a TV-dominated personality politics which is far removed from the traditional concerns and analyses of party politics, lies a commitment to republicanism that is fixed in French political culture so subtly or simply that it goes largely unnoticed. Interestingly, one of the few opinion polls to address the question of the allegiance of the French to the Republic indicated that 68 per cent of respondents said that they would fight for the Republic if they felt it was threatened (Dupoirier, 1987).

We have identified an institutional and possibly cultural

phenomenon which is part of a contemporary republican tradition. Let us here identify and comment, in the context of the socio-economic changes of Fifth Republican France, six elements which contribute to a further assessment of this new or continuing republicanism, and which has been created or consolidated by the Fifth Republic.

The first is that the criteria for measuring allegiance to class or group, or to an established political ideology, should be very different from criteria employed in any earlier period. A large majority of the population in contemporary France is no longer subject to the same channels of family, class, workplace-oriented, or local politico-cultural communication and influence which operated formerly. This does not mean that allegiances to the regime and the political ideas related to it or to the representatives of various political viewpoints within republicanism are weaker than before, but that they are different.

A second and related factor, is that the composition of the workforce has changed with this new urbanised, industrialised social grouping. The influx of women into the urban, industrial workforce in great numbers has coincided with their attainment of formal political equality. In any assessment of French political allegiances and attitudes, it is essential to remember that if the influence of the media and new forms of political communication are, as we have indicated, only 20 or so years old in France, the right of the whole adult population to actively participate in politics is only 20 years older. The entry of women (over half of the population) into the Republic dates only from 1944. Studies have shown, moreover, that it is only recently that this half of the population has begun to vote 'for itself', rather than as prescribed by husbands and fathers (Kergoat, 1982; Mossuz-Lavau and Sineau, 1983). This means that, first, any proper assessment of republicanism in a France where the whole adult population has attained political equality in the Republic can only be of very recent origin, and, second, that the political attitudes of a republican electorate and the political expression of these (women are less involved in political parties, for example) will be very different from former manifestations. Once again, however, a different attitude to politics is no indication of lesser allegiance to the regime or a lesser sensitivity to political reality.

Third, our view that individuals have 'represented' the republican tradition means that any appraisal of contemporary French republicanism must assess this influence as an active constituent of that republicanism. It is incontestable that between 1958 and 1962 de Gaulle as an individual was instrumental in saving (and consolidating) the Republic from other elements (the extreme right) within French political culture who sought to overthrow it. Similarly, the Presidency of François Mitterrand between 1981 and 1986 demonstrated that the entry of the left into the governing elite of the Fifth Republic (and his willingness to bring the French Communist Party into those governing institutions) strengthened the Republic's institutions further, and that his personal comportment in the 1986-88 period influenced significantly the population's perception of the Republic's institutions. And in the case of de Gaulle especially, but also in the cases of the other Fifth Republican Presidents, the allegiance of the French people to the Republic has involved the notion of assurance that a strong Presidency would safeguard the Republic from its tendency in previous periods (particularly in the 1930s and 1950s) to become politically ineffective.

The fourth element in this new republicanism, linked to the left's taking power in 1981 after 25 years of rightist dominance, is that the 'lost illusions' of the post-1981 Socialist experience, that is to say, the left's unwillingness or inability to transform France into a post-republican socialist society, had the effect of strengthening certain elements within republicanism itself. The notion of the transcendence of the Republic, always the ultimate goal of the left, a goal which set it apart from centrist and rightist republicans, ceased to be an issue for the first time since the rise of French socialism in the nineteenth century. In the recent period, moreover, the eclipse, within left republicanism, of the dominance of the idea of the transcendence of the Republic and the establishment of a fundamentally different *République sociale* has created a renewal of interest in the originality of the Republic itself. The popularity of François Mitterrand after the 1986 legislative victory of a right-wing coalition in the National Assembly, a popularity which contributed to his decisive re-election in 1988, was based upon the assumption that his role, in a period of political uncertainty, was to contribute to the Republic's continuing effectiveness and, in the context of a relatively strong Front National, to reaffirm republicanism.

Fifthly, the developing consensus around the Republic has been significantly reinforced by the definitive entry of the Catholic tradition into French republicanism. The political significance of this is not diminished by the reality of France's lessening formal allegiance to practising Catholicism itself. We mentioned above that the French Catholic tradition was historically hostile to the Republic. It is worth pointing out that the reconciliation really began only after 1945 with the active participation of Catholics in Fourth Republican political life. The response to such participation was the diminution of an activist anti-clericalism by republicans and socialists alike. De Gaulle's presidency saw the consolidation of Catholic allegiance to the Fifth Republic via allegiance to him (particularly on the part of the female Catholic electorate), and the leftist Catholic tradition, begun in the 1930s, has been reconciled within the Republic via its insertion into the socialist movement.[15]

The sixth element in an appraisal of this new republicanism is the fact that the republican tradition has two major referential sources which have been drawn upon in the Fifth Republic, as in all republics, the second of which, romanticism, has often been considered in the modern period (though was certainly not in the First, Second, middle years of the Third, or years preceding the Fourth Republic) as anti-republican. The first source is the view that the republic means in practice a rationally informed and established set of political institutions and practices (derived from Montesquieu[16] and, in part, from Rousseau). This set of institutions and practices is negotiable within a set of normative parameters (it ranges from the *régime d'assemblée* idea, through that of the *régime parlementaire* to the *régime présidentiel*). Such a view is underpinned by a belief in the separation of powers and all the checks and balances which flow from this and ensure or enhance social justice, equality before the law, civil rights and, to varying degrees (at different times), liberty and equality. Such a view also takes as self-evident the moral and political rectitude of universal suffrage and freedom of speech. The second source (derived from Rousseau, and in part, from Montesquieu, and fuelled by the vexed question of sovereignty, that is to say, *how* the authority of the people should be exercised) is the romanticism of French republicanism. In the recent period, de Gaulle, in particular, represented himself as possessing a vision which conflated France and the Republic, but which involved ritual sanctification of the exercise of power by democratic institutions. And since de Gaulle, no serious contenders for leadership within the French polity have contested this conflation, and all elected Presidents have underlined it.

It is undeniable that new forms of political allegiance have emerged in the last 30 years; forms created by the nationalisation of politics, the role of the TV, the political 'weight' of the Presidency, the reorientations of and within social class.[17] The relationship of these new forms to political leadership and what they mean to a continuing republican political culture are still to be properly elucidated. How then can we provisionally characterise contemporary republicanism? Old ideas remain strong discursive resources: social justice, civil rights, equality, solidarity, the 'natural' republican reality of France, the strength of France as a Republic. Newer ideas inform older ones: women's rights as a self-evidently justified goal, the state as only one element in an inter-related national reality, the need to incorporate a more sophisticated social dimension into the discourse of republicanism, the need for sensitivity to individualism in the context of a more socially sensitive republicanism. Over the last 30 years a large body of research has developed on media studies and on changes within social class. It is the relation of these areas of research to a continuing republican tradition which remains to be elaborated further.

NOTES

1. See also the articles by the author in *Politics*, 7, 2, October 1987 and *La Revue politique et parlementaire*, 935, May 1988.

2. For discussions of the view that the Left's attainment of power in 1981 was a further legitimation of the Fifth Republic, see M. Duverger (1982) *La république des citoyens*, Ramsay, Paris, and A. Duhamel (1982) *Le complexe d'Astérix*, Gallimard, Paris.

3. The need for political parties to be responsive to the electorate is illustrated by the fact that of 38,000,000 voters fewer than 1,000,000 are active members of a political party.

4. For a good overview of 'Mass Society' theories and their influence, see S. Giner (1976) *Mass Society*, Martin Robertson, London.

5. Perhaps the most influential book on this subject is V. Packard (1957) *The Hidden Persuaders*, Longman, London. Also very influential was the 'cultural pessimism' of the Frankfurt School. For a good contemporary example of this mode of interpretation, see J. Chesnaux (1983) *De la modernité*, Maspéro, Paris.

6. Camilleri argues that youth culture is very different today from what it was in the 1960s; C. Camilleri *et al.* (1983) *Les 'nouveaux jeunes'*, Privat, Toulouse.

7. See also J. Touchard (1971, 1975) *Histoire des idées politiques* (2 vols.), PUF, Paris, 850 pp. In the discussion of the modern period, there is no discussion of republicanism *per se*. It is mentioned briefly (pp. 672-680) as a *version* of liberalism, where the author discusses the Third Republican Radicals. For recent discussion of republicanism, see: E. Dupoirier (1987) in *Opinion publique 1986*, SOFRES, Paris; F. Fonvieille-Alquier (1984) *Une France poujadiste?*, Ed. Universitaires, Paris; C. Nicolet (1982) *L'idée républicaine en France*, Gallimard, Paris; P. Nora (1985) *Les lieux de mémoire: la république*, Gallimard, Paris; A. Rouquié (1984) *La démocratie ou l'apprentissage de la vertu*, Metailié, Paris.

8. We should note, however, that republicanism (in theory libertarian) has made a significant contribution to the repressive aspects of French colonialism, as well as to the repression of the socialist and syndicalist movements.

9. Part of the problem arises because the notion of sovereignty has never and perhaps can never be resolved. This is, in my view, the result of conferring upon 'the people' a form of legitimation which was designed to justify its antithesis, namely, kingship. For a discussion of sovereignty, see Chapter One of J. Hayward (1983) *Governing France*, Weidenfeld and Nicolson, London.

10. For discussion of this idea of blockage or stalemate see M. Crozier (1970) *La société bloquée*, Seuil, Paris, and A. Peyrefitte (1976) *Le mal français*, Plon, Paris.

11. This is the view of the near-totality of the left and is based upon K. Marx (1977) *The Eighteenth Brumaire of Louis Bonaparte*, Progress, Moscow. See also R. Rémond (1963) *La droite en France*, Aubier, Paris.

12. This vacuum is (inadequately) filled with assumptions about 'personality politics', the internal dynamics of which are never properly explained. See for example R-G. Schwartzenberg (1977) *L'état spectacle*, Flammarion, Paris.

13. The multiple significance of republicanism was increased by the interconnections made, in de Gaulle's discourse, between the Republic, the State, and France.

14. For discussions of republicanism and social class in the earlier period, see M. Agulhon (1982) *The Republic in the Village*, Cambridge University Press, Cambridge, and S. Berger (1972) *Peasants Against Politics*, Harvard, Boston.

15. The clearest demonstration of the reconciliation of political Catholicism with the republic was the rise of a strong Christian democratic movement (the Mouvement Républicain Populaire) after the Second World War, and a continuing Christian democrat tradition which has influenced the whole political spectrum.

16. Montesquieu, of course, was a constitutional monarchist and not a republican. His opposition to arbitrary rule, however, is one of the essential sources of French republicanism.

17. We do not, therefore, oppose Wright's view concerning the 'untidy reality' of the distribution of power within the polity, nor Alliot-Marie's identification of near-secret channels of political power, nor the idea that anti-republicanism has enjoyed and, potentially, could enjoy, support, but that republicanism is a significant formative phenomenon in French political culture.

REFERENCES

Adorno, T. *et al.* (1950) *The Authoritarian Personality*, Harper & Row, New York.

Adorno, T. and Horkheimer, M. (1973) *The Dialectic of Enlightenment*, Allen Lane, London.

Alliot-Marie, M. (1983) *La décision politique*, PUF, Paris.

Almond, G. and Verba, S. (1963) *The Civic Culture*, Princeton, New Jersey.

Barel, Y. (1984) *La société du vide*, Seuil, Paris.

Beaud, P. (1984) *La société de connivence. Média, médiateurs et classes sociales,* Aubier, Paris.

Berger, S. (1972) *Peasants Against Politics,* Harvard, Boston.

Bidou, C. (1984) *Les aventuriers du quotidien. Essai sur les nouvelles classes moyennes*, PUF, Paris.

Bourdieu, P. (1973) 'L'opinion publique n'existe pas', *Les Temps modernes*, 38, 317 (Jan.), pp. 1292-1309.

Bourdieu, P. (1982) *Ce que parler veut dire. L'economie des échanges linguistiques*, Fayard, Paris.

Braud, P. (1980) *Le suffrage universel contre la démocratie*, PUF, Paris.

Camilleri, C. and Tapia, C. (1983) *Les 'nouveaux jeunes'*, Privat, Toulouse.

Capedevielle, J. *et al.* (1981) *France de gauche vote à droite*, FNSP, Paris.

Chandernagor, A. (1967) *Un parlement pour quoi faire?* Gallimard, Paris.

Charlot, M. (1970) *La persuasion politique*, Colin, Paris.

Chesnaux, J. (1983) *De la modernité*, Maspéro, Paris.

Club Jean Moulin (1965) *Un parti pour la gauche*, Seuil, Paris.

Crozier, M. (1970) *La société bloquée*, Seuil, Paris.

de Angelis, R. (1982) *Blue-Collar Workers and Politics: A French Paradox*, Croom Helm, Beckenham.

Debray, R. (1980) *Le scribe: genèse du politique*, Grasset, Paris.

Duhamel, A. (1985) *Le complexe d'Astérix*, Fayard, Paris.

Dupoirier, E. (1987) in *Opinion publique 1986*, SOFRES, Paris.

Duverger, M. (1982) *La république des citoyens*, Ramsay, Paris.

Fonvieille-Alquier, F. (1984) *Une France poujadiste?* Ed. Universitaires, Paris.

Gaxie, D. (1978) *Le cens caché*, Seuil, Paris.

Giner, S. (1976) *Mass Society*, Martin Robertson, London.

Gorz, A. (1980) *Adieu au prolétariat*, Galilée, Paris.

Gorz, A. (1983) 'Au-delà du salariat', *Projet*, 177 (Aug.), pp. 679-686.

Grunberg, G. (1979) *L'univers politique et syndical des cadres*, FNSP, Paris.

Habermas, J. (1976) *Legitimation Crisis*, Heinemann, London.

Hayward, J. (1983) *Governing France*, Weidenfeld & Nicolson, London.

Jay, M. (1976) *The Dialectical Imagination: The History of the Frankfurt School and the Institute of Social Research 1923-50*, Heinemann, London.

Kergoat, D. (1982) *Les ouvrières*, Sycamore, Paris.

Kircheimer, J. (1966) 'The Transformation of West European Party Systems'. In: J. Lapalombara and M. Weiner (eds) *Political Parties and Political Development*, Princeton, New Jersey.

Lavau, G., Grunberg, G. and Mayer, N. (1983) *L'univers politique des classes moyennes*, FNSP, Paris.

Lefort, C. (1981) *L'invention démocratique*, Fayard, Paris.

Mallet, S. (1969) *La nouvelle classe ouvrière*, Seuil, Paris.

Marx, K. (1977) *The Eighteenth Brumaire of Louis Bonaparte*, Progress, Moscow.

Marcuse, H. (1974) *Eros and Civilisation*, Beacon Press, Boston.

Mendès France, P. (1962) *La république moderne*, Gallimard, Paris.

Michelat, G. (1964) 'Télévision, moyen d'information et comportement électoral', *Revue française de Science politique*, 14, 5, (Oct.), pp. 877-905.

Michelat, G. and Simon, M. (1977) *Classe, religion et comportement politique*, FNSP, Paris.

Mitterrand, F. (1965) *Le coup d'état permanent*, Plon, Paris.

Mossuz-Lavau, J. and Sineau, M. (1983) *Enquête sur les femmes et la politique en France*, PUF, Paris.

Nicolet, C. (1982) *L'idée républicaine en France*, Gallimard, Paris.

Packard, V. (1957) *The Hidden Persuaders*, Longman, London.

Peyrefitte, A. (1976) *Le mal français*, Plon, Paris.

Riesman, D. (1978, first published 1950) *The Lonely Crowd*, Yale University Press, London.

Rémond, R. (1963) *La droite en France*, Aubier, Paris.

Rouquié, A. (1984) *La démocratie ou l'apprentissage de la vertu*, Metailié, Paris.

Sartre, J-P. (1972) *Plaidoyer pour les intellectuels*, Gallimard, Paris.

Schwartzenberg, R-G. (1977) *L'état spectacle*, Flammarion, Paris.

Thélot, C. (1982) *Tel père, tel fils? Position sociale et origine familiale*, Dunod, Paris.

Touchard, J. (1971, 1975) *Histoire des idées politiques* (2 vols), PUF, Paris.

Touraine, A. (1969) *La société post-industrielle*, Denöel, Paris.

Vedel, G. (1962) *La dépoliticisation: mythes et réalités*, FNSP, Paris.

Wright, V. (1978) *The Government and Politics of France*, Hutchinson, London.

2

Socio-Economic Change and Political Culture in West Germany

Eva Kolinsky

IN SEARCH OF 'HOMO DEMOCRATICUS'

As a concept for analysis, political culture is concerned with the impact on human awareness, value orientations and political behaviour of institutional settings, policy articulation and personal experience (Bogdanor, 1987). In the German context, the question of how National Socialism could sweep through the minds of virtually a whole people, and the follow-on question of how political democracy could subsequently take root in such a country have laid the foundations of political culture research. It is the search for *homo democraticus*, for the conditions and realities of democratic political life.

Over time, the approaches to the study of German political culture have changed as democracy developed in a viable political framework. Early enquiries such as Adorno's *Authoritarian Personality* or Schaffner's *Fatherland* looked for explanations why Germans became National Socialists. They focused on socialisation processes in the family and on decision making in the private and public spheres and argued that the political institutions and attitudes which originated in Imperial Germany produced a personality type with an authoritarian or fascist potential. Democratic or liberal values could not emerge in an environment built on obedience, fear, repression, and on the desire of the apparently powerless individual to himself exercise unlimited power if the opportunity presented itself (Adorno *et al.*, 1950; Schaffner, 1948).

The post-war interest in German political culture had a further and more pragmatic dimension. Since nobody was sure how persistent anti-democratic attitudes and preferences would be, and what needed to be done to establish a democratic government which would command more popular support than its predecessors in the Weimar Republic, keeping track of attitudes and identifying partisan positions seemed all important. Military governments, and especially the Americans, had assumed that the German people were thoroughly 'nazified' and would mount active resistance. These fears proved unfounded but related concerns about the proliferation of anti-democratic leanings were justified. Regular opinion polls were employed to monitor the political climate and assemble a portfolio on preferences and orientations in the no-man's years between the end of the Second World War and the creation of the new German state (Merritt and Merritt, 1970). Opinion polls do not reveal the unspoken assumptions which inform preferences and actions, with their original purpose often only to test the water prior to implementing specific policies. Thus, monitoring public opinion during the occupation period was a means to clarify which groups might oppose democratic government in Germany, and pin-point the acceptance or non-acceptance of policy measures. Despite their pragmatic edge, opinion polls allow a glimpse at attitudes and expectations under specific historical circumstances; they have remained a preferred tool in the study of political culture (Greiffenhagen and Greiffenhagen, 1979: 18 ff; Merritt and Merritt, 1980).

In the 1950s, the focus of political culture research shifted from tracing anti-democratic attitudes to determining which factors would facilitate system stability in any given polity, and how support for democratic political systems could be ascertained. The global context for the new emphasis was the confrontation of two hostile political blocs with different political systems, and the uncertainties in the Western world how the stability or instability of democratic systems could be assessed. Fears of a communist take-over may have played a part in the new interest in system stability. It brought a decisive breakthrough in understanding German political culture since it highlighted that democratic and non-democratic orientations existed simultaneously, and assessing the political culture meant assessing the overall balance of the two sides. The German case was complicated by the apparent tranquility and ease of introducing democracy. The ardent anti-democratic culture of Weimar had virtually disappeared overnight as Germans professed to accept democracy. In *The Civic Culture* (1963) Almond and Verba argued that such acceptance could flow from obedience and reflect authoritarian attitudes, or it could reflect an affective attachment to democratic government and decision making. 'Homo democraticus', they concluded, had to hold such an affective attachment to the democratic political environment. In all democratic polities, including Germany, system stability was seen to rest on affective system support among the people.

West Germans in the late 1950s showed little such affective attachment to their political system. Although they tended to be well-informed about the function of their political institutions, they expressed no particular liking for them, were not 'proud' of them, as Almond and Verba put it. They found affective attachment among West Germans at the time, but it focused on the economic system and the German national character, not on the institutional pillars of democracy (Almond and Verba, 1963; Almond, 1980). In the mid-1960s, Edinger noted in a similar vein that West Germans had accepted democracy as a set of rules and were playing democracy by the book (Edinger, 1968: 81 ff). Both findings imply that democracy worked not because people liked it, but because it performed well. The German term *Schönwetterdemokratie* — fine weather democracy — also underlines the conditional nature of support. 'Foul weather' such as an economic crisis or unemployment might make democracy look unattractive and give rise to extremist parties or movements on the left or the right. The temporary rise and electoral success of the neo-nazi National Democratic Party (NDP) in the mid-1960s is an example for this conditional acceptance of democracy. It followed a slight rise of unemployment and the first ever stagnation of economic growth since the post-war years, and ended as soon as the economic climate had improved. Since then, the impact of economic performance on political orientations and electoral preferences has decreased. The prolonged recession and the endemic unemployment which followed the oil crisis in the early 1970s and which continue to trouble West Germany to this day, have not resulted in large scale shifts against democracy although extra-parliamentary oppositions have gathered momentum, and some anti-system overtones have become audible as the Green party secured a place in parliamentary politics (Kolinsky, 1987; Langguth, 1983).

As a measure of democracy, performance has lost its punch. Similar to other Western democracies, West Germany can now rely on diffuse support among her citizens, a support which retains its democratic orientation even if specific political actions or events are deemed unsatisfactory. The majority of people today are able to reject specific parliamentary decisions or party policies without rejecting parliament or parties as institutions. Or the majority of people are capable of experiencing hard times economically without looking to the right or the left for an anti-democratic solution, a leader, or a revolution to articulate their discontent. A replica study of *The Civic Culture* concluded in 1980 that previous reservations about the affective attachment of West Germans to democracy and its institutions were no longer justified (Conradt, 1980). The economy has, however, retained a specially elevated status. It continues to inspire particular pride and tends to dominate the priority issues of the people and of the political parties. No party has yet won an election at national level if it did not also enjoy the confidence of the voters as the party best able to ensure economic stability, and solve any current or future economic problems the country may face.

The contemporary West German political culture rests on two pillars: the special significance of the economy on the one hand, and on the other, the emergence of a strong and flexible institutional framework which has itself been a guarantor of democratic politics (Sontheimer, 1979; Lepsius, 1982). The socio-economic changes which transformed the economy as a whole and the personal environments of most West Germans during the lifetime of the Federal Republic form the backcloth to the emergence of 'homo democraticus' and the contemporary political culture.

The political significance of generational change in the German political context adds a further dimension. The concept of generations in the study of contemporary political culture highlights the time dimension of attitude changes. The political consciousness of people tends to be shaped by their immediate environments, by the issues which are salient during their youth and early adulthood, by the institutions and the personalities who determine the style of government and the linkage between state and citizens at the time (Fogt, 1982: 109 ff). While generational perspectives exist in all societies, the German case is complicated by the changes of government, ideologies and priorities which occurred during the lifetime of the present day population (Reichel, 1981). For West Germans over the age of 50, the formative years of political socialisation and the concomitant preferences and value orientations date back to Imperial times, to the First World War, to the Weimar Republic, to National Socialism or to the interim years of occupied Germany. All had to adjust their views to embrace democratic principles and practices, and endorse democratic institutions and processes of decision making.

The emergence of West German political culture refers to the emergence among these generations of democratic orientations, values and modes of participation, and to their increased support for West German democracy over the years (Lederer, 1983). For the younger age cohorts, the adolescents and young adults since the mid-1960s, the generational perspective is different. They are democracy's children. They were raised under conditions of political continuity and relative economic prosperity. Their socialising environment was democracy itself. Unlike their parents or grandparents who had to create it or had to adjust to it, they could absorb its ideals and realities. As a generational cohort, young West Germans tend to take democratic government for granted, and also measure the realities of democratic life against the principles of democracy they have absorbed and endorsed. Young West Germans frequently expect different things from their political environment: more participation, more communication, more commitment to innovation (Wasmund, 1982; Hornstein, 1983). Those who have felt that their personal aspirations were frustrated by circumstances, often questioned the legitimacy of established democratic structures. For this segment of the younger generation, endorsement of democracy continues to depend on its perceived performance, and political attitudes have retained a rugged edge of anti-system scepticism (Kolinsky, 1984). Aimed at a new polarisation of issues and modes of participation, this strand of the political culture sets itself against a broadly-based consensus culture which emerged from

37

the 'democracy-by-the-book' approach of the founding years, and embraces the major political parties, political elites and mainstream public opinion. This chapter sets out to trace the two strands of the contemporary political culture — consensus and polarity — and the socio-economic circumstances and political environments in which they arose and which they have influenced.

THE SUSPENDED POLITICAL CULTURE

The brief period between August 1945, when the Potsdam Agreement set the stage for political reconstruction, and September 1949, when the newly elected West German government began its work, was a period of far-reaching adjustments and political innovation. The cornerstones of West German democracy were laid in the 1940s. The major parties were founded or reorganised; local and regional elections helped to shape new electoral legislation and also create elected assemblies, including the Economic Council as forerunner of the Bundestag. The Parliamentary Council as the *constituante* drew up the new constitution which attempted to avoid the pitfalls of Weimar politics, and place the new state on a stable and democratic footing. Newspapers, broadcasting and other media established a communicative culture with a voice for diverse views where National Socialism had forged unison channels to instruct and manipulate the population. Literary products of the so called 'inner exile', were pulled from bottom drawers, writings of real exiles could be published and read, the cultural *Autarkie* of Germany collapsed as international films, music, fiction, journalism became accessible.

One might have expected that breaking from the cultural and political bondage of the Nazi years would cause some excitement, a sense of standing at the threshold of a new era. Such excitement had marked the end of the First World War when it seemed a new world could now be built. Then, writers proclaimed a novel state of liberty for mankind and stood alongside political activists in a variety of apparently revolutionary councils (Kolinsky, 1970). After National Socialism, people or at least those who raised their voice in public, were less certain about the changes they would or could work. The journal *Der Ruf* is a good example for this lack of excitement. Its young editors and many of its authors had been specially prepared in American prisoner of war camps to use media for re-education purposes. Back in Germany, and licensed to write their new paper, they felt that the young generation, the under thirties, should be given a leadership role in uniting the nation and in steering German affairs without the presumed interference by Western or any other Allies. *Der Ruf* blamed military government for violating German national identity, a move which sounded to the Americans like nationalism from the far right, and led to the closure of the paper (Wehdeking, 1971: 13 ff). Others were similarly reluctant to face the past and its legacy directly and proceeded to strip the German language from presumed ideological meanings: the simple naming of objects — a table, a chair, a window — was to combat the infiltration of ideology into language and the brainwashing that went with it. The *Kahlschlag* turned emphatically away from historical or political meanings to an immediately evident present. A similar retreat from troublesome realities made nature a dominant theme. Where fictional works tackled contemporary events, the characters articulated a sense of despair: they were people who had been cheated, who had trusted those in power, had given their best as soldiers, as *Volksgenossen,* as party comrades, mothers, workers, Hitler Youths, and were inexplicably let down (Burdick *et al.*, 1984: 235 ff). There was no enthusiasm, not even a liking for the new times.

The detachment was not confined to disenchanted intellectuals. From the outset, Germans had opted for ignoring the past and resented attempts to remind them of it let alone identify perpetrators of injustice and atrocities. Thus, denazification was widely vilified as unwarranted punishment of loyal and ordinary citizens who had only performed their duties towards the government of the day (Niethammer, 1982). The Nuremberg Trials were rejected as arbitrary; the international tribunal as a court whose rules were devised by the victors and whose sentences were formulated in advance. Once war crimes trials and trials against former Nazis had become the responsiblity of German courts in the mid-1940s, the German judiciary and indeed the German public saw little need to rake up the past by bringing the persecutors and murderers of yesterday to justice (Elon, 1967). The determined detachment from the past was matched by a similarly determined detachment from the present. The political reorientation which was happening in their zones and in their country did not appear to concern a significant segment of the population. The lack of interest in the steps towards a West German state was widespread enough to merit a name of its own: *Ohne Mich Haltung,* a Let-Them-Get-On-Without-Me. The most striking expression of this detachment was the tendency not to voice an opinion. Surveys conducted at the time show that up to half the respondents held no views or better stated no views on political issues. Landmarks of democratic change such as the constitutions being passed at regional level and for the new West German state or the commencement of democratic parliamentary work went virtually unnoticed (Conradt, 1978). In the first year of post-war democratic government, a sizeable segment of the West German population professed not to know whether a one-party state or a multi-party state would be preferable, that the Basic Law had been passed, whether Hitler should be counted among the top statesmen of the world, or whether democracy was the best form of government for their country (Table 2.1).

Table 2.1 The German public and political democracy 1950: the don't knows (in %)

Issue	Don't Know
What is democracy?	33
Is the Bonn government a democracy?	35
Identification with political parties	42
Treatment of former Nazis	29*

Source: A. and R. Merritt (eds) (1980) *Public Opinion in Semi-Sovereign Germany 1945-55*, University of Illinois Press, pp. 64, 16, 11.

*   Two in three of those who voiced an opinion advocated that former Nazis should have the same opportunities for advancement in business and politics as other Germans. ibid., p. 11.

It has been suggested that in the 1940s and 1950s, West Germans were not used to opinion polls partly because demoscopic research was still in its infancy, and partly because governments of the past had told the people what they wanted, not consulted them on their preferences (*Jugendliche und Erwachsene '85: 344*). Voicing an opinion is political participation, the assumption that the individual's views are relevant and will be heard. Social customs in the founding years of the Federal Republic also rendered it unacceptable to express an opinion in public if it was not backed up by information, knowledge, expertise. Having an opinion seemed near identical with understanding what things were about. The less articulate respondents would hold back rather than make a fool of themselves with a wrong answer. Since the mid-1960s, these inhibitions have given way to a communicative culture, where views are voiced more freely and the expectation that solid knowledge should always support them, is beginning to fade.

    The abundance of non-views in the emergent polity and political culture of West Germany also reflected the reluctance of individuals to 'talk politics' especially if these politics might conflict with officially endorsed measures and practices. Non-communication was then a convenient device to signal detachment. It could conceal one's disapproval of the post-war Allied administration; it could hide any resentment about the course of contemporary developments and it could keep the National Socialist past and any questions of national or personal guilt well away from the present. That 98 per cent of West Germans stated in 1951 that they personally and the country as a whole were better off during National Socialism or before, would suggest that they were living on borrowed time, and that political culture as the impact of institutional settings and policy processes on citizens' minds, was strangely suspended (Greiffenhagen *et al.*, 1979: 331).

The language and symbols which were used for the new political developments also show the dilemma of reorientation. National Socialism in Germany had, of course, been defeated from without, by the combined force of the Allied armies. There was no resistance movement to purge and innovate. In retrospect, West Germans refer to the end of the war as the 'total collapse'; this implies that the social and political order before 1945 brought stability, equilibrium and security for the individual. There is no official commemorative occasion to mark the event (Conradt, 1978: 46-8; Weigelt, 1984; Weidenfeld, 1983). In contrast, the East Germans have adopted the prescribed linguistic code of a communist new beginning, and refer to the end of the war as the 'liberation from fascism'. Here, 8 May is celebrated as a national holiday with publicly organised rallies and speeches against fascism and capitalism. The only West German national holiday, the 'Day of German Unity', on 17 June commemorated the workers' uprising in East Berlin in 1953. It was widely observed for nearly two decades as a memorial day of West German democracy, and the liberty it secured. With detente, and a new understanding of both German states, their political systems and their living conditions, the 'Day of German Unity' lost some of its political bite and became just another day off work in the summer for all but adherents of the far right who continue to observe it as a reminder of the lost German *Reich*. In its reluctance to define specific steps which could symbolise the new democratic direction West Germany could draw on anti-communism and the perception of the East as an anti-world. This common rejection developed an integrative momentum of its own (Greiffenhagen *et al.*, 1981: 43-7; Reichel, 1981). The Federal Republic has defined itself as different by defining itself as superior to the severed Eastern part. It also defined its own political culture as the opposite of whatever was on the other side of the Iron Curtain. The negative approach suspended the need to reflect in substance on the aims and workings of democracy.

Political culture as pulling through

When the institutional framework of West German democracy was created, the minds of the people were occupied with other things. The war had not just brought defeat, and transitory military governments with improvised bureaucracies in the various zones, it had also worked disruption and disarray in society and in people's

41

personal lives. An eye witness wrote at the time of a 'migration of peoples', a *Völkerwanderung* which seemed to shift everybody and break traditional, established socio-economic settings (Willenborg, 1978: 189). Between 1944 and 1946, twelve million expellees from the East of the Reich flooded into the Western regions. After 1948, the Soviet zone closed its borders and a further three to four million refugees crossed from one part of Germany into the other. Big cities were unable to accommodate new arrivals since bomb damage had destroyed some 70 per cent of the housing stock. Rural areas, villages and small towns where damage was less severe had to receive the influx, and often doubled in size as newcomers found shelter. Before that, evacuees and people who had lost their homes in air raids had already come to stay. Together these movements of people 'mobilised' the social fabric of small town Germany, and of German society as a whole and brought an unprecedented mix of cultures, religions, regions and origins (Hilger, 1974; Köllmann, 1983). In addition, well over ten million so called 'displaced persons' were stranded in Germany, some looking for a more permanent foothold and all of them needing a roof over their head, food and work. They were survivors of the Nazi slave labour programmes, of work camps and of concentration camps. It has been estimated that in 1945-46, about 30 million people were socially and geographically dislocated. Nobody's life or circumstances seemed unshaken by the war, and the social upheaval which followed it. One might add to this sketch of disruption the so called 'surplus' of women. Through the combined effects of war, captivity and a long list of missing persons women outnumbered men by 7.3 million. About half had been made head of household by the war and were now in charge of securing a living for themselves and for their children (Castell, 1985: 119 ff).

The present was experienced as survival from one day to the next. Compared with war time when Germany deprived the territories she occupied of foodstuffs and consumer goods, living standards began to fall drastically after the war (Jacobmeyer, 1976: 17 ff). Through the Nazi policies of starving other populations, the conscript work force in the country, and all camp inmates, the German population experienced no real hardship during the war. Food rations were adequate, and calorie provisions better than in Britain or France. The food shortages after the war which made even approved rations appear like luxury provisions, hit the population unprepared. Many accused the occupying powers of starving the Germans into submission. Resentment ran high that 'displaced persons' should receive better food rations than the Germans themselves. In the climate of personal concern and political misgivings, the food aid supplied by the Americans was scorned as 'chicken feed', with the undertone that Germans were only good enough to receive animal fodder (Niethammer, 1967; also *Das Parlament,* 32, 8 May 1987, p. 13).

If one were to measure up goodwill and intentions to make the best of difficult conditions, German responses were clearly limited. Once Nazi coercion had disappeared, the farmers were unwilling to co-operate with the new military governments. Although production had not been halted by the war, and the Allies retained the Nazi system of food requisitioning and distribution and also recruited helpers for harvesting, German farmers preferred to barter their goods directly in exchange for labour and valuables, and without regard to the needs of the population. Blame for the shortages, however, was levelled at the Allies, not at German profiteers. When the British had to introduce food rationing in their own country in order to stem some of the hunger in their zone, this measure went unnoticed and politically unrewarded inside Germany (Marshall, 1980). People's attention and resentments were focused on the low calorie counts in the Ruhr district, and their effects on public health.

All accounts of life in post-war Germany confirm that the dominant if not sole purpose which consumed most time and energy of individuals of all ages was obtaining enough to eat. A bartering network emerged (*hamstern*) where belongings could be swapped for food; in addition a black market flourished, and here everything was available which seemed in short supply through official distribution channels (see Schubert, 1984). That the shop windows were laden with hitherto rare and unobtainable goods just one day after the currency reform, has been hailed as the first visible sign of an economic miracle and a major success of Ludwig Erhard's neo-liberalism and, of course, of the CDU/CSU who held the majority in the Economic Council. Beyond the billboard perspective of party politics, the freak affluence reveals the extent to which goods were hoarded for speculative profit with the tacit approval of the German administration, and how such speculative non-distribution had permeated all levels of the fledgling economy. It reveals in particular the productive capacity of post-war Germany and the quick recovery of manufacturing industry even before the West German state was founded. As Abelshauser has shown, despite bomb damage and dismantling, the economy was in fact stronger in 1945 than before the war in capital stock and in stockpiled raw materials (Abelshauser, 1983). That the economy seemed to be crisis ridden was due to transport problems in 1947 but especially to the unwillingness of manufacturers to sell their goods in exchange for a currency which had lost its value. From the perspective of the people, economic uncertainties persisted even after the currency reform which brought price rises, stagnating wages and mass unemployment. On average, 10.3 per cent and regionally up to 28 per cent of the workforce were affected (Gaiser *et al.*, 1985: 181). In the face of real and perceived shortages in the immediate post-war years, public and private worlds were far apart. While political activists of the Weimar years, exiled labour leaders, trade unionists, church men involved themselves in the remaking of politics and articulated the German input into the democracy debate, the people were busy pulling through.

The primacy of the private sphere

'Normalisation', the search for a secure and comfortable private sphere emerged in the 1950s as a dominant current of West German political culture. Latent fears of economic disasters, of galloping inflation like in the 1920s, or the socio-economic dislocations of the 1940s, have never been far from the minds of those West Germans who had lived through those times, or whose families had lost their possessions and status in them. The continued salience of economic security and price stability as political and electoral issues reflects these widespread fears which are embedded in the West German political culture.

Aspirations and activities of the average West German in the 1940s and 1950s were focused on the private sphere, on making a new beginning and on leading a comfortable, normal life. A high divorce rate in the immediate post-war years and a record number of marriages among young couples in 1950 underline the search for a fresh start in the personal environment. Biographical profiles for the 1950s show how finding secure employment, a regular income, a rented flat and furnishing it to conventional standards, earning enough to eat well were prime targets and they were difficult to achieve (Deppe, 1982; Niethammer and von Plato, 1985). Women worked to help finance the *'Anschaffungen'*, the major purchases of goods and appliances. One in three were *mithelfende Familienangehörige*, contributing to the family business as unpaid assistants and saving salary costs in the scramble for an improved living standard (Willms, 1983: 54).

The normalisation of the private sphere consisted of practicalities. It meant improvements, not innovation. A *Freßwelle* — eating and over-eating — seemed to make up for past deprivations; it was followed by a *Reisewelle* — travel to Italy and other foreign countries and countless other waves from car purchase to television ownership, each a visible and symbolic step of normalisation, achievement, personal and economic success. Commercial advertising and the government discovered the family as the pivotal point of social stability and budding consumerism; the German *Heimatfilm* with its idealised world of nature and the wholesome individual enjoyed unparalleled popularity; determination and hard work were seen as a blueprint for personal and national success: on a national level, this meant building a new Germany to 'rejoin the powers' and on a private level, carving a new and better living from the war-time destructions (Jaide, 1983: 49 ff).

Contemporary studies show that West Germans tended to defer expectations of socio-economic or political change until a new generation would take over. Even then, things should not be different, just better. The children especially *sollen es einmal besser haben*; they should start out in life with more money, better jobs, better education and prospects. The 1957 election slogan of the Christian Democrats, *Keine Experimente* — no experiments — catches the popular mood of going along with the government and its policies as long as living standards were good and got better; of going along with democracy and the prescribed ways of participating in it as long as personal circumstances remained comfortable, and a brighter future — at least in material terms — seemed assured for the next generation.

THE POLITICAL CULTURE OF THE MIDDLE GROUND

Once socio-economic changes and the new institutional settings began to mould attitudes and orientations, the middle ground emerged as politically and socially dominant. The new opportunities mellowed ideological partisanships, and modified cleavages which had formerly divided German society into separate and mutually hostile camps. As living conditions became similar across income and status groups, West Germans responded with strong system support. The transition from the suspended and private political culture of the beginning to a consensus culture gathered momentum in the mid-1950s and continues to be relevant into the 1990s.

There were some early signs of change. In 1948, for instance, a study of Berlin families reprimanded the younger women for 'exaggerated self-reliance'. While many men, it was stated, returned from the war dispirited or disabled and devastated by a sense of defeat, women had 'developed sharply rational attitudes, a hardening of their emotions, after years of carrying the burden of full responsiblity and working to the limits of their physical resources' (Thrunwald, 1948: 197). A 1951 study of German families viewed the same changes more favourably and commented on a new equality and partnership, with women often key organisers who held the family unit socially and economically together (Wurzbacher, 1951: 247). While the average West German in the 1940s and 1950s still regarded it as a sign of poverty when a woman *had to* work, an increasing number of married and single women saw working as a new kind of social participation, and preferred it to conventional female roles (Willms, 1983: 112 ff).

Among the young, socio-economic changes opened new avenues of participation. This participation meant above all increased opportunities to develop personal preferences into occupations. Since the 1920s and beyond, training placements and apprenticeships had been in short supply and young people had little occupational choice. If they wanted to learn a trade and qualify, as the majority of Germans including West Germans have always done, they had to take what they could get and make the best of it. In the 1950s, the number of apprenticeships on offer exceeded the number required and for the first time in generations, young people were able to choose from a range of careers (*Berufsbildungsberichte*). After decades of directed or conscripted labour — even the famous *Trümmerfrauen* did not clean up the rubble out of a sense of national duty or enthusiasm for a new beginning but for the practical return of better food rations — the working lives of German adults and adolescents were no longer determined by the state or by the law of scarcity.

Table 2.2 Employment in West Germany by occupational fields, 1950-80 (in %)

Occupational Field	1950	1961	1970	1976	1980
Agriculture	24.6	16.2	8.5	6.8	5.8
Manufacturing	37.0	37.1	36.1	32.2	32.5
Services in manufacturing	9.7	14.0	16.8	18.2	18.4
Services in media, transport and finance	13.9	18.1	20.0	20.3	20.1
Public administration	5.8	6.1	9.1	10.8	11.0
Public service (teaching, medical, social)	3.2	3.6	4.9	7.1	7.9
Domestic/cleaning	5.6	5.0	4.4	4.2	4.4
Total (in 1,000)	23,489	26,527	26,322	25,752	26,874

Source: W. Müller (1982) 'Wege und Grenzen der Tertiasierung: Wandel der Berufsstruktur in der Bundesrepublik 1950-80', *Krise der Arbeitsgesellschaft*, Campus, Frankfurt/Main, p. 148.

The post-war economic boom extended personal opportunities beyond the experiences and living memories of all German citizens at the time. Although there was more scope for choice in industrial and business centres, in big cities and their commuter belts than in remote rural areas or small towns, improvements were felt everywhere. Employees and workers of all types and ages also benefited from reforms of work safety and conditions, better pay which brought West German wages near the top in Western Europe. A new emphasis on qualifications developed, training programmes were modernised and at all levels of skill and seniority, courses were offered for retraining and updating. Locality and tradition became less important for the socio-economic place of the individual than personal inclinations and the mobilisation of the employment sector itself (Glastetter *et al.*, 1983). The economic miracle generated a far reaching shift in the structure of employment. In 1950, close to two in three people worked in agriculture or in manufacturing, the remainder in various services (Table 2.2). By 1980, the proportions were nearly reversed, with a particularly steep decline in agricultural employment.

The working environment changed further as new industries developed and as new administrative structures were introduced. Work changed in content and in its defined occupational status. The new occupations and tasks fitted none of the traditional status groups or clusters of social expectations (Hradil, 1987). New technologies and new fields of expertise loosened social and political patterns of identification, and created novel scope for individual preferences and orientations. Within the overall work force, the proportion of working people in paid employment increased, and within this sector, work shifted from blue-collar to white-collar occupations (Table 2.3).

Table 2.3 The structure of employment, 1950-80 (in %)

Employment	1950	1960	1970	1975	1980
Self-employed	15.9	12.7	10.1	9.9	8.6
Helping family members	15.6	10.1	6.5	5.6	3.4
Paid employment	68.5	77.2	83.4	84.5	88.0
Among these					
Blue-collar workers	-	63.8	56.1	50.1	48.1
White-collar employees	-	28.7	35.1	40.3	42.3
Civil servants	-	7.5	8.8	9.6	9.6

Source: H. Poller (1981) Politik im Querschnitt, *Zahlenspiegel Bonn* (Aktuell), p. 83.

The socio-economic changes may also have fostered democratic change. Although it is impossible to match the working environment directly to the political world, the non-democratic elements seemed to decrease in both. Across employment sectors and occupational fields, mechanisation and innovative technology made working cleaner and lighter for many; traditional command structures and personal authority declined in importance while functional aspects of work organisation shaped patterns of authority in administration and on the shop floor (Matthes, 1983: 141-205). The authoritarian leadership styles which had dominated the West German business world into the 1950s, appear to have been modified by modernisation. Some comparisons of attitudes and expectations over time can be based on opinion polls. Allensbach surveys for instance asked identical questions in 1953 and 1979 (Table 2.4). The replies suggest that acceptance of authority at work has remained stable, but

47

the experience of the individual environment has changed. In the 1970s, more people felt they were doing work of their choice, and felt satisfied with their place of work. The data for the early 1950s indicate that people had not always accepted the involuntary adjustments to a new working environment which had been forced upon them.

Table 2.4 Perceptions of the working environment, 1953 and 1979

Leadership styles. How does your boss generally behave: does he occasionally talk to you, or does he just give you instructions?

	1953	1979
	%	%
Talks sometimes	74	76
Only gives instructions	18	15
Undecided	4	9
Don't know	4	-

Satisfaction with work place: Does it matter to you where you earn your money — in which company you work?

	1953	1979
	%	%
Yes, it matters		
Want to stay with same company, at same work place	41	64
Want to stay with same company, but different work place	5	6
Want to return to my former profession (job)	4	1
No, it does not matter	34	21
Don't know	5	3

Source: E. Noelle-Neumann and E. Piel (1983) *Eine Generation später. Bundesrepublik Deutschland 1953-79*, Saur, Munich, p. 196; 192.

On a more intimate level, the five-day working week, and later the 40-hour or 35-hour week created free time for personal interests and leisure pursuits which had in the past been the prerogatives of the wealthy. In West Germany, this did not mean that work declined in its importance to the individual. Between 80 and 90 per cent consider work an essential part of living (Allerbeck and Hoag, 1985: 70). Or to put it another way: leisure in the West German political culture is linked to employment. The long-term unemployed do not perceive work-free time as leisure time. For them, not working tends to be experienced as isolation, boredom and passivity (Opaschowski, 1983:

36-42). Paired with work, however, leisure has become newly relevant as the time when West Germans of all ages and occupational groups feel they can pursue their personal inclinations and interests or even involve themselves as members in political parties. Preferences are for private participation: in 1985, 72 per cent of men and 45 per cent of women over the age of 18 were members of an association, about one in three in sports or leisure clubs (*Die Zeit*, 3 January 1985; Mohr, 1984: 169). By comparison, an estimated 4 per cent are members of political parties and the same proportion — often the same individuals — are actively involved in citizens' initiatives or groups with specific local grievances or objectives.

Among the effects of socio-economic changes on the political culture, the new perception of the social and political status of white-collar and blue-collar occupations is particularly relevant. In the German past, white-collar employees thought of themselves as socially superior to the working class. Their more prestigious status was legally secured. They were paid monthly salaries, enjoyed some protection from dismissal, holiday rights and special insurance provisions, to name just a few socio-economic pillars of the *Angestellte* (Kocka, 1981). Politically inclined towards anti-socialism, they fell prey to National Socialism once the pay and status differentials seemed in danger of being eroded. *De facto*, National Socialist labour policies further diminished the economic supremacy of white-collar over blue-collar workers. After 1945, two important things happened: although white-collar unionism stayed outside the West German Trade Union Federation (DGB), it cancelled the partisan commitment to the right of its Weimar predecessors. The second change concerns social norms and status demarcation lines. In the post-war era, the social hostility between employees and workers which used to divide occupations and classes, did not become politically salient again (Dahrendorf, 1967: 67 ff). It lingers on in personal expectations, in educational motivation and lifestyles, but it is no longer a political watershed between left and right. The mobilisation in the employment structure allowed children of blue-collar workers to 'rise' into white-collar occupations. Mobility in the opposite direction played an important political part because many members of the new middle class feared it and opted to the right in search of protection; in reality, such mobility from white-collar to blue-collar status remained a trickle even after mass unemployment in the 1920s, and during the life time of the Federal Republic (Kocka and Prinz, 1983). Visible distinctions between occupational and status groups diminished as consumer goods became more widely accessible. The majority of West Germans have become owners of washing machines, television sets, cars and even workers rose to be owner-occupiers. Regardless of a blue- or a white-collar income, West German women have tended to sport no less than a persian lamb coat on special occasions. Across the classes and other cleavage lines, reproduction oak furnishings adorn German sitting rooms (Brunhöber, 1983). Material possessions have become symbols of respectability across socio-economic divides. They point to an unspoken consensus on values and priorities in West Germany society.

Consensus politics

The apparent similarity of blue- and white-collar working people in West Germany also bridged political divisions in the population and fostered broadly based, non-partisan catch-all parties, *Volksparteien* (Smith, 1986: 88 ff). Responding to the new socio-economic blend of occupational and social groups, parties adjusted their policies and communicative styles. The shift towards the centre was particularly painful for the SPD who had to respond to the socio-economic changes by changing its very class focus. By the late 1950s, it had detached itself from its Marxist heritage and the focal points of early opposition. Paired with an innovative approach to East-West relations or educational and social policy, the emphatic consensus with the established political system enabled the SPD to broaden its electoral base in the 1960s and 1970s. The party won new support among an occupationally and politically mobile white-collar population. By comparison, the Christian Democrats enjoyed more continuity and retained their image as the party for practising Christians, especially catholics, for the 'more respectable' and better off people in the country. At times of economic uncertainty, it won additional support from a working-class elite of trade unionists who feared for their socio-economic status. With the exception of 1972, the CDU, together with its permanent partner and sister party from Bavaria, the CSU, has always been the strongest party in parliament (Padgett and Burkett, 1986).

As *Volksparteien*, the big two, CDU/CSU and SPD performed important integrative functions which facilitated the emergence of the consensus culture. Both parties proved sufficiently attractive to hasten the collapse of the political extremes of the left and the right. Both have attempted to offer policies and win backing across society, ranging from the self-employed to pensioners, young people or home-owners. No single party can claim to articulate the specific concerns of any one group. Issues in general lost the cutting edge of ideological alternatives, and became similar between parties (Flanagan and Dalton, 1984). Increasingly, parties consult interest groups and experts of all political camps and base their policies on non-partisan recommendations rather than ideological pre-conceptions. This has been of central importance in the field of economic policy since the Council of Experts (*Sachverständigenrat*) was asked in the early 1960s, to report annually on the state of the economy, and the direction economic policies should take. All governments regardless of political composition followed this practice. In the mid-1960s, consultation between government and the two sides of industry was seen as an optimal means of crisis management, since the parameters of economic policy, of prices, wages, profits could be settled by above-party agreement. The collapse of the Concerted Action indicates that conflicting interests have prevailed underneath the consensus culture; the very attempt at such a broad ranging agreement underlines the intent of the *Volksparteien* to present their own political actions as based on an above party consensus which would give them added legitimacy. Thus, policy formulation in the main parties today is preceded and surrounded by public hearings, by consultation with a range of independent academics and other experts. Issues are no longer articulated according to ideological convictions but they are tuned to people's preferences and perceived priorities; or they are at least packaged to appear as the considered response to such preferences (Beyme, 1985: Chapters 3 and 6).

Since results on election day may be regarded as the ultimate measure of party success, and since the socio-economic mobilisation of West German society means that none of the parties can rely on a ready made and loyal electorate, the link with the citizens has become essential. West German citizens, on the whole, are not given to opting for change as the British, American or French electorates for instance have tended to do in search of better politics (Pedersen, 1983; Lipset and Rokkan, 1967: Part I).With less to choose between parties, West German voters look for continuity and stability. The tendency to confirm governments in office underlines that in electoral politics, West Germans prefer continuity to change. Changes of government normally occur during the lifetime of a parliament as coalition reshuffles. The very existence of coalitions as the backbone of government generates a consensus about core policies among those parties who want a share in government (Bogdanor, 1983). In West Germany, this consensus is facilitated if not prescribed by the constitution. The Basic Law requires political parties to endorse the democratic order and renders opposition of principle illegal (Kirchheimer, 1967; Schumann, 1976). The political scope of opposition is blunted further by the dual role a party may play. It normally is in government and in opposition at the same time, since the federal system allows for the regional and national governments to be of a different political composition (Paterson and Webber, 1987).

The discussion of consensus politics would not be complete without mentioning the role of small parties (Stöss, 1983 I: 145 ff; Rowold, 1974). The composition of the first Bundestag in 1949 with some eleven different political parties holding seats was none too different from the Weimar years, and the partisan splintering which had haunted Germany's first parliamentary democracy. A combination of tightening the electoral legislation to discourage splintering, and the integrative capacity of the *Volksparteien* worked towards consensus politics: by the mid-1950s, only the two major parties, CDU/CSU and SPD had remained, flanked by the small Free Democratic Party (Freie Demokratische Partei — FDP) which carved out a distinctive political role for itself as the near perennial coalition partner. Each time the FDP changed sides at the national level, it underwent a programmatic reorientation. From an emphasis to the right in the 1950s and 1960s, to a left-liberal profile in the 1970s, and back to the right in the 1980s and a role as the vanguard of small and middle-sized business, the self-employed, and, above all, those who favour a voice of moderation. This latter function has been crucial to the consensus culture: West German voters have been reluctant to give any one party an absolute majority at national level. Despite its political predicaments of changing programmes, electorates and members, the FDP has been perceived as the political force to prevent any one of the big parties to govern without restraint. The voice of moderation has been intended as a means of preventing the bigger coalition partner of the day from following party political and ideological priorities unchecked.

With more experience in government than any of the other parties, the FDP has been a catalyst of political continuity and consensus (Beyme, 1985: 333). It is firmly rooted in the first and still dominant phase of political culture change, the emergence of system support and consensus after disaffection and the suspended political culture of the early years. In the 1980s, small party politics became more varied than they had been for decades. After small parties seemed to be on the decline in the regions, and nearly doomed at national level, the Green party appeared to reverse the trend towards a two party system when it emerged as a viable electoral party at all political levels. If the FDP is firmly rooted in the consensus culture, the Greens are a product of a political culture change towards conflict and dissent (Bürklin, 1984; Papadakis, 1984; Roth, 1985). Their ambivalent attitudes towards parliamentary and coalition politics, their focus on extra-parliamentary action and a radicalisation of issues draws on a diverse protest culture which can be traced to the 1950s and 1960s. Alongside and in open hostility to the prescribed consensus of West German society, youth cultures such as *Halbstarke* or 'rockers' set out to shock the burghers in the 1950s; in the 1960s, the student movement pressed for political innovation where the ubiquitous consensus seemed to breed stagnation; since the 1970s, action groups, initiatives, new social movements and also terrorism on both political extremes have pointed to an increased willingness to participate, and to an increased scepticism that established channels of participation were suited to bring about change (Raschke, 1985; Kolinsky, 1987). The duality of consensus and dissent characterises the West German political culture of the 1980s.

GENERATIONAL PERSPECTIVES ON POLITICAL CULTURE

When Conradt took stock of the 'changing German political culture', he observed for the late 1970s, that 'ways of thinking had been reshaped to provide a basis for a democratic political system' but that this system and its institutions could not fully satisfy the 'participatory needs and policy demands of a population no longer in its democratic infancy' (Conradt, 1980: 263). Twenty years earlier, West Germans seemed more contented with their scope for political involvement. They were less interested in politics (Table 2.5) but did not appear to perceive their environment as restrictive. In the 1950s, more people thought they could express their opinions freely than did in the 1970s when the under 25s were particularly sceptical regarding freedom of speech in their personal environment (Greiffenhagen, 1979: 354). Party identification which had grown in the founding years of the Federal Republic now began to decline among the youngest age cohorts (Hofmann-Göttig, 1984; *Jugend '81*, 1982; *Die verunsicherte Generation*, 1983; *Jugend privat: Verwöhnt? Hedonistisch? Bildungslos?* 1983). Politicians and parties were accused of neglecting the concerns of ordinary people and of having nothing relevant to offer to the young.

Table 2.5 Interest in politics since the 1950s (in %)

Generally speaking, are you interested in politics?

	1952	1959	1962	1965	1969	1972	1973	1977	1983
Yes	27	29	37	39	45	46	49	50	58
Not much	41	36	39	43	42	34	34	41	37
No	32	35	24	18	13	20	17	9	6

Sources: D. Conradt (1980) 'Changing German Political Culture'. In: G. Almond and S. Verba, *The Civic Culture Revisited*, Little, Brown & Co., Boston, 239; *Generationen im Vergleich* (1985) Jugendwerk der Deutschen Shell, vol. 3, Leske, Opladen, p. 369.

Parteiverdrossenheit, a blanket rejection of parties and politics seemed to proliferate. The fear that young people had cancelled their loyalty to the democratic system and to the consensus in the political culture generated a government inquiry, a library of research, and an intensive public and parliamentary debate on the political attitudes and the political preferences among West Germany's young generation (see Wissmann and Hauck, 1982; *Jugendprotest* I, 1982; II, 1983). In the background of all this stood and stands the old fear that Weimar and its anti-democratic activism might re-emerge among the young and in their politics.

Democracy's children, the adolescents and young adults of the 1980s are no longer preoccupied with accepting and securing democracy, and with creating a blanket consensus which might cushion disparities and mellow social and political conflicts. The younger generations show a different commitment. They tend to be more emphatic about democratic values and objectives than their elders, and also more doubtful that these values and objectives are best served in the West German political environment. The conventions about the contents and the participatory forms of politics which guided the founding generations from a non-democratic to a democratic political culture, are no longer seen as binding by West Germans whose experiences reach back no further than the Federal Republic. A new volatility, and a duality of consensus and dissent or protest characterise today's political culture. The difference between the two strands points to a polarisation and a formation of camps which perceive themselves as juxtaposed and virtually separate political cultures.

Compared with the 1950s, the socio-political make-up of young West Germans has changed noticeably. Then, young West Germans were authoritarian in international comparison, and moulded by yet unchanged attitudes of Nazi vintage to political and social life. In the 1980s, they tended to defy authority, to assert themselves, to challenge established institutions and conventions (Lederer, 1983: 94 ff). Attitudes of young West Germans had changed faster and moved further away from authoritarian traditions than those of young people in other Western democracies.

As consensus cohorts whose views and attitudes were formed under similar socio-economic and political conditions, generations are important milestones for the nature and the changes of the political culture. If one assumes that the formative years for political orientations are those under the age of 30, every polity contains a number of distinct political generations. In the Federal Republic, the changes of political system and the transition from non-democratic to democratic government add a further dimension. The children of the German Empire, now well into their seventies, may have retained some pre-democratic views; the cohort between 50 and 65 on whom National Socialist political socialisation made a lasting impression may be prone to call for a strong leader at times of crisis (Sinus, 1981: 77 ff). Age cohorts appear to share a perspective on politics. There is plenty of evidence to show that in West Germany, age cohorts have remained distinctive, and that their views and attitudes also changed as they experienced democratic government and the new socio-economic mobility. The 1985 Shell study, for instance, compared young people today with young people 30 years ago and also examined how their views had changed in the interim. Perceptions of National Socialism have been regarded as a yardstick of democratic orientations and identical questions asked since the early 1950s. Table 2.6 records some of them.

Table 2.6 Core characteristics of National Socialism: a comparison of young people, 1955, young people, 1984, and adults, 1984

	Youth 1955 15-24 years %	Youth 1984 15-24 years %	Adults 1984 45-54 years %
Overall characteristics of NS			
Negative	77	87	84
Positive	16	6	15
Ambivalent	7	6	1
Negative characteristics (Multiple answers)			
Dictatorship	39	64	48
War	11	27	34
Racialism	9	74	41
Terror, Concentration camps	7	27	12
Godlessness	4	-	-
Nationalism/fanaticism	9	9	7
Positive characteristics (Multiple answers)			
Social/economic/cultural success	11	7	14
German unity	2	-	-
Others	4	8	12
Ambivalent characteristics	8	15	2

Source: *Jugend und Erwachsene*, 3, p. 343; 346

It suggests that young people of today have on the whole negative views of National Socialism and can mention a number of characteristics to back these up. The over 45s in 1984 found more acceptable features in National Socialism than young people did, but compared to their own youth, they have become more critical. The segment of the generation cohort which saw National Socialism as a positive experience in the past remained virtually unchanged. Older West Germans have changed their views somewhat, but have retained socio-political evaluations which set them apart from younger age cohorts.

If we take political culture to characterise an underlying consensus of values, priorities and attitudes, West Germany has several consensus cohorts. They are cohesive internally, and distinct from one another. Table 2.7 takes national consciousness as an example and shows the generational rifts on issues such as national pride or the notion of 'fatherland'. It also shows how young West Germans have become more detached from worn symbols of German nationhood, and the consensus culture. They were less emphatically 'German' than the population as a whole, or their elders, and contrary to other age groups, their views of the term 'fatherland' have become more negative since the 1970s.

Table 2.7 Issues in a generational perspective

Q. Are you proud to be German? (December 1979/January 1980)

	Population	Age cohorts		
	%	16-29	30-59	60 and over
Yes, definitely	44	31	41	66
Yes, predominantly	35	38	39	25
Not really	6	7	7	2
Not at all	5	9	4	2
Undecided	10	15	9	5

Q. Does the word 'fatherland' sound good to you or do you think it no longer fits into today's world? (1975 and 1981)

	Population %		16-29 %		30-44 %		45-59 %		60 and over %	
	1975	1981	1975	1981	1975	1981	1975	1981	1975	1981
Sounds good	60	59	41	35	55	54	63	69	82	81
Does not fit	38	39	56	61	42	44	35	29	17	17
No answer	2	2	3	4	3	2	2	2	1	2

Source: E. Noelle-Neumann (1981) 'Brauchen wir eine Fahne?', *Allensbach Berichte*, 23, Table 14, p. 26; Table 8, p. 30.

The twin effects of a reduction in the birth rate since the early 1960s and an increase in average life expectancy have combined to make the older cohorts proportionately more important: in 1950, just over 33 per cent of the West German population were aged 45 and over; in 1970, 37 per cent, with projections of nearly 40 per cent for the year 2000 (Köllmann 1983, 98; Neumann and Schaper, 1982: 105). In a generational perspective views and attitudes which are based on pre-democratic environments are likely to remain salient influences in the present and future. Politically, these influences have been slanted towards the right. In their self-perception, older West Germans see themselves as politically in the centre or on the right while the under thirties see themselves as in the centre or on the left of the political spectrum (Bürklin, 1980: 228).

Electoral preferences confirm this generational divide. Older people have tended to give above average support to conservative or right-wing parties. The self-perception of young people as located on the political left, has shaped recent election results. Between 1969 and 1980, the Social Democrats won the lion share of the young vote. Since 1980, the new Green Party drew over two-thirds of its support from the under 35s attracting 4.8 per cent of the 18-25 year olds in 1980, 13.9 per cent in 1983 and over 20 per cent in 1987. The SPD won 39 per cent of that electorate in 1983, and about one-third in 1987. Counting the two parties together, the centre/left has been supported by about 54 per cent of the young electorate, the same proportion as the SPD obtained on its own in 1972 (Kolinsky, 1986: 42). The CDU/CSU, which had dominated the young voters' sector up to the mid-1960s lost some of that support in the 1970s. Starting in 1976, it has regained ground and in 1983 the CDU/CSU emerged with 41.2 per cent as the largest party among young voters. In 1987, its share had declined again to under 40 per cent.

The changing fortunes of the parties among the young electorates point to a re-emergent left-right divide among the under 25s in the 1980s. The youngest age cohort is in itself divided into partisan segments on the ends of the political spectrum, and a sizeable centre whose attitudes and orientations blend in with the mainstream political culture and its preoccupations with consensus, stability and a secure personal existence.

New educational divides

Education has always been a political divide in German history. Generally speaking, up to the 1950s, the higher educated would be inclined towards the political right, the lower educated towards the political left. After that, this correlation no longer fits.When Habermas and his team of authors analysed the social and political attitudes of West German students at the end of the decade, they noted that the majority held views ranging from the centre to the far left (Habermas et al., 1961). In the 1960s, the student movement hurled criticism and protests at a range of institutions and issues from facilities for higher education to the policy priorities of Western capitalism or the war in Vietnam (Baeyer-Katte et al., 1982). Since then, the 'restless generation' (Wildenmann and Kaase, 1968) of West German students has located itself more clearly on the left or among the emphatic democrats for whom existing channels are not sufficiently democratic. Young academically trained West Germans have been the backbone of the new social and political movements whose tendency towards radicalisation has been mentioned earlier (Raschke, 1985).

Reminiscent of the anti-system fervour of oppositions in the Weimar Republic, the Federal Republic has been branded as a fascist state, no different from its Nazi predecessor and arguably more dangerous since its repressive character is less apparent. Political activity has become dramatised as 'resistance' aimed not at change but at destruction of the cluster of institutions and attitudes which forms mainstream West German political culture. The tendency among West German students to measure their political and social expectations against their image of reality and find it wanting, has created an enclave of 'protest consensus'. Within it, new modes of opposition — such as the Greens or the new social movements — find fertile ground.

The new volatile orientations among young and educated West Germans are interesting not only because the radicalism of yesteryear seems to have swung the other way. Educational policies, and increased affluence which allowed young people to delay their entry into the labour market and remain in education worked an educational transformation of an impressive scale. In the 1950s, about 3 per cent of an age cohort would qualify for university entry; nearly 80 per cent had only basic schooling (Kloss, 1985: 118-19). Thirty years laters, 25 per cent of an age cohort were qualified to commence higher education and the proportion of young people with only basic schooling had declined to 39 per cent. From a slim segment, the young and educated West Germans have grown into a sizeable quarter of their generation.

At the opposite end of the social and political spectrum, the changes have been similarly far reaching. Right extremism among the young is now largely located among the poorly educated (Noelle-Neumann and Ring, 1984: 42 ff). An analysis of pupils' essays showed for instance that those with more advanced education were able to distance themselves from their parents' or relatives' narratives about the Nazi period and its meanings. By contrast, those with little education had accepted in good faith the memories and the usually positive evaluations passed on through oral history (Boßmann, 1977).

Among the young and comparatively uneducated, neo-nazism has become a small but volatile protest culture on the right. The recourse to Nazi language, symbols, snippets of ideology such as anti-semitism, enmity against foreigners or a leadership cult has been interpreted in two different ways. Some argue that all this has been dormant in the West German political culture, an unspoken part of social milieux, and ready to be activated at will (e.g. Niethammer,

1969; Kühnl *et al.*, 1969; Dudek and Jaschke, 1984). Others have pointed out that neo-nazism deliberately uses language, symbols, meanings which have been perceived as unacceptable and as officially outlawed. Stigmatised by mainstream politics and at least shunned by most West Germans, it became a ready tool of protest like punk, pop and other distinctive and aggressive gestures against adult society. In this perspective, neo-nazism demonstrates detachment from the democratic consensus, not right-extremist or racist convictions (Stöss, 1986).

In the rise of neo-nazism remnants of past ideologies and contemporary protest potential come together. Aspects of a dormant political culture have been re-activated. The new little Nazis tend to amuse rather than anger the average West German bystander; it seems a radicalisation to the right is less alien to the German public mind and perceived as less of a threat than a similar one to the left. Of course, anti-communism has been part of the German political culture since the 1920s, perhaps the only part with a high degree of continuity across the changes of political system. A negative predisposition towards communism and things related to it has remained a powerful current of the contemporary political culture. What has changed is the social and educational origin of the perpetrators of radical politics among the young: the new would-be Nazis have low levels of education and low levels of skill while the politically active and organised left includes a substantial number of academics. From their respective vantage points, both challenge the institutional setting, the consensus culture, and each other's political orientations.

The new anti-system radicalisms cannot be explained without recourse to the socio-economic conditions surrounding them. Both were responses to uncertainties about employment and the socio-economic integration of the individual. It is important to remember that access to universities broadened and more young West Germans graduated at the very time when the labour market could no longer absorb the new numbers at a status level to which graduates had been used in the past. In addition, the state, who had been the biggest employer of graduates with at least 60 per cent entering some kind of public service, reduced its recruitment. In 1985 only 20 per cent of graduates became civil servants or public employees. With the exception of specialist courses, West German university education has also not been tailored to serve the needs of industry and just 5 per cent of university graduates found employment in industry or business (*Der Spiegel*, 20, 1985, p. 42). In 1985, an estimated 100,000 academics were unemployed and the numbers would have been higher had it not been for special bridging — and retraining programmes and for the fact that 180,000 graduates decided to stay at university and study for an additional degree. Although graduate unemployment is low compared with unemployment in other occupational sectors, uncertainties about employment and especially about employment at the appropriate level of expertise and pay are widespread. Radicalisation, then, can be seen as a reponse to these uncertainties; even opting out into a so called alternative culture which defies social conventions and political values can be considered a step away from, if not against, the mainstream political culture. In 1983, most students (87 per cent) saw themselves as adherents of such an alternative culture; so did 62 per cent of university graduates, and 42 per cent of West Germans under the age of 30 (*Die verunsicherte Generation*, 44-6).

A similar link exists between socio-economic constraints and the radicalisation to the right. Adherents of neo-nazism tend to belong to social groups who have been hit especially hard by unemployment in the 1970s and 1980s. In line with their modest educational qualifications, many are unskilled or semi-skilled. Those who completed apprenticeships tend to work as artisans in small businesses, a sector which has traditionally been close to the right. Here, the perceived threat of unemployment is as potent a radicalising factor as the actual experience of unemployment. On the left, the notion of an 'alternative culture' functions as counter-ideology and can make not working an accepted part of a political style. On the right, with its emphasis on manhood and leadership, unemployment is experienced more directly as defeat, and as a fundamental loss of status and personal dignity (Neidhardt, 1982; Kolinsky, 1988). In both instances, radicalisation follows disappointment. To quote from a comparison of extremist attitudes on the left and the right: 'reality is seen as lagging behind the ideal and this justifies the call for changing the system, the refusal to defend this state, and the willingness to use violence' (Noelle-Neumann and Ring: 104).

The limited impact of unemployment on the democratic equilibrium of the Federal Republic is the really striking facet of contemporary political culture in all this. Although electoral studies have shown that the Greens have been perceived as a protest party and gained some support from unemployed who opted in an anti-system gesture against all established parties, the electoral effect of unemployment has been limited. In most cases, the unemployed and those who feared unemployment rallied around the party they normally supported, or around the party they saw as more competent in creating and securing employment.The radicalised anti-system gesture has remained at the side-lines of politics, at the non-party and extra-parliamentary level.

CONCLUSION

West German political culture in the 1980s refers to the broad consensus whose origins lie in the suspended and private political culture of the 1940s and 1950s. Its key tenor is agreement with the institutions, the policy directions, the place of the citizen in the political process. Political culture also refers to the various divides across generations, across educational lines and protest milieux which gained momentum since the children of democracy came of age in the 1960s. None of these accepts any of the others as a valid response to their socio-economic or political environment. And none would see any of the others as a legitimate — if different — contribution to the political process of the country as a whole. To question the legitimacy of the other side always implies that it has no legitimacy and is a danger, not an asset to the polity. Such de-legitimation has been an entrenched feature of German political culture in pre-democratic times, and has survived into democratic ones. Legitimacy tends to be denied on both sides of the consensus divide, and between factions. The scramble to either manage conflicts in legalistic channels, or to dramatise them as all-challenging catastrophes, kept the sides apart. It also ensured that mechanisms or customs of tolerance and of accepting multiplicity did not emerge. In this either-or-world, political protest or radicalised political action declares the whole political framework in which it operates, the parties, parliaments and administrative structures of democracy deficient (Veen, 1987). On the other side, political leaders and the proverbial man in the street, i.e. the official and the dominant political culture, are given to criminalising protesters and activists as a danger to the survival of the state and democracy itself.

Contemporary political culture embraces a dominant consensus culture and a divided protest camp with left-wing and right-wing factions. There is little communication or tolerance across the divide. To give an example: in 1975, the Federal Constitutional Court was called upon to deliberate on the duties of public servants, after a decree had ruled three years earlier that radicals were not eligible to hold civil service positions (Röhrich, 1983: 259 ff). The court pronounced that a civil servant has 'to feel at home in the state whom he serves' (BVerf GE 39/349). It was found to be insufficient if only actions complied with the law of the land. 'The political duty of loyalty — loyalty to the state and the constitution — demands more than a merely formally correct, but on the whole disinterested, cool and internally distant attitude towards state and constitution; it requires from a civil servant in particular that he distances himself clearly from groups and intentions which attack, undermine and vilify this state, its constitutional organs and the existing constitutional order' (BVerf GE 39/348). The pronouncements summarise what civil servants should do and they also spotlight the image of the loyal citizen and his place in state and polity.

The attempt by the federal and the regional governments to block possible critics, dissenters and radicals from entering public service was perceived by the left, and in particular by students and intellectuals, as the heavy handed attempt by the state to enforce consensus from above. The German authoritarian state tradition seemed to have surfaced again as surveillance methods were perfected and data collected to combat political radicalisation. The Federal Republic was portrayed as a 1984 state, a *Schnüffelstaat* where everbody spied on everybody else, a surveillance society without regard for individual liberties, or room for political dissent. Both sides accused each other of destroying democracy, and questioned each other's legitimacy. The same syndrome prevailed in the terrorism scare in the mid-1970s when West German politicians, the press and the public suspected as sympathisers and co-terrorist everybody who appeared left of centre or who dared to advocate that imprisoned terrorists should be treated humanely (*Frankfurter Allgemeine*, 17 December 1977).

The response consisted of non-cooperation, of 'undermining, of destruction and of a real break with society', a complete opting out of and opting against society and political conventions (*Betrifft*, 1985: 111). With the same degree of inflexibility, each side accused the other of endangering democracy. This inflexibility, the inability to accept a diversity of political positions as constituent components of the political process, is at the core of German contemporary political culture. The socio-economic constraints of the last decades brought sharper into the open that the two processes of change in the political culture have remained separate and essentially juxtaposed into a mainstream consensus and a polarised and polarising protest culture.

REFERENCES

Abelshauser, W. (1983) *Wirtschaftsgeschichte der Bundesrepublik 1945-80*, Suhrkamp, Frankfurt.

Adorno, T.W. *et al.* (1950) *The Authoritarian Personality*, Harper & Row, New York.

Allerbeck, K. and Hoag, W. (1985) *Jugend ohne Zukunft? Einstellungen, Umwelt, Lebensperspektiven*, Piper, Munich.

Almond, G. (1980) 'The Intellectual History of the Political Culture Concept'. In: G. Almond and S. Verba (eds) *The Civic Culture Revisited*, Little, Brown & Co., Boston, pp. 1-36.

Almond, G. and Verba, S. (1963) *The Civic Culture. Political Attitudes and Democracy in Five Nations*, Little, Brown & Co., Boston.

Baeyer-Katte, W. von, Claessens, D. Feger, H. and Neidhardt, F. (1982) *Gruppenprozesse. Analysen zum Terrorismus*, vol. 3, Westdeutscher Verlag, Opladen.

Der Bundesminister für Bildung und Wissenschaft (ed.) (1973 ff) *Berufsbildungsbericht*, Ministerium für Arbeit und Soziales, Bonn.

Der Bundesminister des Inneren (ed.) (1986) *Betrifft: Verfassungsschutz 1985*, Bonn.

Beyme, K. von (1985) *Political Parties in Western Democracies*, Gower, Aldershot.

Bogdanor, V. (ed.) (1983) *Coalition Government in Western Europe*, Heinemann and Policy Studies Institute, London.

Bogdanor, V. (ed.) (1987) *Dictionary of Political Institutions*, Blackwell, Oxford.

Boßmann, D. (1977) *'Was ich über Hitler gehört habe ...' Folgen eines Tabus*, Fischer, Frankfurt.

Brunhöber, H. (1983) 'Wohnen'. In: W. Benz (ed.) *Die Bundesrepublik Deutschland, vol. 2: Gesellschaft*, Fischer, Frankfurt, pp. 183-208.

Bürklin, W. (1984) *Grüne Politik. Ideologische Zyklen, Wähler und Parteiensystem*, Westdeutscher Verlag, Opladen.

Bürklin, W. (1980) Links und/oder demokratisch? *Politische Vierteljahresschrift*, 21,3, pp. 220-47.

Burdick, C., Jacobsen, H-A. and Kudszus, W. (1984) *Contemporary Germany. Politics and Culture*, Westview, Boulder.

Castell, A. zu (1985) 'Die demographischen Konsequenzen des Ersten und Zweiten Weltkriegs für das Deutsche Reich, die Deutsche Demokratische Republik und die Bundesrepublik Deutschland'. In: W. Dlugorski (ed.) *Zweiter Weltkrieg und sozialer Wandel*, Vandenhoeck und Ruprecht, Göttingen, pp. 117-37.

Conradt, D.P. (1978; 1986) *The German Polity*, Longman, London.

Conradt, D.P. (1980) 'Changing German Political Culture'. In: G. Almond and S. Verba (eds) *The Civic Culture Revisited*, pp. 212-72.

Conze, W. and Rainer Lepsius, M.R. (eds) (1983) *Industrielle Welt. Sozialgeschichte der Bundesrepublik*, Klett-Cotta, Stuttgart.

Dahrendorf, R. (1967) *Society and Democracy in Germany*, Weidenfeld & Nicolson, London.

Deppe, W. (1982) *Drei Generationen Arbeiterleben. Eine sozio-biographische Darstellung*, Campus, Frankfurt.

Die verunsicherte Generation. Jugend und Wertewandel (1983) Leske & Budrich, Opladen.

Dudek, P. and Jaschke H-G. (1984) *Entstehung und Entwicklung des Rechtsextremismus in der Bundesrepublik. Zur Tradition einer besonderen politischen Kultur*, 2 vols., Westdeutscher Verlag, Opladen.

Edinger, L. (1968; 1986) *Germany*, Little, Brown & Co., Boston.

Elon, A. (1967) *Journey Through a Haunted Land. The New Germany*, Deutsch, London.

Flanagan, S.C. and Dalton R.J. (1984) 'Parties Under Stress: Realignment and Dealignment in Advanced Industrial Societies', *West European Politics*, 7,1, pp. 7-23.

Fogt, H. (1982) *Politische Generationen. Empirische Bedeutung und theoretisches Modell*, Westdeutscher Verlag, Opladen.

Gaiser, W., Tully, C.J. and Wahler, P. (1985) 'Arbeitsmarkt — Risikoschwelle fürs Erwachsenwerden'. In: Deutsches Jugendinstitut (ed.) *Immer diese Jugend*, Kösel, Munich, pp. 180-98.

Glastetter, W., Paulen, R. and Spörel, U. (1983) *Die wirtschaftliche Entwicklung der Bundesrepublik 1950-80*, Campus, Frankfurt.

Glatzer, W. and Zapf, W. (eds) (1984) *Lebensqualität in der Bundesrepublik. Objektive Lebensbedingungen und subjektives Wohlbefinden*, Campus, Frankfurt.

Greiffenhagen, M. and Greiffenhagen, S. (1979) *Ein schwieriges Vaterland. Zur Politischen Kultur Deutschlands*, List, Munich.

Greiffenhagen, M., Greiffenhagen, S. and Prätorius, R. (eds) (1981) *Handwörterbuch zur politischen Kultur der Bundesrepublik Deutschland*, Westdeutscher Verlag, Opladen.

Habermas, J., von Friedeburg, L. Oehler, C. and Weltz, F. (1961) *Student und Politik*, Luchterhand, Neuwied.

Hilger, D. (1974) 'Die mobilisierte Gesellschaft'. In: R. Löwenthal and P. Schwarz (eds) *Die zweite Republik*, Seewald, Stuttgart, pp. 95-122.

Hofmann-Göttig, J. (1984) *Die jungen Wähler*, Campus, Frankfurt.

Hornstein, W. (ed.) (1983) *Jugend ohne Orientierung?* Beltz, Weinheim.

Hradil, S. (1987) *Sozialstrukturanalyse in einer fortgeschrittenen Gesellschaft*, Leske & Budrich, Opladen.

Jacobmeyer, W. (1976) 'Die Niederlage 1945'. In: *Westdeutschlands Weg zur Bundesrepublik 1945-49*, Beiträge von Mitarbeitern des Instituts für Zeitgeschichte, Beck, Munich, pp. 11-24.

Jaide, W. (1983) *Wertewandel? Grundfragen zur Diskussion*, Leske & Budrich, Opladen.

Jugend '81. Lebensentwürfe. Alltagskulturen. Zukunftsbilder (1982) (ed.) Jugendwerk der Deutschen Shell, Leske & Budrich, Opladen.

Jugendliche und Erwachsene '85 (1985) *Generationen im Vergleich.* vol. 3: Jugend der Fünfziger Jahre — Heute. Studie im Auftrag des Jugendwerks der Deutschen Shell, Leske & Budrich, Opladen.

Jugendprotest im demokratischen Staat I (1982) Zwischenbericht der Enquête Kommission des 9. Bundestages, *Zur Sache,* 1.

Jugendprotest im demokratischen Staat II (1983) Schlußbericht der Enquête Kommission des 9. Bundestages, *Zur Sache,* 1.

Kirchheimer, O. (1957) 'The waning of opposition in parliamentary regimes', Social Research, 24, 2, pp. 127-56.

Kloss, G. (ed.) (1985) *Education Policy in the Federal Republic 1969-84,* UMIST, Manchester.

Kocka, J. (1981) *Die Angestellten in der deutschen Geschichte 1850-80,* Vandenhoeck & Ruprecht, Göttingen.

Kocka, J. and Prinz, M. (1983) 'Vom "neuen Mittelstand" zum angestellten Arbeitnehmer. Kontinuität und Wandel der deutschen Angestellten seit der Weimarer Republik'. In: W. Conze and R. Lepsius (eds) (1983) pp. 210-55.

Köllmann, W. (1983) 'Die Bevölkerungsentwicklung der Bundesrepublik'. In: W. Conze and R. Lepsius (eds) (1983) pp. 66-114.

Kolinsky, E. (1970) *Engagierter Expressionismus. Literatur zwischen Weltkrieg und Republik,* Metzler, Stuttgart.

Kolinsky, E. (1984) *Parties, Opposition and Society in West Germany,* Croom Helm, London.

Kolinsky, E. (1986) 'Youth Parties and Democracy in West Germany', *Politics,* 6, 1, pp. 41-6.

Kolinsky, E. (1987) The transformation of extra-parliamentary opposition in West Germany and the Peace Movement. In: E. Kolinsky (ed.) *Opposition in Western Europe,* Croom Helm and PSI, London, pp. 318-52.

Kolinsky, E. (1988) 'Terrorism in West Germany'. In: J. Lodge (ed.)*The Threat of Terrorism in Western Europe,* Wheatsheaf, Brighton, pp. 57-88.

Kühnl, R., Rilling, R. and Sager, C. (1969) *Die NPD. Struktur, Ideologie und Funktion einer neofaschistischen Partei,* Suhrkamp, Frankfurt.

Langguth, G. (1983) *Protestbewegung. Entwicklung, Niedergang, Renaissance. Die Neue Linke seit 1968,* Wissenschaft und Politik, Cologne.

Lederer, G. (1983) *Jugend und Autorität. Über den Einstellungswandel zum Autoritarismus in der BRD und in den USA,* Westdeutscher Verlag, Opladen.

Lepsius, R. (1982) 'Institutional Structures and Political Culture'. In: H. Döring and G. Smith (eds) *Party Government and Political Culture,* Macmillan,

London, pp. 116-31.

Lipset, S.M. and Rokkan S. (eds) (1967) *Party Systems and Voter Alignments. Cross-National Perspectives*, The Free Press, New York.

Marshall, B. (1980) German Attitudes to British Military Government 1945-47, *Journal of Contemporary History*, 15, 1, pp. 655-684.

Matthes, J. (ed.) (1983) *Krise der Arbeitsgesellschaft?* Campus, Frankfurt.

Merritt, A.J. and Merritt, R.L. (1970) *Public Opinion in Occupied Germany*, The OMGUS Surveys, 1945-49, University of Illinois Press, Urbana.

Merritt, A.J. and Merritt, R.L. (1980) *Public Opinion in Semi-sovereign Germany*, The HICOG Surveys, 1949-55, University of Illinois Press, Urbana.

Mohr, M. (1984) 'Politische und soziale Beteiligung'. In: W. Glatzer and W. Zapf (eds) (1984) pp. 157-176.

Müller, W., Willms, A. and Handl, J. (1983) *Strukturwandel der Frauenarbeit 1880-1980*, Campus, Frankfurt.

Neidhardt, F. (1982) 'Linker und rechter Terrorismus. Erscheinungsformen und Handlungspotentiale im Gruppenvergleich'. In: W. von Baeyer-Katte *et al.* (1982) pp. 434-77.

Neumann, L.F. and Schaper, K. (1982) *Die Sozialordnung der Bundesrepublik*, Campus, Frankfurt.

Niethammer, L. (1967) 'Die amerikanische Besatzungsmacht zwischen Verwaltungstradition und politischen Parteien in Bayern 1945', *Vierteljahreshefte für Zeitgeschichte*, 15, pp. 153-210.

Niethammer, L. (1969) *Angepaßter Faschismus. Politische Praxis der NPD*, Fischer, Frankfurt/Main.

Niethammer, L. (1982) *Die Mitläuferfabrik. Die Entnazifizierung am Beispiel Bayerns*, Dietz, Berlin/Bonn.

Niethammer, L. and Plato, A. von (eds) (1985) *Wir kriegen jetzt andere Zeiten. Auf der Suche nach der Erfahrung des Volkes in nachfaschistischen Ländern*, Dietz, Bonn.

Noelle-Neumann, E. and Piel, E. (1983) *Eine Generation später. Bundesrepublik Deutschland 1953-79*, Saur, Munich.

Noelle-Neumann, E. and Ring, E. (1984) *Das Extremismus-Potential unter jungen Leuten in der Bundesrepublik Deutschland 1984*, Allensbach.

Opaschowski, H.W. (1983) *Arbeit, Freizeit, Lebenssinn? Orientierungen für eine Zukunft, die längst begonnen hat*, Leske & Budrich, Opladen.

Padgett, S. and Burkett, A. (1986) *Political Parties and Elections in West Germany*, Hurst, London.

Papadakis, E. (1984) *The Green Movement in West Germany*, Croom Helm,

London.

Paterson, W.E. and Webber, D. (1987) 'The Federal Republic of Germany: The Re-Emergent Opposition?' In: E. Kolinsky (ed.) *Opposition in Western Europe* (1987) pp. 137-68.

Pedersen, M.N. (1983) 'Changing Patterns of Electoral Volatility in European Party Systems, 1948-77'. In H. Daalder and P. Mair (eds) *Western European Party Systems. Continuity and Change*, Sage, London, pp. 29-66.

Raschke, J. (1985) *Soziale Bewegungen. Ein historisch-systematischer Grundriß*, Campus, Frankfurt.

Rausch, H. (1980) *Politische Kultur in der Bundesrepublik*, Colloquium, Berlin.

Reichel, P. (1981) *Politische Kultur in der Bundesrepublik*, Leske & Budrich, Opladen.

Röhrich,W. (1983) *Die verspätete Demokratie. Zur politischen Kultur der Bundesrepublik Deutschland*, Diederichs, Cologne.

Roth, R. (1985) 'Neue soziale Bewegungen in der politischen Kultur der Bundesrepublik — eine vorläufige Skizze'. In: K.-W. Brand (ed.) *Neue soziale Bewegungen in Westeuropa und den USA. Ein internationaler Vergleich*, Campus, Frankfurt, pp. 20-82.

Rowold, M. (1974) *Im Schatten der Macht. Zur Oppositionsrolle der nicht-etablierten Parteien in der Bundesrepublik*, Droste, Düsseldorf.

Schaffner, B. (1948) *Fatherland: A Study of Authoritarianism in the German Family*, Columbia University Press, New York.

Schubert, D. (1984) *Frauen im Nachkriegsdeutschland*, Schwann, Düsseldorf.

Schumann, H.-G. (ed.) (1976) *Die Rolle der Opposition in der Bundesrepublik*, Wissenschaftliche Buchgesellschaft, Darmstadt.

Schwab-Felisch, H. (ed.) (1962 reprint) *Der Ruf. Eine deutsche Nachkriegszeitschrift*. Fischer, Frankfurt.

Sinus Institut (1981) *5 Millionen Deutsche: 'Wir wollen wieder einen Führer haben ...' Die Sinus Studie über rechtsextremistische Einstellungen bei den Deutschen*, Rowohlt, Reinbek.

Smith, G. (1986) *Democracy in Western Germany. Parties and Politics in the Federal Republic*, 3rd edition, Gower, Aldershot.

Sontheimer, K. (1979) *Die verunsicherte Republik. Die Bundesrepublik nach 30 Jahren*, Piper, Munich.

Stöss, R. (ed.) (1983; 1986) *Parteien Handbuch*, 2 vols., 2nd edition, Westdeutscher Verlag, Opladen.

Stöss, R. (1986) 'Pronazistisches Protestverhalten unter Jugendlichen'. In: A. Silbermann and J.H. Schoeps (eds) *Antisemitismus nach dem Holocaust,*

Wissenschaft und Politik, Cologne, pp. 163-92.

Thrunwald H. (1945) Gegenwartsprobleme Berliner Familien, Colloquium, Berlin.

Veen, H.-J. (1987) *Die Grünen als Milieupartei*, Manuscript.

Wehdeking, V.C. (1971) *Der Nullpunkt*, Metzler, Stuttgart.

Weidenfeld, W. (ed.) (1983) *Die Identität der Deutschen*, Hanser, Munich.

Weigelt, K. (ed.) (1984) *Heimat und Nation. Zur Geschichte und Identität der Deutschen*, Hase & Köhler, Mainz.

Wildenmann, R. and Kaase, M. (1968) *Die unruhige Generation. Eine Untersuchung zu Politik und Demokratie in der Bundesrepublik*, (Forschungsgruppe Wahlen), Mannheim.

Willenborg, K.-H. (1978) 'Überleben nach dem Zusammenbruch. Die Not der Besiegten'. In: J. Weber (ed.) *Auf dem Wege zur Republik 1945-47*, Landeszentrale für politische Bildung, Munich, pp. 187-210.

Willms, A. (1983) 'Grundzüge der Entwicklung der Frauenarbeit von 1880 bis 1980'. In: W. Müller *et al.* (1983) pp. 25-54.

Willms, A. (1983) 'Segregation auf Dauer? Zur Entwicklung des Verhältnisses von Frauenarbeit und Männerarbeit in Deutschland', 1882-1980. In: W. Müller *et al.* (1983) pp. 107-82.

Wissmann, M. and Hauck, R. (eds) (1982) *Jugendprotest im demokratischen Staat. Enquête Kommission des Deutschen Bundestages*, Edition Weitbrecht, Bonn.

Wurzbacher, G. (1952) *Leitbilder gegenwärtigen deutschen Familienlebens*, Enke, Stuttgart.

3

The Politics of Disaffection: France in the 1980s

James G. Shields

When history comes to judge the French political culture of the 1980s, it will have to take account of a singular paradox. At a moment when the 'middle ground' appears to be at a premium, when the terms *cohabitation, consensus* and *ouverture* are the currency of political commentators (Duverger, 1987; SOFRES, 1987: 47-74; Cayrol, 1988: 9-10; Lancelot, 1988: 40-44), a new extremist factor has become firmly established within the French political equation. Polling between 8 and 11 per cent nationally in every major election since its emergence in 1984, Jean-Marie Le Pen's extreme right-wing Front National has staked out and occupied the political space to the right of Jacques Chirac's Rassemblement pour la république (RPR). Le Pen's astonishing 14.4 per cent in the first round of the presidential elections on 24 April 1988 took the French extreme Right to a level of electoral support unprecedented under the Fifth Republic. Such a result for a far-right candidate in a presidential election testifies to important changes in political values and predispositions in France, and raises issues whose significance carries far beyond the boundaries of Le Pen's own electoral constituency.

One cannot hope to understand the Le Pen phenomenon without taking account of the changes which have been wrought in the French political landscape over the course of the 1980s. For the dramatic decline of the Communist power base, the unrepentant conversion of the Socialists to the politics of *rigueur*, the radicalisation of mainstream conservatism on a number of important social issues, and the emergence of a potent new force on the far-right fringe are all evidence of a substantial shift in the centre of political gravity in France. The notion of a broad-based opening of French politics towards the centre may be valid insofar as it reflects the 'diluted radicalism' which, it is argued, has come to characterise the economic debate on both sides of the political divide (Levy and Machin, 1986: 274-5). There remain, however, areas of discourse and policy within which the French political establishment, far from being engaged in any 'race for the centre' (Cotteret and Mermet, 1986: 22), has shifted significantly to the right. It is the purpose of this chapter to examine the new radical right-wing tendency in

France and to offer some corrective to the view, upheld by a number of commentators (Duverger, 1986: 120; July, 1986: 16-17; Duhamel and Jaffré, 1987: 37-42), that a moderating spirit of consensus is at work in French political debate.

The electoral rise of the Front National is the most remarkable political development in France since the Left won its historic mandate in the presidential and parliamentary elections of 1981. When François Mitterrand succeeded Valéry Giscard d'Estaing as President of the Republic, the extreme Right was little more than an amalgam of irreconcilable factions, condemned in the post-Gaullist era, it seemed, to a spiral of political alienation and decline. The derisory performance of the extreme Right in national and local elections had been a constant of French political life for almost a quarter of a century. Le Pen's own bid for the Elysée in 1981 came to grief when he failed to muster the 500 *signatures de parrainage* required in support of his candidature. In the legislative elections which followed Mitterrand's victory in June l981, the Front National laid claim to a token share in the extreme Right's 0.36 per cent of the first-round vote (Charlot, 1986: 33). Though hindsight lends its own irony to the timing of the remark, J.-C. Petitfils articulated the conviction of political commentators in general when, in 1983, he offered the following assessment of the extreme Right as a force in French politics:

> The extreme Right has disintegrated. It has ceased to be of any electoral significance, except in the purely negative sense of contributing, for example, through its calls for abstention, to the defeat of Valéry Giscard d'Estaing. Reduced to a myriad of tiny isolated groups, powerless factions and shadowy associations, it constitutes nothing more today than a historical relic (1983: 123).

In order to explain the abject failure of the far Right previously to exercise even the most modest political appeal under the Fifth Republic, one must take account of a number of separate but related factors: the opprobrium attaching to extreme-right politics in post-war France (the stigma of Vichy proved a powerful and enduring legacy in the isolation of the far Right by the political establishment as a whole); the perennial divisions of the 'nationalists' into ideologically entrenched and mutually hostile *groupuscules*; the failure of the latter to mobilise support around a set of coherent and electorally viable themes; and the critical role played by the Gaullist regime. While decolonisation and economic modernisation did, as Malcolm Anderson observes (1974: 275), provide a short-term stimulus for extreme-right activism in the late 1950s and early 1960s, the same factors proved, in the longer term, to be the very agents of its suppression. By resolving the Algerian crisis and responding with uncompromising vigour to the threat of the OAS, de Gaulle deprived the right extremists of a unifying cause and reduced their hard-core to 'little more than a collection of heroes and martyrs in Gaullist prisons' (Tucker, 1968: 87). More importantly, the establishment of a climate of political and economic stability under the Fifth Republic left the malcontents on the far Right with no prospect of exploiting the sort of dissension which had favoured the remarkable though short-lived success of the Poujadist movement in the mid-1950s.

In his study of French political parties and elections, John Frears identifies among the principal reasons for the failure of the extreme Right in the 1960s and 1970s 'the much higher level of consensus and legitimacy that [. . .] the Fifth Republic, with its stable and accepted institutions and its background of great economic development, has known' (1977: 165). If the same author is correct in his further assertion — and few political scientists would take issue with the point — that 'it is economic crisis and political instability that are the recruiting sergeants of extremist movements', then the recent surge of support for a radical party on the far-right fringe raises compelling questions about the nature and course of French political culture in the 1980s. For in a remarkably short space of time Le Pen's movement has emerged from the wilderness to become a powerful component of the French Right and a fully fledged rival to the Communists as the party of the disgruntled. Its success attests to an *aggiornamento* of right-extremist political strategy and appears to herald a new phase in the historically fraught relations between the French far Right and its mainstream political neighbours, the Gaullist RPR and centre-right Union pour la démocratie française (UDF) (Vaughan, 1987).

The performance of the Front National in the legislative elections of March 1986 confirmed the new-found strength of a movement which burst onto the national political stage in the European elections of June 1984. With its populist rhetoric and its appeal to national-chauvinist sentiment, the Front National has succeeded in wooing one voter in ten away from the established parties. It has shown a remarkable capacity to adapt itself to the exigencies of campaigning on all levels, from national to local. In the cantonal elections of 1982, the extreme Right had fielded 65 candidates and mustered 0.2 per cent of the first round vote; in the corresponding elections of 1985, Le Pen's party was in a position to contest close on 1,500 of the 2,044 cantonal seats at stake and to command 8.7 per cent of the overall national vote in the first round of balloting. This dramatic swelling of the Front National's grass-roots support was all the more remarkable since local elections of this sort provide a far from congenial platform for strident nationalist politics. Such politics were to find a more propitious forum in March 1986, when the election of 35 parliamentary *députés* and 135 regional councillors gave Le Pen's party representation for the first time in the National Assembly (with some 2.7 million votes, or 9.7 per cent of the national ballot), together with a new and influential role in a number of France's regional councils (Shields, 1987a). While the Front National's support reached its peak (22.5 per cent) in the Bouches-du-Rhône, where it emerged as the most powerful party of the Right, its new national strength was confirmed by the fact that its share of the vote fell below 5 per cent in only 14 of France's 96 metropolitan *départements* (Dupoirier and Grunberg, 1986: 248-9).

The presidential elections of 1988 provided more dramatic evidence still of the Front National's new role in French politics. With 14.4 per cent of the first round vote, Le Pen came close to equalling the score of Raymond Barre and fell only 5.5 per cent short of Jacques Chirac. In the legislative elections which followed, the Front National, with 9.65 per cent, repeated its performance of 1986, though the two-ballot majority system ensured its virtual exclusion from the National Assembly. These results illustrate the extent to which Le Pen has galvanised what appeared at first to be an aberrational protest vote into an effective electoral constituency. Though the long-term significance of Le Pen's achievement is far from clear, the rise of the Front National poses a number of pressing questions for the political analyst. What, in the France of the 1980s, has provided a seedbed for the growth of a movement such as Le Pen's? What changes have been brought about in the social and political value-system which have allowed the entry into the mainstream political theatre of a tendency that was hitherto excluded? What is the nature of Le Pen's electoral appeal, and what has been its impact upon the contemporary political debate in France?

In attempting to address these questions, political commentators have concentrated upon the social and economic *conjoncture* within which the Front National has attained its new and startling level of support. Mounting unemployment and inflation rates, a shrinking manufacturing and industrial base, the erosion of purchasing power, increased taxation, a spiralling budget deficit and a weakened franc have all been features of the French economy's attempt to grapple with the realities of recession in recent years. Since its foundation in 1958, the Fifth Republic has played host to an era of great economic and sociological change. The optimism which marked the early years of modernisation and prosperity have given way to a deepening pessimism about France's ability to emerge from a perceived cycle of socio-economic decline (SOFRES, 1985: 112-27). In a climate where radical solutions commend themselves ever more readily to the public imagination, the immigrant in particular has become an object of resentment. Analysis of the Le Pen vote reveals a striking correlation between the three variables of urbanisation, industrialisation and immigration. Support for the Front National is strong in the highly industrialised regions of France — notably

Ile-de-France and Rhône-Alpes — where Le Pen has been adept at exploiting tensions over unemployment, immigration and a rising inner-city crime rate. The real bastions of Front National support, however, are the *départements* of the south (Bouches-du-Rhône, Alpes-Maritimes, Vaucluse, Var, Pyrénées-Orientales, Hérault and Gard) where a high proportion of North African immigrants coexist with large numbers of *repatriés* from Algeria who are receptive to Le Pen's nationalist rhetoric and his undying nostalgia for *Algérie française*.

The *pied-noir* vote, however, represents but a fraction of an electorate which is characterised above all by its heterogeneity. For Le Pen has made inroads into areas where his success cannot be readily ascribed to factors such as immigration and unemployment. While he draws support mainly from the RPR and UDF parties, the evidence is that he has capitalised on an electoral volatility that spans the political spectrum (Perrineau, 1985; Charlot, 1986; Mitra, 1988). The appeal of the Front National cuts across conventional socio-professional and ideological boundaries. The findings of a number of surveys indicate that a very considerable percentage of those who voted Front National in the European elections of June 1984 or in the legislative elections of 1986 had supported François Mitterrand in the second ballot of the 1981 presidential election (Lorien *et al.*, 1985: 222-3; Jaffré, 1986: 215; Ysmal, 1986: 22; Schain, 1987: 234). Between the two rounds of the 1988 presidential election, as many as one in four Le Pen voters are estimated to have switched their support to Mitterrand rather than to his right-wing opponent, Jacques Chirac (*Le Monde: Dossiers et Documents*, May 1988: 82-3). There are, of course, severe limits to what such extrapolations tell us about the character of the Le Pen vote: firstly, because presidential elections are such highly personalised affairs; secondly, because the *rapports de forces* between Right and Left in the 1981 and 1988 presidential elections is indicative of a significant though by no means definitive — witness the legislative elections of 1986 and 1988 — shift in the voting pattern (Grunberg, 1985); thirdly, and most importantly, because the Front National has become the vehicle for what Jérôme Jaffré calls an 'electorate of refusal', with no firm ideological anchor in any one political camp (*Le Monde*, 26 May 1987). Such partial indices, however, for all their shortcomings, do serve to underline the fact that Le Pen's breakthrough has been achieved within a context of electoral instability in which a number of commentators see signs of a significant dealignment in French political allegiance (Grunberg, 1985; Inglehart and Rabier, 1986; Eatwell, 1986).

While examination of the Front National electorate reveals a striking social, professional and ideological diversity, a much greater coherence emerges on the question of voting motivation. Among the major preoccupations expressed by Front National voters, opinion polls consistently indicate the overriding importance accorded to the dual themes of law and order and immigration. In surveys conducted after the European elections of June 1984, the percentage of voters citing immigration as a priority was up to nine times higher among Front National voters than among those of any other party; on the question of insecurity, it was considerably higher than that of the traditionally security-conscious RPR and UDF electorate (Lorien *et al.*, 1985: 221). The term *insécurité* has, in the course of the 1980s, taken on a new dimension of meaning in French political parlance. A broad and increasingly emotive catchword which finds no ready translation into English, *l'insécurité* is, as J. Marcus observes, 'a short-hand term for the fear and uncertainty prompted by economic recession and social change. It embraces fears of juvenile delinquency, growing street crime, unemployment and racial tensions' (Marcus, 1984: 510). While current 'liberal' themes — such as the free-market economy and the evils of *étatisme* — have their place in Le Pen's rhetoric, they are subordinated to the ready political capital that can be made from crime and unemployment figures, or estimates of the illegal immigrant population in France.

In response to the anxieties aroused by such issues, Le Pen extols a lost age of family morality, civic order and patriotic virtue. The restoration of capital punishment, the abrogation of the 1975 Abortion Law and an active policy of immigrant repatriation are central to the political message of this self-styled Cassandra who offers the vision of a nationally debilitated and spiritually degenerate France falling prey to the insidious forces of Marxist ideology and Islamic Arab influence. The French, intones Le Pen, are no longer at home in a country where medical, educational, housing and prison facilities are increasingly the preserve of a foreign population. In a ringing denunciation of the policies of former governments, he calls for the withdrawal of welfare benefits from immigrants and argues a simple equation between the unemployment and immigration statistics. For Le Pen, however, the immigrant issue is as much a symptom as a cause of the spiral of moral and cultural decadence into which France has sunk. Abortion, sexual promiscuity, homosexuality, and, more recently, the AIDS virus, he charges, are all features of a 'genocide' perpetrated by the French upon themselves. *La dénatalité*, the relative decline of the birth-rate within France's changing demographic profile, is a common enough theme in French political discourse; but Le Pen has given it a new and sharper edge by presenting it within the perspective of a relentless colonisation of France by Islam.

Yet, for all their critical importance, the factors referred to above — economic recession, unemployment, urban tension and immigration — provide only a partial response to the questions raised by the Le Pen phenomenon. The reason for this is, quite simply, that none of these issues is specific to the 1980s. The so-called '*crise*' has been with France for close on two decades; Giscard d'Estaing presided not over a reversal of unemployment in the 1970s, but over a dramatic three-fold increase in its level; the Barre Government (1976-1981), when it relinquished office, left a panoply of measures to protect public '*sécurité*' against what the then Minister for Justice, Alain Peyrefitte, described as an 'alarming' increase in violent crime (*L'Année politique, économique et sociale en France 1980*, 1981: 69); the immigration issue, with all its racist concomitants, had already become a question of national political import in 1974, when the onset of recession and the ensuing polemic over immigrant labour forced Giscard d'Estaing to call an official halt to further immigration on any meaningful scale. The rejection reflex towards North African immigrants in particular, far from being a new phenomenon in France, has been evident in some of its least edifying aspects since the 1960s (Freeman, 1979: 99-284 *passim*; Schain, 1987: 238).

While these enduring social and economic issues provide the cutting edge of Le Pen's electoral success, and while they remain essential to any analysis of it, they must be viewed within the developing *political* context of the Fifth Republic. A scion of the Poujadist movement, Jean-Marie Le Pen, has been present throughout the post-war history of the French far Right; the Front National has been in existence and doggedly campaigning since 1972. Yet it is only now that Le Pen and his party have found a forum for their ideas. Consideration must be given, therefore, to the political climate within which Le Pen's recent success has been achieved, if one is to understand that success and take account of any light which it has to shed upon the current relationship between civil and political society in France.

When the Socialists came to power in 1981, 'hope' and 'change' were the two notions which best summed up the political mood. Mitterrand stood as the 'candidate of hope' and won what was widely acknowledged to be a mandate for sweeping reform (Hainsworth, 1981; Northcutt, 1982). Of his chief rival for the Elysée, the outgoing President Giscard d'Estaing, the converse was true. He was perceived as a pragmatic and able technocrat, but one who had run short of reformist zeal (Machin and Wright, 1982). The contest between 'Mitterrandism' and 'Giscardism' was seen not just as a political choice but as a *choix de société*. 'There was only one winner on May 10', declared the new Socialist President in his inaugural address: 'it was hope' (*Le Monde*, 22 May 1981).

This desire for change, which Mitterrand invoked as the basis for his own election, seemed to be confirmed by a landslide majority for the Socialists in the parliamentary elections that followed in June 1981. For the second time only in the history of the Fifth Republic, a single party could lay claim to an overall majority in the National Assembly. 'Social' and 'political' France were at last, according to the President, in tune. In the opening session of the new Parliament in July 1981, Prime Minister Pierre Mauroy stressed the tide of popular expectation which had borne his party into office. 'By electing [. . .] a broad parliamentary majority in keeping with the presidential majority, the French wanted to give the force of law to change. This hope, or rather this demand for change [. . .], reflects the will of the majority of the people' (*Le Monde*, 10 July 1981).

Such was the prelude to the Left's first period of office under the Fifth Republic. A 23-year political tradition had been broken. Until then, the business of government had been the preserve of the Right, while the Left remained the repository of hope for a better future. In that very fact, however, lay the seeds of an intractable problem. After almost a quarter of a century of right-wing rule and left-wing promise, too much was expected too soon from the Mitterrand regime. Ill-prepared for the reality of wielding power in a period of deepening international recession, the Mauroy Government set about implementing a neo-Keynesian policy of 'reflation in one country', or the construction, as one commentator put it, of 'a socialist island in a capitalist world' (McCormick, 1983: 50). To an electorate weary of Barrist austerity, Mitterrand offered not only social justice but economic recovery too (Northcutt, 1985a: 91-116). The early 'state of grace' (1981-82) saw the introduction of a series of important social and economic reforms which were to herald a new political departure: a programme for the nationalisation of banks and industrial groups was set in train; a large number of public sector jobs were created; workers' rights were extended through the *Lois Auroux*; the working week was reduced to 39 hours and the retirement age lowered to 60; a fifth week of annually paid holiday was introduced; the national minimum wage (SMIC), family allowances and old age and disability benefits were increased; a wealth tax was imposed, and the reimbursement of abortion costs became statutory.

Whatever the initial popularity of these and other reforms, their net effect was to deliver a powerful shock to the French economy (Harrison, 1983: 27-39). The public spending programme required to sustain the Government's policy of reflation sent the budget deficit soaring, pushed inflation above 14 per cent and forced a devaluation of the franc. While investment levels fell, unemployment remained obdurately high. Between 1974 and 1981, unemployment had risen from 2.3 per cent to 7.4 per cent; by March 1982, it had passed the politically damaging two million mark and stood at 8.7 per cent (McCormick, 1983: 47, 58). Inflation, unemployment, living standards and social justice had been the most severely indicted areas of Giscard's *septennat* (Machin and Wright, 1982: 23). After a year in office, it was on the latter only that the Socialists' record could be seen as an improvement upon that of their predecessors.

To this extent, one can contend, the Socialists were caught in a spiral of their own creation. The more vigorously they had inveighed against the causes of popular discontent while in opposition, the more they had raised the stakes against their own eventual failure to resolve these when in government. The politically emotive issues of unemployment and inflation were to rebound with unforeseen effect upon the Mauroy administration. As the official language changed from optimism to 'realism', a series of deflationary and austerity measures — for which 'discipline', 'rigour' and 'efficiency' became euphemistic by-words — recalled the much maligned Barre Plan of the late 1970s. Measures introduced to redress the economic deficit included an income tax surcharge, a temporary wage and price freeze, special levies on petrol, tobacco and alcohol, and higher energy and public transport costs. The abrupt switch from reflation to economic retrenchment suggested vacillation and incompetence on the part of the Government, while calling into question its whole reformist strategy (Northcutt, 1985b). To the ranks of disenchanted Socialism were added those voters who, having deserted the 'liberal' Right more out of impatience than conviction, witnessed with increasing dismay the early fruits of the so-called *'rupture avec le capitalisme.'*

As the loss of governmental credibility led to a generalised disenchantment, French public opinion began to swing massively away from the Socialists. The defeat of the Left in the cantonal elections of March 1982 signalled the loss of an electoral majority that the Government would fail to regain in any of the subsequent municipal (1983), European (1984), cantonal (1985), regional or parliamentary (1986) elections. The popularity ratings of Mitterrand and Mauroy provide a graphic measure of the collapse in public confidence. In June 1981, fully 74 per cent of those polled in a SOFRES survey registered confidence in Mitterrand's capacity to resolve France's problems, while 71 per cent accorded a similar confidence to Pierre Mauroy. By the summer of 1984, Mitterrand's confidence rating had dropped as low as 38 per cent, while Mauroy's plummeted to a dismal 25 per cent prior to his resignation in July (SOFRES, 1984: 36, 50; 1985: 132, 143).

As growing industrial unrest and public protest (most notably over a controversial bill to extend state control to private schools) conspired to dramatise the Government's unpopularity, the slump in the personal stock of the President and Premier was compounded by a sharp decline in the image of the Left as a whole. Though the Socialists' austerity policy did, from 1984 under the new Prime Minister, Laurent Fabius, induce positive signs of economic recovery (a striking reduction in inflation, a stabilising of the unemployment rate, a much reduced budget deficit, higher corporate profits, an increase in economic growth, industrial investment and purchasing power), the disenchantment had gone too far to be readily reversed. A number of polls conducted after 1983 suggested that words and concepts generally associated with the Left ('nationalisation', 'trade unions', 'Socialism') had become increasingly negative in their connotations. Terms and values, on the other hand, traditionally held to be the preserve of the Right ('competition', 'free enterprise', 'profit') appeared to enjoy a new-found popular currency (SOFRES, 1984: 85-7; Perrineau, 1986: 42-3; Rizzuto, 1987: 154-6; Duhamel and Jaffré, 1987: 53). The most telling index of such a shift in political attitudes was the new and unabashed frankness with which the voting public seemed prepared to embrace the word *'droite'* itself (SOFRES, 1985: 93; Rémond, 1987: 131-2). It is a peculiar fact of French political life that, 'unlike politicians of the left, who revel in the title, those of the right never like to be described as such. They have always preferred a label such as *modéré*, *indépendant* or even *centre-gauche*; only the very muscular right likes to call itself *'la droite'* (Hanley *et al.*, 1979: 135). Notwithstanding the continuing importance of the 'liberal' qualification in the contemporary Right's definition of itself, the 1980s saw distinct signs of a reversal in this trend. As the Socialists were forced increasingly to abandon the old redoubts of Leftist ideology and discourse, to turn instead to economic pragmatism and the 'management of the status quo' (Cahm, 1983: 60), the notion of 'the Right' gained a new legitimacy in the French political conscience (Rémond, 1987: 131-2). Indeed, it is one of the more paradoxical legacies of the Left's term of office that, from 1981 to 1986, it presided over the renewed expression of a hard core conservatism which had been forced onto the retreat in the years preceding the Socialists' victory. The qualified espousal by Raymond Barre of the Pétainist maxim *'Travail, Famille, Patrie'* during the 1986 legislative election campaign is but one aspect of a resurgent appeal to traditional conservative values which would have paid few political dividends in 1981 (*Le Monde*, 17 December 1985).

What is striking, however, is the fact that this clear shift in political dispositions did not rebound automatically to the advantage of the mainstream Right. In the period from autumn 1982 to summer 1983, when polls showed public confidence in the Left to be sliding from 40 per cent to 26 per cent, confidence in the traditional right-wing parties rose only marginally from 40 per cent to 43 per cent (SOFRES, 1984: 73-4). The reasons for this are undoubtedly related to the perceived disunity between and within the RPR and UDF, and to the fact that their defeat in 1981 had dealt a severe blow to their credibility as a viable alternative to the Left in government. A more fundamental reason, however, why the mainstream Right did not benefit more comprehensively from the *déçus du socialisme* can be identified in the deep-seated scepticism which has come to characterise current attitudes in France towards the political class as a whole. Political disaffection among the French voting public is, of course, nothing new; de Gaulle himself both exploited and scorned what he saw as the readiness of the French to turn against those whom they elect to political office. Such disaffection, however, appears to have reached new depths in the 1980s and to have contributed to what a number of commentators describe as the 'widening gap between civil and political society' in France (Rizzuto, 1987: 155; Perrineau, 1986: 49; SOFRES, 1985: 111). Recent opinion polls abound in accusations that politicians are divorced from the realities they purport to represent, that they lack competence, integrity and, above all, the capacity to resolve France's problems (SOFRES, 1985: 11-29; 1987: 162). In a survey conducted for *Le Monde* in August 1984, no fewer than 82 per cent of the respondents claimed that politicians were not to be believed in what they said (*Le Monde*, 6 September 1984). In the light of such unsparing censure, the first address by Prime Minister Laurent Fabius to the National Assembly in July 1984 takes on a fuller meaning and contains what appears to be more than a tacit acknowledgment of the previous Government's failure to keep faith with its public. I promise, pledged Fabius, 'one thing to the French: I shall tell you the truth' (*Le Monde*, 26 July 1984; Northcutt, 1985b: 159).

It is within this context that the Le Pen phenomenon must be interpreted. The sweeping victory and equally sweeping discredit of the Left destabilised the voting pattern and contributed greatly to the electoral volatility from which the Front National subsequently benefited. The high-water mark of the extreme Right's fortunes between 1981 and 1986 — 10.95 per cent of the vote in the European elections of June 1984 — coincided with the nadir of the Left's popularity in government. In an election where the Socialist Left fell from almost 38 per cent to just over 20 per cent, and the PCF from 16 per cent to 11 per cent, the RPR and UDF — at 43 per cent — showed barely any advance on the performance which had seen their parliamentary representation decimated in 1981. Nor was the traditional Right to do significantly better in the legislative elections which returned it to power with a wafer-thin majority in 1986 (*Le Monde: Dossiers et Documents*, March 1986: 67-8).

This does not, of course, argue any uniform transfer of votes from the Left to the extreme Right, but rather a generalised upset in the pattern of voting allegiance which permitted the Front National in the 1980s to benefit from the 'discredit' of Left and Right alike. Le Pen's place on the periphery of the political establishment, his freedom to attack at will the 'Band of Four' (RPR, UDF, PS, PCF), was a valuable asset in his mobilising of the *mécontents*. His extra-parliamentary status before 1986 allowed him to harness this protest vote and to capitalise much more readily than the institutionalised parties on the changing political mood. Such is the optimal posture for the demagogue, and Le Pen was able fully to exploit it by his tireless insistence on the populist themes of unemployment, law and order, immigration and anti-Communism.

The Front National electorate, we have argued, is a composite constituency which cuts across class and socio-professional boundaries. For R. Inglehart and J.-R. Rabier, the success of the Front National in France is indicative of a long-term shift in the advanced industrial societies of Western Europe from class-based to 'value-based', or 'issue-based', politics (Inglehart and Rabier, 1986). It is impossible, certainly, to define the Le Pen vote in strictly economic terms. Though unemployment, for example, constitutes a powerful theme in the Front National's rhetorical arsenal, it appears most effective when presented in its broadest, least 'economic' terms: as a *symptom* of a generalised climate of insecurity, or as a *consequence* of immigration. The unemployment question in itself, when divorced from the security and immigration issues, appears as an altogether weaker mobilising factor in the Front National vote (Lorien *et al.*, 1985: 221; Perrineau, 1985: 27; Schain, 1987: 237-8), though Le Pen's performance on 24 April 1988 indicates that he has succeeded in extending considerably his appeal to blue-collar workers and the unemployed (*Le Monde: Dossiers et Documents*, May 1988: 41, 44).

In the run-up to the 1986 legislative elections, a SOFRES survey indicated that Front National voters were markedly less motivated than any other electorate by questions such as employment, economic recovery, purchasing power and social equality. In the importance accorded to 'security', immigration, 'the restoration of order' and France's world role, however, Front National voters outdistanced by far the constituencies of all the other parties (SOFRES, 1987: 107). 'Today', claim Inglehart and Rabier, 'the most heated issues tend to be non-economic' (Inglehart and Rabier, 1986: 473). Though the premise itself is subject to some considerable caution, it is arguable that the inability of the mainstream parties to respond adequately to the initial challenge of the extreme Right stemmed from their failure to appreciate what truth there was in this point when applied to the case of the Front National. Caught up in the economic debate of the *alternance*, they failed to take the full measure of the issues, or 'value priorities', for which Le Pen's party was to become a focus. The rise of the Front National is, within this perspective, an example of what can happen when the established parties are perceived to have failed in addressing 'concerns in such areas as safety from crime, and problems linked with immigration and cultural change' (Inglehart and Rabier, 1986: 473). Schain makes an important point in this respect when he asserts that 'the issues of race and crime, around which the National Front has mobilised large numbers of voters, are the kinds of 'quality of life' issues the potential of which has been generally ignored in the literature on post-industrial values' (1987: 229).

After taking stock of the Front National's new-found appeal, the political class shifted its orientation in order to meet Le Pen on his own ground. This had serious implications in terms of the ensuing political debate. We have made a distinction between economy-based and value-based politics; and it is here that we should return to the question of 'consensus' posed at the outset. For if it is the case, as Levy and Machin claim, that the 1980s have seen the emergence of a 'moderate, managerial consensus' between Right and Left on economic questions (Levy and Machin, 1986: 275), the same is by no means true of those issues which — though central to the current *political* agenda — lie outside the strictly 'economic' debate, and where Le Pen has brought to bear a radicalising influence far beyond the boundaries of his own electoral province.

When the Socialist Government took office in 1981, civil liberties had a foremost place on the agenda. Among the first measures implemented by the Mauroy administration were the abolition of capital punishment and the dismantling of the controversial *Cour de sûreté de l'Etat*, a special tribunal set up by de Gaulle to deal with State security offences in the wake of the Algerian crisis and subsequent OAS terrorism. Two highly contentious public order Acts from previous legislatures — the *Loi anti-casseurs* and the *Loi sécurité et liberté* — were also repealed. The powers of search available to police were strictly regulated, and the conditions under which suspects could be held without charge were redefined. The underlying intention of these reforms was to curtail the intrusion of police powers upon the citizen and to shift the long-term emphasis from a punitive to a preventive philosophy. A presidential amnesty was granted to a large number of prisoners, the right of political asylum was reaffirmed, the legal aid system was improved and new measures were implemented to halt discrimination against certain marginalised groups such as homosexuals (Wright, 1981: 423-4).

Nowhere, however, was the new libertarian spirit which informed the early period of Socialist rule more apparent than in the series of measures which were effected to improve the lot of France's 4.5 million strong immigrant population. In an attempt to correct the excesses of previous legislation, the Government placed tight new restrictions on the guidelines for the expulsion of immigrants and abandoned the scheme of voluntary repatriation which the Giscard regime had sought to promote by a system of financial incentives. The right of association was granted and an amnesty extended to illegal immigrants who could give evidence of secure employment. Most potentially far-reaching of all was the presidential undertaking — spelt out in proposition 80 of Mitterrand's 1981 manifesto — to extend voting rights in municipal elections to immigrants who had been resident in France for five years or more.

After 1981, however, the political climate underwent a profound change. The importance accorded to the question of public security brought about a sharp reversal in law and order policy and prompted a hardening of attitudes towards the immigrant community

(SOFRES, 1985: 75-88; 1986: 121-9; Perrineau, 1986: 45-7). While France had a conservative Government which could be seen to be tackling the issues of crime and immigration, the discourse of the hard Right was effectively neutralised. The accession to power of a left-wing Government which could readily be accused of 'laxism' in the fight against crime and of pursuing an overly liberal policy towards foreigners in France (SOFRES, 1984: 125) provided an expedient focus for the far Right's 'strategy of tension' on the breakdown of law and order and the dangers of immigration (Hainsworth, 1982a: 158, 162). While Le Pen made the running on these issues, the other parties became engaged in an electoral 'auction' which moved the debate rightwards and forced the Socialists radically to revise their original stance. Having insisted initially on the link between insecurity and unemployment, the Socialists were obliged ultimately to address the former as a problem in itself and to adopt a posture which, by its own former standards, would have been deemed repressive. Identity controls and special judicial procedures, while they might be anathema in principle, were found to have their place in the world of *realpolitik* (Hainsworth, 1982b: 220). In the months following the Left's heavy defeat in the European elections of June 1984, the Fabius Government placed increasing emphasis on the need to bolster law and order and to reassure French public opinion (*Lettre de Matignon*, 1984, nos. 127, 133). The new will with which the Socialists came to address the security question culminated, in summer 1985, with the bizarre spectacle of a left-wing Government proposing a massive increase in the police budget and pushing it through, at a time of comprehensive cutbacks in public spending, against opposition from the RPR and UDF benches (*Le Monde*, 12 July 1985).

On the immigration question, the rightward shift of Socialist policy was even more pronounced. The exploitation of the immigrant issue by the Right and, more notably, the extreme Right in the municipal elections of 1983 prompted a revision by the Government of the policies articulated two years earlier. The launch of a resolute campaign to combat illegal immigration was accompanied, in 1984, by the reintroduction of financial incentives to encourage the repatriation of 'regular' immigrants. Border security was tightened and the rate of deportations stepped up. Stiffer penalties were imposed on the employers of illegal immigrants, whilst the *'regroupement familial'* of immigrants and their dependents became subject to stringent new conditions (*Lettre de Matignon*, 1983, no. 71; 1984, no. 123). In an interview for *Les Temps Modernes* in spring 1984, the then Minister of the Interior, Gaston Defferre, having lamented the disquieting turn which the immigration debate had taken, proceeded to depict France as a seedbed of Islamic fundamentalism and a logistical haven for international terrorism. In terms that might have been borrowed from the discourse of Le Pen himself, the Socialist Interior Minister claimed that France had become a refuge for illegal immigrants from the 'four corners of the globe', whose arrival was nothing short of an 'invasion' threatening the very fabric of French society and the value-systems on which it was founded (Lanzmann, 1984). The new Prime Minister, Laurent Fabius, far from denouncing such sentiments, appeared, on his arrival in office in summer 1984, to give them his endorsement. In a televised interview in September 1984, Fabius caused consternation among a number of his political colleagues when he referred to the rise of the far Right as a response to real questions which had to be addressed. To concede as much was, of course, both to endorse Le Pen and to suggest that the Government had been slow in taking cognizance of the issues upon which the latter had constructed his electoral platform.

Such instances provided clear evidence of a deviation by the Socialists from the trajectory upon which they had embarked in 1981. As for the pledge to grant immigrants a vote in local elections, it was — despite Mitterrand's continued allegiance to the *principle* — quite simply dropped from the Socialist agenda, in deference to a French public opinion which showed itself increasingly ill-disposed towards any such enfranchisement of the immigrant community (SOFRES, 1985: 84). What is striking about the measures introduced by the Government in 1983 and 1984 is not that they were new, but rather that they resembled so closely in their intention the Giscardian reforms which the Socialists had been at such pains to overturn. While the latter remained keen to mark themselves off from a number of the Right's more radical proposals, there were several aspects of the immigration debate upon which the Socialist Left and the mainstream Right moved, in the course of the 1980s, so close as to become almost indistinguishable. This fact was never better dramatised than in October 1985 when the then Prime Minister, Laurent Fabius, and the leader of the opposition, Jacques Chirac, met in a televised *face-à-face*. On that occasion, the Socialist Fabius' treatment of the immigration issue differed neither in tone nor in substance from that of his Gaullist counterpart. As evidence of his Government's resolve in responding to the mounting public concern over what he termed an 'incontestable problem', Fabius found himself reeling off the numbers of immigrants who had been deported or who had taken up the offer of subsidised repatriation (*Le Monde*, 29 October 1985). The conspicuous absence of any reference to egalitarian values or civil liberties suggested that the Socialists had relinquished much of the ground over which they once boasted an undisputed ideological hegemony.

The return of the Right to power in 1986 gave new impetus to the rightward swing of the political debate on the security and immigration issues. Confident that its policies would be endorsed by French public opinion, the Chirac Government set about implementing an electoral platform where the social emphasis lay squarely on strong-arm law and order. The appointment of the belligerent Charles Pasqua as Minister of the Interior, and the creation of a special minister with responsibility for public security, signalled the vigour with which Chirac intended to tackle the immigration and public order issues. Police identity controls, abolished as a widespread practice and made subject to strict guidelines under the Socialists, were brought back as a vital weapon in the fight against crime. While random police spot-checks became the order of the day, broader powers were granted for the surveillance and detention of suspected criminals and terrorists. The application of legal penalties was stiffened, and special courts without juries were set up to try terrorist offences. Controls on non-EEC foreigners entering France were made more stringent, together with the conditions governing political asylum and extradition. Police were given wider powers to deal with illegal immigrants, whose summary expulsion could be effected as an administrative rather than a judicial exercise. The Government also drew up a bill to reform the Nationality Code. The express purpose of the proposed reform was to tighten the procedures whereby immigrants could acquire French citizenship (Shields, 1987b). The bill was based on the principle, outlined in the joint RPR-UDF 'Platform for Government', that French citizenship for second generation immigrants should no longer be granted automatically but should be applied for through legal channels and should presuppose an undertaking on the part of the candidate to abide by the laws of the Fifth Republic (*RPR-UDF: Plate-forme pour gouverner ensemble*, 1986: 14). The Government did, it is true, stop short of enacting an RPR proposal to restrict to French households only the introduction of a special family allowance intended to promote the national birth-rate (*L e Renouveau: Pacte RPR pour la France*: 85; *Le Monde*, 17 January 1986). The fact, however, that proposals such as this featured openly in the programme of France's largest right-wing party illustrates the extent to which previously marginal, hardline policies had found a new currency in mainstream political debate.

The Chirac Government's reforms, between 1986 and 1988, provoked criticism from the Socialist President Mitterrand, the left-wing opposition in the National Assembly, human rights organisations, the French episcopacy and the immigrant community at large. France was, charged ex-Socialist minister Yvette Roudy, taking on some of the aspects of 'a fascistic police state', where a law-and-order mentality was in danger of subverting democratic values (*Le Monde*, 27 May 1986; Hainsworth, 1987: 35-6). Another stern critic of the Chirac Government was Harlem Désir, leader of the anti-racist movement *SOS-Racisme*. This organisation, while it proved instrumental in mobilising a cross-section of public support, lacked the *political* dimension required to provide an adequate counterweight to the rightward swing of the immigration and public order debates. Harlem Désir's decision not to stand as a candidate in the 1988 presidential election was perhaps in part a recognition of the limits within which such a movement could operate, given that a significant proportion of its support resided in a disenfranchised immigrant community.

Within the French public as a whole, the Chirac reforms met with remarkably little resistance. The brutal wave of terrorist bombings which disrupted the capital in September 1986 did much to vindicate the Government's muscular stance and to make French public opinion amenable to any measures which would ensure the 'normalisation' of daily life. France's reaction to the resurgence of terrorist activism within its borders provided a classic example of what Cerny sees as the power of the terrorist phenomenon to threaten liberal-democratic norms by prompting a collective reflex which, 'far from evoking a mass outcry or protest, not only carries public opinion along with greater repression but also creates public — "democratic" — pressure for tougher measures still' (1982: 94).

This is one reason why the Left, for all its protestations, was unable to mount an effective challenge to what it denounced as the excesses of a reactionary administration. In the first place, public perceptions of crime, terrorism and immigration made it difficult — not to say electorally imprudent — to contest too strongly the Chirac Government's objectives in these areas. Mitterrand's role as the champion of egalitarian ideals and civil liberties, it might be further argued, was undermined by his choice for the 1986 parliamentary elections of a system of proportional representation which, while weakening the conservative mainstream, opened the doors of the National Assembly to an extreme Right that kept up a relentless pressure on Chirac to implement radical reform. This raises the wider question of the role which the Left can now aspire to play in the public order and immigration debates. For the Socialists in 1986 lost not only their electoral majority: they lost also, in some considerable measure, the claim to moral ascendancy which had been the prerogative of an opposition that had never, prior to 1981, been called upon to exercise power under the Fifth Republic. While the non-Communist Left may congratulate itself on having emerged from office in 1986, and been returned to it in 1988, with considerably more realism than it evinced in 1981, its new *culture de gouvernement* has, in this sense, been bought at a price. The Socialists' reversion to their historic oppositional stance proved a temporary phenomenon; but they are no more the bearers of a millennial political vision. This has damaged the power of the Left to dictate the terms of political debate on a number of sensitive issues. What consensus there is on the law and order and immigration questions is built largely on the Right's terms — and it is a far cry from what the Socialists of 1981 would have considered to be 'moderate'. This gives some point to the view of Garnier and Janover, who argue that the dividing line between 'Left' and 'Right' in France has come increasingly in the 1980s to denote not two essentially distinct visions of the social order, but rather 'two types of conservatism, . . . the one reactionary, the other progressive' (1986: 19).

The political realities of France in the 1980s are complex and ambiguous. While the Socialists have traded their radical-left rhetoric for a new language of managerial pragmatism, the Right has found it prudent not to campaign for any crude *retour en arrière* that would systematically undo the reforms of the 1981-86 legislature. Hence the retention by the Chirac Government of a number of popular — if costly — Socialist reforms, such as the 39 hour week, the fifth week of annual holiday and retirement at 60. Such an apparent spirit of accommodation must, however, be interpreted with care. Whilst the experience of the Socialists since 1981 points up the current fragility of voting allegiance in France, the groundswell of popular disenchantment which has favoured the growth of a powerful far-right constituency has opened new areas of political and ideological uncertainty to parties and electorates across the political spectrum. What *is* certain is that the emergence of a radical new force to the right of Jacques Chirac's RPR has seriously altered the balance of French politics on those issues where Le Pen has seized the political initiative. The wooing of a disaffected and increasingly disaffiliated voting public, moreover, has revealed a disquieting element of opportunism within the major parties. The Right has, between 1983 and 1988, been subject to the political dilemma posed by the extreme Right's success. While the clear rightward shift in mainstream debate on the issues of cultural pluralism and public order has done much to accredit Le Pen's political message, a number of electoral deals with the traditional conservative parties have helped to consolidate the Front National's newly acquired political legitimacy. In those municipal and regional councils where the Right owes its majority to the support of the Front National, the latter has been rewarded by a number of influential posts. The ambivalence of the RPR and UDF in responding — both politically and tactically — to the challenge issued by Le Pen has served to obscure a once clear demarcation line between the 'moderate' and 'extremist' currents in French right-wing debate.

The Chirac government proved to be no more than a two-year interregnum in the politics of the Fifth Republic. With the period of *'cohabitation'* being replaced by a period of coalition-type 'government from the centre', French politics have entered a new and uncertain phase. The return to a two-round majority voting system all but eliminated Le Pen's party from the National Assembly in the legislative elections of June 1988; but this in itself offers no solution to the long-term problems posed by the rise of the extreme

THE POLITICS OF DISAFFECTION: FRANCE IN THE 1980S

Right in the 1980s. That some 4.4 million electors — 14.4 per cent of the total national vote — should have endorsed Le Pen's candidacy for the presidency on 24 April 1988 demonstrates clearly the extent to which the mainstream parties have failed to mobilise a very significant proportion of the French voting public. The 1988 presidential election, unlike its 1981 and 1974 predecessors, was fought not on the theme of change but on that of continuity. New societies are no more the vogue. Any talk of consolidation, consensus or *ouverture*, however, must take account not only of the 80 per cent of voters who stand, broadly speaking, on the so-called 'middle ground'; it must also seek to embrace those 20 per cent on the far Right and far Left who refuse their confidence to the only parties who have a realistic prospect of holding office. While the Communists have been reduced to the role of a junior partner on the Left, the Front National poses for the parties of the Right a problem for which the solution is yet to be found. The challenge for the mainstream Right and Left alike lies in eschewing the politics of disaffection and in endeavouring to redefine a political vision for a France which has undergone more profound political change in the 1980s than in any other period in the history of the Fifth Republic. The success with which this challenge is met may do more to determine the future of the Front National than all the efforts of Jean-Marie Le Pen and his far-right *confrères*.

REFERENCES

Anderson, M. (1974) *Conservative Politics in France*, Allen and Unwin, London.

L'année politique, économique et sociale en France, 1980 (1981), Moniteur, Paris.

Cahm, E. (1983) 'Political Parties'. In: J.E. Flower (ed.) *France Today*, 5th edition, Methuen, London, pp. 31-64.

Cayrol, R. (1988) 'Gauche, droite et tentation centriste', *Le Journal des Elections*, 3, pp. 9-10.

Cerny, P.G. (1982) 'Non-Terrorism and the Politics of Repressive Tolerance'. In: P.G. Cerny (ed.) *Social Movements and Protest in France*, Frances Pinter, London, pp. 94-124.

Charlot, M. (1986) 'L'émergence du Front national', *Revue française de Science politique*, 36 (1), pp. 30-45.

Cotteret, J.-M. and Mermet, G. (1986) *La bataille des images*, Larousse, Paris.

Duhamel, O. and Jaffré, J. (1987) *Le nouveau président*, Seuil, Paris.

Dupoirier, E. and Grunberg, G. (1986) *Mars 1986: la drôle de défaite de la gauche*, PUF, Paris.

Duverger, M. (1986) *Bréviaire de la cohabitation*, PUF, Paris.

Duverger, M. (1987) *La cohabitation des Français*, PUF, Paris.

Eatwell, R. (1986) 'The French General Election of March 1986', *Political Quarterly*, 57 (3), pp. 315-21.

Frears, J.R. (1977) *Political Parties and Elections in the French Fifth Republic*, Hurst and Co., London.

Freeman, G.P. (1979) *Immigrant Labor and Racial Conflict in Industrial Societies. The French and British Experience, 1945-75*, Princeton University Press.

Garnier, J.-P. and Janover, L. (1986) *La deuxième droite*, Robert Laffont, Paris.

Grunberg, G. (1985) 'France'. In: I. Crewe and D. Denver (eds) *Electoral Change in Western Democracies. Patterns and Sources of Electoral Volatility*, Croom Helm, Beckenham, pp. 202-29.

Hainsworth, P. (1981) 'A Majority for the President: The French Left and the Presidential and Parliamentary Elections of 1981', *Parliamentary Affairs*, Autumn.

Hainsworth, P. (1982a) 'Anti-Semitism and Neo-Fascism on the Contemporary Right'. In: P.G. Cerny (ed.) *Social Movements and Protest in France*, Frances Pinter, London, pp. 146-71.

Hainsworth, P. (1982b) 'France under Mitterrand: Domestic Problems', *The World Today*, 48, June, pp. 215-23.

Hainsworth, P. (1987) 'From Opposition to Office: The French Right After the March 1986 Legislative Elections', *Contemporary French Civilization*, XI (1), pp. 26-38.

Hanley, D.L., Kerr, A.P. and Waites, N.H. (1979) *Contemporary France: Politics and Society since 1945*, Routledge & Kegan Paul, London.

Harrison, M.M. (1983) 'The French Economy in Disarray', *Contemporary French Civilization*, VII (1), pp. 27-39.

Inglehart, R. and Rabier, J.-R. (1986) 'Political Realignment in Advanced Industrial Society: From Class-Based Politics to Quality-of-Life Politics', *Government and Opposition*, 21 (4), pp. 456-79.

Jaffré, J. (1986) 'Front national: la relève protestataire'. In: E. Dupoirier and G. Grunberg, *Mars 1986: la drôle de défaite de la gauche*, PUF, Paris, pp. 211-29.

July, S. (1986) *Les années Mitterrand. Histoire baroque d'une normalisation inachevée*, Grasset, Paris.

Lancelot, A. (1988) 'L'électorat français s'est-il recentré?' In: P. Habert and C. Ysmal, *Elections législatives 1988: résultats, analyses et commentaires*, Paris, Le Figaro/Etudes politiques, pp. 40-4.

Lanzmann, C. (1984) 'Entretien avec Gaston Defferre, Ministre de l'Intérieur et de la Décentralisation, Maire de Marseille', *Les Temps Modernes*, 40 (452-454), pp. 1561-80.

Lettre de Matignon (1983) no. 71; (1984) nos. 123, 127, 133.

Levy, D.A.L. and Machin, H. (1986) 'How Fabius Lost: The French Elections of 1986', *Government and Opposition*, 21 (3), pp. 269-85.

Lorien, J., Criton, K. and Dumont., S. (1985) *Le système Le Pen*, EPO, Antwerp.

Machin, H. and Wright, V. (1982) 'Why Mitterrand Won: The French Presidential Elections of April-May 1981', *West European Politics*, 5 (1), pp. 5-35.

Marcus, J. (1984) 'France: The Resurgence of the Far Right', *The World Today*, December, 507-13.

McCormick, J. (1983) 'Thorns Among the Roses: A Year of the Socialist Experiment in France', *West European Politics*, 6 (1), pp. 44-62.

Mitra, S. (1988) 'The National Front in France: A Single-Issue Movement?' In: K. von Beyme (ed.) *Right-Wing Extremism in Western Europe, West European Politics: Special Issue*, 11 (2), pp. 47-64.

Le Monde: Dossiers et Documents (March, 1986) *Les élections législatives du 16 mars 1986: le retour de la droite.*

Le Monde: Dossiers et Documents (May, 1988) *L'élection présidentielle: le nouveau contrat de François Mitterrand.*

Northcutt, W. (1982) 'The Election of François Mitterrand and the *Parti socialiste* in France: The Making of a *phénomène socialiste*', *Australian Journal of Politics and History*, 28 (2), pp. 218-35.

Northcutt, W. (1985a) *The French Socialist and Communist Party under the Fifth Republic, 1958-1981: From Opposition to Power*, Irvington, New York.

Northcutt, W. (1985b) 'The Changing Domestic Policies and Views of the Mitterrand Government, 1981-1984: The Crisis of Contemporary French Socialism', *Contemporary French Civilization*, IX (2), pp. 141-65.

Perrineau, P. (1985) 'Le Front national: un électorat autoritaire', *Revue politique et parlementaire*, 918, pp. 24-31.

Perrineau, P. (1986) 'Glissements progressifs de l'idéologie'. In: E. Dupoirier and G. Grunberg, *Mars 1986: la drôle de défaite de la gauche*, PUF, Paris.

Petitfils, J.-C. (1983) *L'extrême droite en France*, PUF, Paris.

Rémond, R. (1987) 'The Right as Opposition and Future Majority'. In: G. Ross, S. Hoffmann and S. Malzacher, *The Mitterrand Experiment: Continuity and Change in Modern France*, Polity, Oxford.

Rizzuto, F. (1987) 'Anti-Political Politics: The Barre Phenomenon', *Government and Opposition*, 22 (2), pp. 145-62.

Schain, M.A. (1987) 'The National Front in France and the Construction of Political Legitimacy', *West European Politics*, 10 (2), pp. 229-52.

Shields, J.G. (1987a) 'Politics and Populism: The French Far Right in the Ascendant', *Contemporary French Civilization*, XI (1), pp. 39-52.

Shields, J.G. (1987b) '*Jus soli* and *Jus sanguinis*: French Nationality in the Scales', *Patterns of Prejudice*, 21 (3), pp. 34-6.

SOFRES (1984) *Opinion publique 1984*, Gallimard, Paris.

SOFRES (1985) *Opinion publique 1985*, Gallimard, Paris.

SOFRES (1986) *Opinion publique 1986*, Gallimard, Paris.

SOFRES (1987) *L'état de l'opinion: clés pour 1987*, Seuil, Paris.

SOFRES (1988) *L'état de l'opinion: clés pour 1988*, Seuil, Paris.

Tucker, W.R. (1968) 'The New Look of the Extreme Right in France', *Western Quarterly Review*, 21, pp. 86-97.

Vaughan, M. (1987) 'The Wrong Right in France'. In: E. Kolinsky (ed.) *Opposition in Western Europe*, Croom Helm and PSI, Beckenham, pp. 289-317.

Wright, V. (1981) 'The Change in France', *Government and Opposition*, 16 (4), pp. 414-31.

Ysmal, C. (1986) *Le comportement électoral des Français*, La Découverte, Paris.

4

Language and Politics: The Case of Neo-Gaullism

John Gaffney

The textual analysis which takes up the bulk of this chapter is based upon two assumptions. The first is that organised politics as a hard-nosed, calculating, 'profane' activity, the domain of career politicians who operate in a climate of corridor dealings and public cynicism, co-exists with another politics which makes appeals to a moral order and a sacralised sense of community, and that this relationship can be apprehended through an analysis of political discourse. The second assumption is that this moral dimension in contemporary politics is more significant than is often assumed in traditional political analysis, and in French political culture is linked to the notion of heroic leadership. In order to demonstrate these points, I shall examine the case of the contemporary figure who is perceived as perhaps the most careerist major political figure in contemporary France, namely, Jacques Chirac, leader of the Gaullist Party (RPR), Prime Minister (1974-76, 1986-88), and Mayor of Paris since 1977.

On the question of the heroic status of leaders, Alexandre Sanguinetti once remarked that de Gaulle himself would never, as Chirac did, diminish himself by attempting to become Mayor of Paris. And it is true that opportunist calculation has been one of the hallmarks of Chirac's career. He has, moreover, always been associated with sectional interests, whether those of big business or else electorally crucial sections of the middle and lower middle classes, in a way that de Gaulle never was. Moreover, Chirac has been involved to a far greater degree than de Gaulle ever needed to be with electoral and other negotiations with the other main parties of the French right. And the notion of Chirac's political trajectory being motivated more by petty personal calculation than by the desire to 'serve' France in a Gaullian manner was compounded by a series of political interventions which were perceived as those of an out-and-out careerist. We have already mentioned the Mayorship of Paris (which gave Chirac not only a strong local powerbase but also sustained access to the media). His organised opposition to the Gaullist Party's candidate in the 1974 presidential elections, his resignation from the premiership in 1976, his divisive opposition to Giscard d'Estaing as President (which was never 'bold' enough to bring down the government in the 1976-81 period), the assumption of his having, as if deliberately, contributed to Giscard's defeat in the 1981 presidential elections, thereby allowing the *'socialo-communiste'* arch enemy to take power, in order that he, Chirac, become the exclusive leader of the right, and his calculated ambivalence towards the extreme right in the 1988 presidential election campaign all gave credence to the idea that his political life was motivated by a personal ambition which had little relation to Gaullism's claim to rally the people of France. His clear defeat in the 1988 presidential elections was, in part, public confirmation of the view that Chirac 'ne faisait pas le poids' of a national leader. An analysis of Chirac's discourse, however, will demonstrate how his political career is informed by a complex set of ideas which have involved him in an attempt to re-create symbolically the notion of a heroic 'quest' analogous to the legend of his predecessor, de Gaulle, and that, to a large extent, his 'opportunism' can only be properly understood in this context.

Chirac's strategy, however, along with his claim to heroic status, were undermined in the 1980s by three factors which could not have been foreseen, and all of which are illustrations of the risks involved in the use of highly personalised political strategies within a party system. The first is that Chirac's ability to present himself as *'le recours'*, the sole guardian of the rightist interpretation of French republicanism, was seriously undermined by the dramatic rise in popularity, after 1981, of Giscard's second Prime Minister, Raymond Barre, who, moreover, was able to exploit to advantage his apparent major disadvantage, the absence of a substantial political power base, by presenting himself, in a Gaullian manner, as coming from *outside* established political circles. The second is that Chirac felt forced to take the premiership in 1986 because he was the leader of the largest single party in the wake of the 1986 legislative elections. The result of this was double. This meant that he would be associated with *la politique politicienne* which all governments become associated with when in power, as well as with the failures of that government in the run-up to the contest for the ultimate prize of the 1988 presidential election. It meant also that he would be seen as 'collaborating' with a leftist President (something which Barre exploited) thus further diminishing any claim Chirac could make to a heroic exclusive status. We should add the observation that Chirac did, in fact, hesitate in the months preceding the 1986 elections over the question of accepting the premiership. The third unforeseen factor was that the electoral system, proportional representation, which had been introduced by the Socialist government in order to minimise the Socialist Party's losses in the 1986 election, had a secondary effect of diminishing the RPR's strength *vis-à-vis* both the Socialists and its coalition partner, the UDF. If the *scrutin uninominal à deux tours* had been operative in 1986, the RPR-UDF coalition would have enjoyed a much larger majority thus almost certainly forcing the resignation of President Mitterrand and catapulting Chirac into the presidency in the ensuing elections. The proportional representation system introduced in 1986 also facilitated the national representation of the extreme-right Front National, thus allowing for the national exposure of *its* 'heroic' leader, Jean-Marie Le Pen, who was to bite a significant chunk out of Chirac's potential electorate in the 1988 presidential elections.

Nevertheless, we can demonstrate how the 'mythical' or 'transcendental' register of political discourse survives in contemporary French politics, and how Chirac attempted to construct a heroic persona *alongside* his more party political one (the second being a function of the first), in order that he represent himself initially to his party and later to the people as waiting to be called to presidential power as a providential leader. We shall demonstrate this in our analysis of Chirac's discourse. We can note here that the prerequisite to this was the establishing of a loyalty among RPR members which went beyond his party leadership role, and well beyond the affection enjoyed by the historic Gaullist 'barons'. We shall thus demonstrate that Chirac's 'breaks' with the political establishment (1974, 1976, 1981) were part of this strategy, and involved the transformation of the Gaullist Party from a governing party into a crusading one. Such an undertaking involved a recapitulation of the essential elements of Gaullist myth (which we shall explain below), a recapitulation which involved only one modification: the identity of the providential leader.

For the purposes of illustration, I have chosen to analyse a text from the European elections of 1979, and this for two reasons. First, because the European elections, unlike in the UK, are high-profile 'national' elections, akin to legislative elections but, until the 1986 legislative elections, the only ones in France conducted under the proportional representation system. This meant that the RPR was able for the first time, in the absence of constraining alliances and in the context of Europe, to deploy a Gaullist discourse remniscent of the Rassemblement du peuple français (RPF), the crusading Gaullist Party of the Fourth Republic. Second, focusing upon 1979 will demonstrate how the claim to a particular mythical status involved a very elaborate undertaking which was to be measured in decades rather than weeks (as most electoral and media observers would have it). As will be shown in our analysis, such a time span was crucial if Chirac were to lay claim to the Gaullist heritage and, eventually, to the Presidency of the Republic.

Before analysing the text of Chirac's main speech of the European elections at Bagatelle (Bois de Boulogne, Paris),[1] brief reference to three major contexts of contemporary Gaullism is necessary: 1) political representation in Gaullism; 2) the significance of de Gaulle; 3) Gaullism as organisation. Analysis of these will also explain why and how the notion of *time* is essential to the claim in French political culture to national leadership.

REPRESENTATION AND THE STATE

Chirac as leader of the Gaullist Party, like de Gaulle before him, has always emphasised that a Gaullist organisation has an approach to the task of political representation which is different from that of other political parties and associations. Although a Gaullist organisation may resemble other political parties in establishing and maintaining local units and providing alike for internal elections and regional and national conferences, and for participation in representative institutions, it differs from them in its readiness to claim transcendence of such activities, to treat them as ephemeral and to acknowledge, sometimes implicitly, sometimes explicitly, that the essential political relationship is that between the leader of vision and a rally of the people. In this way, any organised form of Gaullism is recognised as an imperfect or as yet unrealised attempt to enact the mystical idea of 'true' political representation, that is, national allegiance to a political visionary who is able to envisage an ideal France.[2]

In Gaullist mythology, the concept of the State has considerable complexity and range, and it links up in one universally applicable context with a mystical idea of France and, circumstantially, with the idea of the Republic. The three terms — France, State, and Republic — constitute a hierarchy, with France, a mystical, though historically-grounded, apolitical ideal, as the highest term. The Republic is the lowest and denotes the constitutional arrangements that the people and their visionary leaders have accepted as best adapted to France's historical tradition. Therefore, just as the Gaullist vision is directed towards France as an ideal, so the Gaullist mission is expressed in the modern period as a series of tasks within the republican tradition.[3] The middle term, the State, stands in a complex relation to the other two. In Gaullist discourse, the State is called into being by the nation and thereafter becomes the custodian of national self-expression. It is neither a better kind of republic, nor an imperfect reflection of France, but denotes the idealism necessary if the former is to serve France's interests, and the materiality necessary if the latter is to find political expression. The State and the Republic in modern France are therefore in an equilibrium, and the role of Gaullism as a political force varies according to shifts in that equilibrium. As sectional and special interests progressively gain power, Gaullism is driven first to warn of the decline, then to restore the State to proper equilibrium within its particular regime expression.

It is the tension between the mystification of representation, on

94

the one hand, and a determined effort to treat the State devotionally, on the other, which underlies the atemporal character of Gaullism. And it is this which impels it to seek temporalisation in and through a person. In this way, the ineffable vision of an ideal State becomes the property of the visionary leader. Logically, the vision and the envisioning precede both representation and political action, and are themselves dependent only upon an unarticulated sense of nationhood. The experience of the vision by the visionary leader, recognition of the leader's claim, and the restoration of the State therefore follow one another chronologically within the Gaullist myth. Within this logical and chronological series, the plebiscite becomes the temporal expression of the subsequent legitimation of the leader, even though mythically his legitimacy predates the plebiscite. Once the plebiscitary event enters the series, however, the people, as well as the leader, become responsible for the fate of the State. Subsequent rejection of the leader by the people withdraws his right to continue his task — he cannot govern without the people's allegiance — but does not remove mythical legitimacy from him, because this logically precedes, and chronologically predates, his political acceptance by the people.

THE SIGNIFICANCE OF DE GAULLE

Although it is possible to derive the significance and interrelationships of the central terms in de Gaulle's view of the State from an elaborated Gaullist political philosophy, the principles and rules governing constitutional practice were always difficult to grasp. When translated into political objectives, the idea of what de Gaulle's vision entailed is reducible to national independence on the one hand and *grandeur* on the other.[4] The identifiable elements of the vision are few, even doctrinally inconsequential. But to argue that the ideology or the themes of Gaullism are so disparate or general that they cannot claim a doctrinal coherence is to miss the point. Like all visions, Gaullism's true content is incommunicable. The only certain focus of allegiance in Gaullism is not the vision itself, but the envisioning, is not a specific cause, but the person who espouses it, is not a particular strategy, but an idea of mission. At the level of myth, the visionary leader is the central character in an epic cycle, the essential moments of which are: the patient bearing of witness, sudden and tumultuous acceptance, the lonely exercise of power, and final acclaim or rejection. The myth of de Gaulle was elaborated within this framework: the lonely, visionary certainty of 1940; the banding together of the first disciples; the first total acceptance by the people in the Liberation period (1944-45); self-imposed isolation in the name of the mission that had been thwarted by sectional interests (January 1946); the renewed but unheeded calls (Bayeux, June 1946;

Strasbourg, April 1947); the long period in the wilderness (the 1950s); the second tumultuous acceptance (1958-62); the lonely exercise of power (the 1960s); and the final rejection (1969).

Given the range of this myth, the scope of Gaullist activity at any moment in political life is potentially very wide: from the maintenance of small groups of the faithful in times of adversity, to determined intervention in public affairs by, or in support of, a great leader. The Gaullist principle of leadership rests, therefore, upon the identification of an inspired person whose status is derived from his awareness of the needs of the State and the Republic in present time and the nature of France in mythic time. There is, therefore, a series of elements within the Gaullist myth which informs political action: France, the State, vision, the visionary, his mission, and the eventual rally of the people. In the 1970s and 1980s, many of the elements which would sustain the myth were missing: the republic which de Gaulle had founded was accepted, effective and enduring; France was not threatened by military invasion; and Chirac was an ordinary party leader, a product of the Administration and a young man lacking the authority and presence of de Gaulle. In addition, the political organisation inspired by Gaullism appeared to have become an integral unit of the party system of the Fifth Republic and to have acquired sectional characteristics, and other non-Gaullist leaders were laying claim to de Gaulle's heritage. For these reasons, any contemporary Gaullist leader intending to lay some form of *mythical* claim to the Gaullist heritage had to restore the myth to its general form and rescue the Gaullist organisation from its dependence upon the regime.

GAULLISM AS ORGANISATION

As leader of the RPR, Chirac created and justified his own advocacy of a new mission for the Gaullist movement and, ultimately, for France. His personal position had to be defined, not only within the movement, but in relation to the myth. If he disclaimed any special vision and remained one of a number of Gaullist 'barons', he risked being downgraded within the leadership hierarchy with no claim to the myth greater than that of older and still politically active *compagnons* of de Gaulle. The alternative was to enact, discursively and symbolically, the Gaullist myth, thereby claiming an original vision.

After resigning the premiership, in 1976, Chirac was able to treat the Gaullist Party not as a party of government, integral to the regime, but to take it, under his leadership, into partial opposition, changing its name and transforming its internal structures into an overt personalist rally around himself.[5] He thus offered it the opportunity to transcend its recent past and dissociate itself from the institutions which had robbed it of its original purpose.[6] From this point, Chirac and his party were able to effect a new exile, the first phase of the ultimate rally of the French people around the visionary leader which was to take place at some point in the future.[7]

THE TEXT

The essential quality of Chirac's discourse, which we shall illustrate in our analysis, is the creation of a sense of community allegiance to a personalist leader. In the 1979 speech, this was facilitated by the occasion itself. As the climax of a series of provincial meetings, the speech marks the moment when RPR followers from all over France and abroad came to commune with the leader in a symbolic response to his own tour of France. At the beginning of the speech, Chirac welcomes the people gathered region by region, a device which implies the speaker's summoning of an eternal, immutable France, most of the regions bearing the names of the old French provinces (see Appendix, paragraphs 1 and 2).

In order to demonstrate the relationship between Chirac, as an inspired leader, and the people, represented in microcosm by the 50,000 strong audience, we shall examine the speech from three related perspectives. The first concerns the status of the audience. The second concerns the myth of Gaullism itself. The third perspective concerns the status of the speaker, both implicitly and explicitly, *vis-à-vis* both the audience and the myth. We shall, therefore, make three readings of the speech.

The audience

Chirac refers to the purpose of the occasion in his first sentence. The assembled have come 'pour communier dans la même ferveur' ('in order to commune in the same fervour') (1). Both the nature of the occasion and the status of the audience are thereby established. The members of the audience are there in order to commune (with one another and with the speaker). The 'dans' of 'dans la ferveur' (rather than 'avec', with) indicates, moreover, that the presence of the audience and 'ferveur' are interdependent. To commune 'dans la ferveur' has an enfolding quality which not only makes 'ferveur' a prerequisite to communion but also underlines the fact that the 'being there' of the audience is also a prerequisite to communion. Communion and fervour are therefore mutually reinforcing. The audience's self-awareness is also encouraged by the constant repetition of 'vous' ('you') at the beginning of the speech. (In the first 300 words, for example, — and apart from the use of the second person plural verb form and words such as 'votre' ('your') — 'vous' occurs 14 times.)

The component parts, as it were, of the audience, correspond, as we have seen, to those of France itself. And although they are welcomed one by one, now 'réunis à Paris, dans la joie du printemps' ('reunited in Paris in the joy of springtime') (3), they constitute an organic or transcendent whole. The audience, moreover, is considered as being identical to a previous one: 'Souvenez-vous de Pantin' ('Remember Pantin') (3), which had assembled the previous February in the rigour of winter (3). This reference to a previous occasion refers to a Gaullist rally (and to a speech made by Chirac) during the campaign for the legislative elections of March 1978, elections which were themselves credited with exceptional historic significance. The outgoing government's majority was successful in those elections. The Pantin speech and rally, therefore, are here depicted as having been necessary to that success. The particular treatment of the previous Pantin meeting therefore indicates the role of the Bagatelle meeting by making it the prerequisite to future success. As we shall see, however, the impending European elections do not correspond to the 1978 legislative elections. The projected success here is a future one which lies at a point well beyond the 1979 European elections.

There occurs at the beginning of the speech, by naming and by inference, the endowment with symbolic significance of geographical location. The third essential place mentioned after the provinces and Paris is France; 'avenir digne de la France' ('a future worthy of France') (4). There is, then, a developmental chain of terms: Auvergne, Limousin, Aquitaine . . . ; Paris; France. Within this immutable geography lie specific historic locations (Pantin, Bagatelle) which hold together the chain which maintains or constitutes France. This use of geographical terms to denote spiritual qualities corresponds in Gaullist mythology to a wider nationalist-Catholic mythology in French life represented by such places as the sites of religious revelation such as Lourdes (the Virgin to Bernadette) or Domrémy (the voice of God to Joan of Arc). Within Gaullism, reverence for place is well-represented; for example, by London (June 1940), and by Strasbourg (April 1947) where de Gaulle founded the RPF and violently attacked the Fourth Republic. In Gaullism, therefore, the sacred nature of geographical location is always associated with a political speech. Through Chirac's speech, Bagatelle is being lent the significance of a geographic site of revelation, and the discursive creation of such a sacred site confers upon the speech itself a historic quality. In this way, the audience is being depicted in the speech as being present at what will become in the future a historic site whose significance will retrospectively be drawn from its founding character. The audience is thus endowed with the quality of a founding rally. Within Gaullism, participants at a rally such as this are always perceived, initially, as a minority whose faith and optimism eventually triumph over apparently overwhelming odds. The reference to the Pantin/Bagatelle audience elevates those present to the status of this minority: 'les seuls à croire encore à la victoire de la liberté' ('the only ones to go on believing in the victory of liberty') (3). In the case of the 1978 elections, such faith was justified. Here, however, such faith is presented as being rewarded at some future time, on condition that those *given* such status accept the *consequences* of such status. The future victory is not simply electoral, for, as we shall see, the European elections will be depicted not as the moment of victory but as the first step in a journey to a more historic victory. Pantin and Bagatelle in this way signify moments of crisis where the true patriots are called upon to come to the rescue of a threatened France, as they have been throughout history:

> Une fois encore, il nous appartient de changer le cours d'une apparente fatalité. (4)

> Once again, it falls to us to change the course of the apparently inevitable.

This 'encore' refers not only to Pantin but to the course of history itself. The changing of an apparently inevitable course of events not only implies the mythical future as well as the European elections themselves, but also makes the Bagatelle rally the first practical step towards such a change; just being at Bagatelle and making the choice, within the context of a spiritual occasion, to accept an elevated status, charges the audience with the power to change history.

Having established the surreal quality of both the people present and the site of assembly and their close relationship to one another, questions are implicitly created: why do they constitute such a rally? What is the political function of the meeting? These interrogations are presented in the speech as being, not those of the speaker or those of the audience, but those of an imaginary figure who will ask tomorrow:

> 'Vous étiez à Bagatelle. Et alors ?' (5)

> 'You were at Bagatelle. So what?'

We shall come back to this imaginary French person who appears again during the speech. Here we must simply note that the discursive invention of this figure allows the actual audience to retain the attributes of an elect rather than be discursively depicted as a series of audiences or aggregate of differentiated listeners who facilitate the exposition of ideas but lose their own elect status and profound sense of presence.

The audience's status is conferred by two terms: 'compagnons' ('companions') (2 and 5) and 'amis' ('friends') (2 and 5), terms which Chirac uses in all his speeches to RPR activists. 'Compagnons' is, firstly, a term of affection which indicates that the political relationship involved is more than contractual. The term is, moreover, a non-party one and so adds an unrestricted quality to the speaker/audience relationship. 'Compagnons' also carries a deeper, more mystical meaning. It is non-party but in a precise way. It distinguishes those present from certain aspects of organised Gaullism, that is to say, from the party which formed for the purpose of supporting de Gaulle in November 1958. The 'compagnons' in 1979 are depicted in this way as *compagnons d'armes, compagnons de route* or *compagnons d'exil* and are therefore pre-party. They thus enjoy the same moral and affective ties with Chirac that de Gaulle's *gaullistes de la première heure* enjoyed with him. The whole party is given the collective status of a group of apostles rather than that of the *organisational* inheritors of Gaullism. There is implied here a parallel between Chirac/RPR and de Gaulle/*compagnons*. Both the audience and the speaker are therefore given mutually dependent mythical status. The term 'amis', moreover, is used many times in the speech, confirming and re-confirming the privileged relations between speaker and audience. Another indication of the intimacy of the gathering is the early profusion of personal pronouns in the speech. 'Je' ('I') and 'vous' ('you') create, as it were, 'nous' ('we') (see paragraphs 1 to 5) and underline the notions of the presence of the participants and the creation of community.

Because of the way the audience at Bagatelle is addressed and mythified, therefore, the meeting is given certain qualities which themselves reinforce both the status of the audience and the audience's privileged relationship to the speaker: it is extra-constitutional and communitarian; it is historically sensitive and quasi-religious; and it is a meeting of companions and is therefore akin to the roll-call of a brotherhood. It is, within Gaullism, the most exclusive form of rally or *rassemblement* of those who believe in France and have the perspicacity and sense of history necessary to know the way forward.

Once the speaker has established the status of the audience, asserted its participation in an act of communion, and introduced the idea of preparation for the tasks of consistent witness and the coming 'journey', the tone is set for the discursive enactment of the central themes of the Gaullist myth.

Having referred to the need to overcome 'une apparente fatalité', the speaker prepares the audience for the deployment of the myth by reaffirming the former's special status:

> Voilà, mes amis, voilà chers compagnons, pourquoi au milieu de la fête et de l'enthousiasme populaire que vous avez su créer depuis ce matin, nous devons maintenant marquer un moment de réflexion et de

gravité. Si votre choix est fait, songez à tous ceux qui cherchent encore et qui demain vous diront:

'Vous étiez à Bagatelle. Et alors ?' (5)

That's why, my friends, why, my dear companions, in the middle of the festivities and celebrations that you've created since this morning, we must pause now for a moment of deep reflection. If your choice is already made, think of all those who still search and who tomorrow will say to you:

'You were at Bagatelle. So what?'

The elaboration of the myth

As we have seen from the way in which the audience is depicted in the Bagatelle speech, it is clear that the speech involves, from the beginning, ideas fundamental to the Gaullist myth. The speech elaborates four of them: inevitability (*fatalité*); truth; betrayal; and voluntarism, before going on to use these ideas to develop the vision/mission theme and the role of leadership judgement.

We saw above how the issue which provoked the rally was the need to challenge 'une apparente fatalité' (4). This notion of resisting *fatalité* is fundamental to Gaullism's philosophy of action. De Gaulle despised governments which failed to surmount difficulties, and, for this reason, condemned both the Vichy regime for accepting the Armistice of 1940 and the Fourth Republic for tolerating governmental *immobilisme*. In both cases, the acceptance of *une fatalité* by others was assumed. Gaullists themselves had the assurance of the vision and will of their leader. The Bagatelle audience, like the Gaullists of 1940 and 1947, is represented in Chirac's speech as refusing *fatalité* in favour of a voluntarism, despite the fact that these two related choices involve the acceptance of isolation and powerlessness in the first instance as prerequisites to eventual triumph.[8] To dramatise this point, the classic metaphor of a *chemin* or journey is introduced (and will reoccur) through reference to 'la porte étroite' and all that this connotes of self-sacrifice, self-denial, (and elitism):[9]

la porte étroite qui ouvre sur le seul avenir digne de la France. (4)

The strait gate which leads to the only future worthy of France.

We have, therefore, the idea of a mission evoked, with the audience as the chosen people who must 'montrer' ('show') (4) the strait gate to 'ceux qui cherchent encore' (those who still search) (5). This notion of mission is lent the sense of urgency and drama characteristic of Gaullism. Chirac reminds the members of the audience that they have only one week to reveal what is at stake for

101

France and for Europe (6). This immediacy both increases the idea of an impending defeat and lends to the notion of mission the idea of effort and determination. The image used here to describe the act of persuasion is also a dramatic one and involves Gaullists going out to the people at large to 'déchirer devant leurs yeux le voile' ('tear the veil from their eyes') (6).

This act of tearing away a veil brings us to the second evocation of Gaullist mythology after that of *fatalité*, the theme of *vérité*. The word 'vérité' ('truth') occurs 16 times in the speech and is supported by other words: 'vrai que' ('true that'), 'cela est faux' ('that is false'), 'ne faut pas croire' ('do not believe'), 'c'est particulièrement vrai' ('this is particularly true'), 'vraies' ('true'), 'véritables' ('true'), 'véritable' ('true'). The *vérité* that Chirac refers to, however, is not that of the rational conclusion of articulate political debate. Several times the *vérité* is qualified in order that the speaker indicate what it really refers to: *une vérité historique*. The notion of historic or historical truth is in fact the opposite of a purely rationally established truth. Defined as *historique*, it exists within its own logical realm. This paradox is explained by Gaullism's mythification of history itself. It is not linked to what happened in the past but to the ineffable vision of what lies *behind* past events, on a metaphysical plane. However, since it can only be apprehended intuitively, and not grasped intellectually, there is a constant danger that it will be misunderstood and distorted by those who lack vision. The moral obligation here to cherish *une vérité* is akin to that of ensuring that the State does not deteriorate within the Republic.

In Gaullism, the characteristic idea of *vérité* (sensed by the nation, believed in by the *compagnons*, understood by the visionary leader) is the opposite of an equally characteristic idea of falsehood which derives either from neglect or from deliberate human misrepresentation or deviation from the truth. Although falsehood, like truth, is metaphysical in Gaullism,[10] all the words used in the speech emphasise its human agency. The implied opposite of truth, therefore, has two aspects: either it is the lies of those who wish to undermine truth, or else is the error of those who have allowed themselves to be misled or cannot help but be so. Chirac draws attention to 'une extraordinaire entreprise de mystification' ('an extraordinary scheme to mystify') (9), and blames all the leading personalities (Marchais, Mitterrand, Chevènement, Mauroy, Lecanuet, Barre, Veil (7-9)) for participation in it. He warns that 'certains brouillent les pistes !' ('some people create smokescreens!') (7). Behind such personalities he identifies the amorphous and anonymous agencies such as 'une armée de plusieurs milliers de bureaucrates' ('an army of several thousand bureaucrats') (12), 'un pseudo-parlement, une commission apatride' ('a pseudo-parliament, a stateless commission') (14), 'l'Europe. . . à vague forme humaine' ('Europe . . . ghostlike') (30), 'la propagande bruxelloise' ('Brussels propaganda') (30), and to the even less specific 'on' ('they'): 'on nous a beaucoup parlé' ('they often tell us'), 'On prétend' ('they pretend'), 'On nous parle' ('they tell us') (7). This treatment of 'on' as despicable is used again later in a string of 'Qu'on ne vienne pas me raconter' ('I don't want to hear about') (20, 21, 22, 23) and 'On pourra bien nous dire/expliquer/démontrer' ('they can try and tell/explain/show us') (57, 58).

The two examples of *vérité* given at this point in the speech involve, first, an attack upon the Left's conceptions and contradictions (7), but, more importantly, a second *vérité* (10): that that which divides the Gaullists ('nous') from the Giscardian UDF is incomparably deeper than that which unites them; that the UDF is engaged in an attempt to mystify not only the people in general but also the Gaullist faithful (23). The point here is that the dishonourable bond which unites *all* of those outside Gaullism is deliberate mystification or else the veiling of truth. Chirac returns to this near-Manichean idea when he declares how such opposing views are represented on the question of European organisation:

> La vérité historique, c'est que, depuis trente ans au moins, s'opposent deux idées nettement tranchées de l'organisation européenne. (10)

> The historical truth is that, for 30 years or more, there have been two fundamentally opposed conceptions of European organisation.

These two ideas are, of course, a supra-national one and 'la nôtre' ('our idea') (12). Chirac then gives examples of Gaullist Europeanism: confounding attempts at supra-nationalism in 1965, effecting Franco-German reconciliation and a sound agricultural policy, and the creation of the European Airbus (15-17). These examples of international co-operation, based upon the principle of the nation-state, are each prefaced with a juxtaposing 'Croyez-vous ?' ('Do you believe?') ('que la paix en Europe et la réconciliation . . . sont nées par décret de la Commission de Bruxelles' ('That peace and reconciliation in Europe are born by decree from the Bruxelles Commission') (15); 'que la politique agricole . . . soit l'oeuvre des experts' ('that agricultural policy . . . was produced by experts') (16); 'que l'Airbus soit le fruit d'une politique . . . sortie des tiroirs communautaires' ('that the Airbus was the product of a policy . . . pulled out of some Common Market drawer') (17). Such a rhetorical device not only evokes scorn for those who do not understand Chirac's message (for the audience, the only implied answer to 'do you believe' can be a derisory 'bien sûr que non') ('of course not!') but is also a direct reference to the idea of the adversaries' perpetual attempts to dissimulate the truth. Within this context of *vérité*, and its capacity for distortion or mystification in certain political forms, a third related idea emerges which is introduced into the speech and lends it much of its sense of outrage: that of betrayal.

Chirac refers to the dangers of a false Europeanism and the danger that its advocates will 'bloquer' ('block'), then 'casser', ('break') everything which has been built up over a period of 25 years (19). What is also significant in this evocation of a 25 year period is that, because they both began at the same time, Chirac is able to allude to the Fifth Republic while referring to the EEC, thus making it possible discursively to imply that the strength of the State in the Fifth Republic and the maintenance of the EEC in a form compatible with Gaullism are mutually dependent.

It is in this context that the personal accusations of the betrayal of France/de Gaulle are made one after another against 'la plupart des ténors de la liste Veil' ('those on Veil's list' (the UDF)) (19). The greatest scorn is reserved for Jean Lecanuet who 'se faisait un honneur d'avoir mis le Général de Gaulle en ballottage avec le soutien d'un comité où siégeait d'ailleurs M. Barre' ('who thought it an honour to have forced General de Gaulle to a second round [in the 1965 presidential elections], and this with the support of a committee which included Mr Barre') (23). The base nature of such a collection of unworthy conspirators is further alluded to in the following quotation which underlines both their cunning and their cowardice:

> La vérité historique, c'est qu'après s'être mis en sommeil le temps d'une campagne électorale, pour ne pas effaroucher notre électorat et se prêter à une odieuse entreprise de récupération, les co-listiers de Mme Veil qui se répartiront à Strasbourg entre divers groupes politiques, espèrent bien prendre leur revanche. (23)

> The historical truth is that, after having lain low for the duration of an election campaign, in order not to affront the French electorate and then have to explain their odious scheme, those on Mme Veil's joint list will disperse at Strasbourg hoping then to take their revenge.

In the final words of the quotation the accusation of betrayal is explicit. The speaker goes on:

> Ce serait, si nous les laissions faire, la revanche sur la thèse gaulliste. (24)
> It would be, if we let them do it, their revenge on Gaullism.

In this use of the word 'gaulliste', de Gaulle himself and the present thesis (Chirac's) are conflated so that a synonymity between Chirac and the European elections, de Gaulle and his EEC policy is established. Gaullist voluntarism is also strengthened by the use of the conditional and imperfect tenses quoted above. The implication here is that there would be revenge if the Gaullists allowed it but that Gaullists will not allow it just as they did not allow it in the past. The responsibility this puts upon the RPR activists is considerable in that it implies that the strengthening of the French State is dependent upon their acquiescence in the re-enactment of the Gaullist myth as exposed by the speaker.

The theme of the desire for revenge on the part of those who wish to weaken France is extended. Three times in rapid succession Chirac refers to such a desire on the part of others (and the word 'revanche' is used four times in seven lines): that of Mme Veil's associates; that of a disordered Europe over an efficient one; that of a motley coalition of Centrists over the Fifth Republic (24-26). Furthermore, Chirac makes this unmasking of the desire for revenge itself a 'vérité' to 'rétablir' ('re-establish'). And here he makes reference to the covert connection between discourse and action:

Mais une fois la vérité rétablie, notre tâche n'est pas finie pour autant. (28)

But having re-established the truth, our task is still not completed.

It is at this point in the speech that Chirac introduces a fourth element of the Gaullist myth, that of voluntarism.

The voluntarist argument is developed at length (32-56). Chirac offers his followers the missionary task of convincing the French people that much of what they have been told about Europe is misleading. The argument is directly related, therefore, to the themes already elaborated or alluded to: the overcoming of *fatalité*, the reestablishment of truth, the exposure of betrayal, and the determination to act. He warns against taking the illusion of European unity for reality, speaks of the need for a strong France, and draws attention to the threat of Germany's economic superiority, and to the need for the French economy to be strengthened.[11] Concerning the internal political perspective, the speaker stresses the dangers of a Left victory, while refusing to accept the Prime Minister's (Raymond Barre) claim that the government's policies are the only alternative to those of the Left. He speaks also of the need for investment, for the fight against unemployment and foreign interference, and for a proper application of the Community's customs tariffs and agricultural policy. He ends by affirming that it is they, the Gaullists, who are the real Europeans (53).

What is significant about this argument is not the complexity of its substance — the argument is straightforward, characteristic and uncontentious — but the intricacy of its form and the sense of the complexity of argumentation which it evokes.[12] A closer analysis of this argument-within-the-argument reveals much about the manner in which the Gaullist myth is deployed in political discourse.

The argument contains three warnings each of which is elaborated in turn. The formal elaboration of the argument can be well illustrated in schematic form.

The first warning ('avertissement') is this:

Il ne faut pas croire les marchands d'illusions qui cherchent à vous vendre l'Europe comme je ne sais quel remède miracle à tous vos maux. (32)

Don't believe the illusion sellers who are trying to sell you Europe like some kind of miracle remedy for all your ills.

This is then followed by three illustrations or observations:

Ce n'est pas parce qu'on fera l'Europe qu'on pourra du jour au lendemain travailler 35 heures par semaine, sans craindre pour notre compétitivité . . . (33)

Just constructing Europe won't mean the 35-hour week overnight without threatening our competitiveness . . .

C'est n'est pas parce qu'on fera l'Europe . . . qu'on fera reculer le chômage . . . (34)

Just constructing Europe won't reduce unemployment . . .

Ce n'est pas parce qu'on fera l'Europe que les jeunes médecins, les jeunes avocats, les jeunes agriculteurs français trouveront à s'installer plus facilement . . . (35)

Just constructing Europe won't mean that young doctors, lawyers, and farmers will find it easier to get established . . .

Each of these observations is concluded by a 'bien au contraire' ('on the contrary'), and the whole is summed up thus: 'Tout cela est un leurre' ('The whole thing is a trap') (36). In this way, each observation is a dramatic extension of the initial warning itself.

The second warning is that:

Pour bien faire l'Europe, il faut que la France soit forte. (38)

To really make Europe, France must be strong.

This is amplified to indicate that a strong France means having the means to be strong on the demographic, economic, defence, diplomatic and social levels. (39)

This amplified second warning is then divided into a *constatation*:

Force est de constater que la France qui, au début des années 70, était bien partie pour rattraper l'Allemagne . . . ne cesse . . . de s'en éloigner; (39)

It's clear that France which, at the beginning of the 1970s, was well on the way to catching up with Germany, is falling back all the time;

two comparisons: between France in 1979 and France in 1976, (39), and between France in 1979 and its competitors, (40); and an observation: that the reasons for France's failure can be seen in the gulf between 'le discours de nos gouvernants' ('the discourse of those who govern us') (41) and the reality concerning France's energy, expenditure, administrative spending and social policy.

All of these observations lead to the conclusion that the French people deserve to know the truth (42):

> Or la verité, que l'on cache au pays, la voici. Elle tient en deux constatations. (43)

> But the truth that they hide from the country, is this. It is summed up in two observations.

These are:

1) That there is a need for change in economic policy.

   This 'première constatation' (44) is divided into three more observations which we can paraphrase: (i) broken government promises and the humiliation of the French will lead to social instability (45), (ii) The rise of the Left will lead to collectivism (46), (iii) France's economic weakness will be compounded by its position in Europe (47);

2) That there is an alternative to present economic policy. This 'deuxième constat' (48), the Gaullist alternative, is divided into six 'moyens' ('means') (48): (i) the fight against unemployment, (ii) investment, borrowing and the provision of credit facilities, (iii) help for key industries, (iv) help for small industries, (v) proper planning, (vi) a properly functioning State apparatus (49).

The third warning is that:

> Le rôle de nos représentants à Strasbourg ne doit pas être de se prêter au jeu du régime de l'impuissance et de la technocratie, mais d'agir en défenseurs intransigeants des intérêts de la France dans une Europe en marche. (52)

> The role of our representatives in Strasbourg must not be that of lending themselves to the game of powerless and technocratic rule, but to act as the intransigent defenders of France in a Europe that is on the move;

and that other members of the Community behave like American satellites, and to this end have blocked its development (53). Two examples are given: 1) the Community's customs barriers have been dismantled because of American and Japanese pressure (54); 2) since de Gaulle's agricultural policies, no other Community policy initiatives have been elaborated; not for energy, steel, transport, textiles, 'ni pour rien' ('nor for anything'). (54)

The characteristic feature of this method of argument is that the audience is addressed at two quite different levels even though the form of the argument resembles that of a closely reasoned case. The sources of complexity are the three warnings. These 'avertissements' are not simply cautions but cries of alarm, a claim to the attention of the audience who, though at one with the speaker, need to be put on their guard against the insidious, yet apparently reasonable, arguments put to them by outsiders. Warnings of this kind are not intended to persuade but to dramatise, in rhetorical form, a truth already accepted. Gaullists and, at a second remove, the French as a whole are being alerted to the fact that the adversaries of France are surreptitiously leading the French into error.

At the second level, and expressed with much less intensity than the three warning calls, the speaker offers advice which takes the form of a long series of prudential rules and maxims which are variously presented as observations, comparisons, reasons, means to given ends, and examples. In this way, the three observations which follow the first warning, concerning the illusion that Europe is a miracle cure for all France's ills, are disguised maxims which may be expressed thus: 1) Do not believe that the length of the working week can be reduced without reference to external competition. 2) Do not believe that unemployment can be solved by outsiders. 3) Do not believe that the young people of France can depend for career openings upon outsiders.

The second warning, that a strong France is a prerequisite of a strong economy, is based upon three maxims which can be represented thus: 1) Remember that a non-Gaullist French government's promises are meaningless. 2) Remember that a non-Gaullist French government allows the Left to gain strength. 3) Remember that a non-Gaullist French government cannot defend France's interests in the wider community.

Such an argument indicates that the basic structure of argumentation is that of strong Cassandra-like warnings followed by sets of illustrative maxims and rules concerning how to respond to outsiders' claims. The style is, therefore, both didactic and anti-analytical (or, rather, prescriptive within a given frame of reference). The organising terminology of the argument centres upon the proposition that an underlying truth and an inspired mode of interpreting reality have been discovered by the speaker. In this way, 'constater' comes to mean to unmask and expound a 'vérité'; 'raisonner', to explain a 'vérité' through factual examples. The facts themselves, however, are incidental to, in that they are only indicative of, a much more far-reaching 'vérité historique'. The exercise of reason within the logic of this Gaullist perspective is to distinguish the true from the false, the enduring from the ephemeral, the inner from the surface reality; and the basis of this inspired reasoning is the imagination, judgement and certainty of the speaker. In this way, the concluding appeal of the 'argument':

> Voilà, mes amis, ce que nous appelons avoir une politique européenne. (56)

> That, my friends, is what we call a real European policy

refers not only to the argument elaborated but to the mode of reasoning of the speaker. And the 'mes amis' and the ambiguous 'nous' here reinforce the personal nature of the reasoning.

Bearing this in mind let us return and comment upon the quotation which prefaces this long argument-within-the-argument, and observe how it refers to all the essential elements in the Gaullist myth with the exception of one: that of the final victory:

> Mes amis, dans l'immense rassemblement de ce 2 juin où se mêlent toutes les régions de France, tous les métiers de France, tous les niveaux de la société française, oublions pour un temps les listes et les sièges, les pourcentages, les partis et leurs états-majors. Songeons à la route qu'il nous faut faire ensemble, demain et chaque jour. Sur ce chemin, je voudrais placer quelques repères, en forme d'avertissements que je vous demande d'entendre, pour agir et, s'il fallait, pour témoigner. (31)

> My friends, in the immense rally of this 2 June, where all of France's regions, all of France's professions, all the levels of French society, are gathered, let us forget for a little while the lists and the seats, the percentages, the parties and their HQs. Let us think of the road we must take together, tomorrow and each day. On this road, I would like to place a few signposts in the form of warnings that I would like you to heed, in order to act and, if necessary, in order to bear witness.

Personal vision: 'France' (x2), 'je voudrais placer quelques repères' ('I would like to place a few signposts').

Leadership claim: 'Oublions pour un temps', 'Songeons', 'je vous demande d'entendre' ('Let us forget for a while', 'Let us think', 'that I would like you to heed').

Sacred location: 'l'immense rassemblement de ce 2 juin' ('the immense rally of this 2 June').

Communion: 'Mes amis', 'Songeons', 'oublions' ('My friends', 'Let us think', 'Let us forget').

Organic community: 'où se mêlent toutes les régions de France, tous les métiers de France, tous les niveaux de la société française' ('where all of France's regions, all of France's professions, all the levels of French society, are gathered').

Mission: 'la route qu'il nous faut faire ensemble' ('the road that we must take together').

Soulless adversary: 'les listes et les sièges, les pourcentages, les partis et leurs états-majors' ('the lists and the seats, the percentages, the parties and their HQs').

Voluntarism: 'l'immense rassemblement', 'agir' ('the immense rally', 'to act').

Thankless witness: 'la route', 's'il fallait, pour témoigner' ('the road', 'if necessary, to bear witness').

We can see, therefore, that the exposition of Chirac's own claim to vision (the elaborated argument-within-the-argument) is prefaced, and thereby strengthened, by a brief recapitulation of Gaullist myth itself.

This brings us to the notion, absent in the above quotation, of a Gaullist victory. At the end of his central argument, Chirac declares:

> Plus les gaullistes sortiront renforcés du scrutin du 10 juin et plus la France aura de chances de prendre enfin le chemin du redressement. (50)

> The stronger Gaullists come out of the 10 June election, the greater France's chances of taking once again the road to recovery.

Given the impending and widely-predicted failure at the polls in 1979, the opposite is equally implied: if the Gaullists emerge weakened from the elections, the road to recovery will be tortuous. The audience, therefore, is endowed with the status of an original Gaullist community on the eve of an election in which the Gaullist party is unlikely to achieve success (the Gaullists were to gain only 16 per cent of the vote). The 'redressement', therefore, is not temporally situated in the aftermath of the elections but well into the future/in mythic time. The European election campaign is thus presented as the first stage in the voluntarist Gaullist struggle against the imagined *fatalité* advocated or represented by rival leaders, and in the creation, through discourse, of a privileged minority of believers and in the clarifying of their relationship to the leader at the outset of a mission which will eventually create the great rally of the French people.

The voice of the speaker

As we have shown, both the status and the identity of the audience signified in the text are of a particular kind. Moreover, these are relatively constant, that is to say, the movement of *je* in relation to *vous* is relatively constant. Furthermore, *nous* invariably signifies, in a straightforward manner, a collective *moi* and *vous* united in mission. These features are unusual in political discourse. Normally, the identity of 'vous' is ever-changing in order that political speakers address several discursively invented audiences consecutively or simultaneously. This straightforwardness in Chirac's discourse, where slides of meaning within the first person singular and plural pronouns are virtually non-existent, is possible because the *je/vous* hierarchy is a tenet of Gaullist doctrine and therefore needs no manipulation. According to the myth, moreover, the Gaullist leader draws his inspiration not from his followers (although the opposite is true) but from the original vision itself. The emergence of *nous*, where this occurs, therefore, is always posterior to the formulation of the vision and the personal experience of the visionary leader. When, for example, at the very beginning of his speech, Chirac greets the assembled: 'je vous adresse mon salut !' ('I offer you my greeting') (1), he is claiming a certain form of relationship. In one sense, the speech is, to use a military metaphor, the pre-battle address of the warrior-king in which the reasons for assembly and the strategy of the conflict have been elaborated in advance, and where the forms and degrees of allegiance are not ambiguous. At the very beginning of the speech, immediately after welcoming the audience, Chirac declares: 'nous sommes venus faire entendre la voix forte de l'espoir.' ('We have come to make heard the strong voice of hope') (3). Whether the 'voix' is his or a combination of his and the rally's is not an issue, that is, not an issue unless he fails to present himself as a personalist leader in terms of the Gaullist myth.

This personalism-in-discourse is effected initially by the manner of greeting, the welcoming of *vous* by *je*, which both emphasises the difference in status and posits *je* (Chirac) as logically preceding *vous* (the audience) in terms of the myth. The spatial or hierarchical distance between speaker and audience need not therefore be overstressed, as distance already exists temporally or sequentially within the myth itself. Therefore, when the *je/vous* distinction is expressed:

> Amis venus de toutes les régions . . ., je vous adresse mon salut ! A vous, compagnons . . . A vous, Normands et Bretons . . . A vous . . . A vous tous enfin . . . j'adresse mon salut ! (1-2)

> Friends who have come from all the regions . . . , I give you my greeting! To you, companions . . . To you Normans and Bretons . . . To you . . . To you all, then . . . I offer my greeting!

the essential quality of the Gaullist form of communion is emphasised automatically: the 50,000 members of the audience have, in the last analysis, come to commune with Chirac rather that with one another.

After the initial welcome, the presence of Chirac's persona is maintained not only by the act of speaking itself but is maintained rhetorically within the speech. The first indication of this is Chirac's immediate portrayal of opposing doctrines in terms of their leaders. The Communists, Socialists and Giscardians are introduced in the speech, identified, described, and belittled in terms of their leaders: 'M. Marchais dresse un absurde constat' ('Mr Marchais makes an absurd claim'); ('M. Mitterrand prône l'Europe socialiste' ('Mr Mitterrand extols Socialist Europe'); 'Tout en ayant à se garder . . . du supranational Mauroy . . . de l'anti-européen Chevènement' ('While all the time having to guard himself against the supranational Mauroy, the anti-European Chevènement'); 'une extraordinaire entreprise de mystification de la part des responsables de la liste officielle conduite par Mme Simone Veil et parrainée par M. Barre' ('an unbelievable attempt at mystification on the part of the official list led by Mrs Simone Veil and supported by Mr Barre'). In this way an alternative leader — Chirac — is implied. A contrasting device of personification is used later where individuals represent in a positive way whole nations: de Gaulle or Pompidou, France; Adenauer, Germany. Moreover, we do not have in these examples merely the notion of the personification of a state power. Within Gaullism, effective power and true authority themselves derive ultimately from individuals, and the greatness of the state that such individuals represent is both a reflection of and is reflected in their own greatness. Early in the speech, Chirac's reference to Franco-German reconciliation is an illustration of this view; such reconciliation was effected by 'deux gouvernements souverains et leurs chefs: le Chancelier Adenauer et le Général de Gaulle !' ('two sovereign governments and their leaders: Chancellor Adenauer and General de Gaulle') (15).[13] All of these references imply just such another figure of international reconciliation, the speaker himself.

The unmistakable presence of the speaker, over and above the fact of the speech's delivery, is sustained by the frequent occurrence in the speech of 'je' (x23) and 'mes', 'me', 'ma', and 'mon' ('me', 'to me', 'my') (x24) and by the contexts in which these pronouns are often used: 'Voilà, mes amis, voilà, chers compagnons' ('that, my friends, that dear companions'), 'je n'hésite pas à affirmer' ('I don't hesitate to affirm'), 'Je redoute — et je le dis ici solennellement' ('I fear, and I say here solemnly'), 'Qu'on ne vienne pas me raconter' ('Don't tell me'), 'Je songe aussi aux jeunes' ('I think too of the young'), 'Mais, par moment, je me demande' ('But, sometimes, I ask myself'), 'je voudrais placer quelques repères' ('I would like to place a few signposts'), 'Tel est mon premier avertissement' ('that is my first warning'), 'Et je lance maintenant aux Françaises et aux Français mon troisième avertissement' ('And to French women and men I give my third warning').

Apart from the personae of the speaker, the audience, de Gaulle, and the adversaries of Gaullism, there is another character in the discourse: an unnamed French citizen who plays a particular rhetorical role *vis-à-vis* the speaker and the speaker's relationship to his audience. He/she appears as the interlocutor of the members of the audience after they have rejoined ordinary time, that is, after they have gone back to their homes and jobs. As we have seen, he/she will ask of them: 'Vous étiez à Bagatelle. Et alors?' Later on in the speech he/she is presented as asking a longer, more puzzled question:

> 'En fin de compte, cette Europe dont on nous rebat les oreilles, faut-il être pour ? Faut-il être contre ? Les communistes sont contre, et vous n'êtes pas d'accord avec eux. Les socialistes et l'UDF, semble-t-il sont pour, et vous n'êtes pas d'accord avec eux. Que voulez-vous donc ?' (28)

> 'All said and done, this Europe that they bomb our ears with, should we be for it? Or against it? The Communists are against it, and you don't agree with them. The Socialists and the UDF seem to be for it, and you don't agree with them either. What exactly do you want?'

Apart from allowing the speaker to introduce and elaborate upon certain arguments, this character serves several purposes. First, his/her presence indicates that Chirac himself is aware of him/her and knows the questions that the mythical man or woman-in-the-street asks him/herself, his/her colleagues and the political elites. Second, Chirac is able to offer to the audience a task; that of converting to Gaullism those amongst whom they live and work. Third, the discursive presence of the imaginary citizen enables the speaker to imply that there is a major difference between the audience and the outside world. Fourth, because the ordinary person is confused, the speaker is able to imply that Gaullism, and his own reasoning, is not only complex but revelatory. We can see, therefore, that the creation of a range of characters in the speech enables the speaker to suggest a particular form of relationship between himself and the audience.

*

From our analysis so far we can see that an essential feature of Chirac's discourse is the posited relationship between the speaker and the audience and the respective status of these; Chirac must treat his audience as if he drew strength to act, though not vision, from them. It is for this reason that he treats them as a chivalric brotherhood. It is interesting to note in this context that Chirac dates the beginning of France's decline from 1976 (39), the year in which he resigned from the premiership. In terms of normal political polemic this is not at all surprising. In the context of Chirac's reenactment of the Gaullist myth, it makes Chirac's resignation in 1976 a symbolic recreation of de Gaulle's resignation of January 1946.

In the last moments of the speech, Chirac employs the oratorical register and the themes of traditional Gaullist *appel* speeches. This qualitative change begins with the claim:

La France, ce n'est pas un Etat européen comme les autres. (61)

France is not a European state like the others.

France, Chirac claims, is the reference point for all those who throughout the world need a champion to speak out 'par dessus l'opposition des blocs' ('above the opposition of the blocs') (62). France 'demain encore, peut étonner le monde' ('France can tomorrow once more startle the world') (63), that is to say that it does not do so today. The emphasis here is characteristically Gaullist in that the claim stresses defeat as much as the certainty of eventual triumph:

Dix fois au cours de son histoire, elle a su explorer des voies nouvelles et retrouver force et audace quand certains la voyaient prostrée. (63)

Ten times in the course of its history, it has been able to find new ways, and to find strength and nerve when others considered it prostrate.

At this point, and for the first time in the speech, there is a conflation of audience and people:

Français, Françaises, mes amis, le 10 juin, tout le peuple de France sera interrogé . . . (64)

French men and women, my friends, on the 10 June, the whole of the French people will be questioned.

The issue is not partisan (64) but personal and patriotic, and is depicted as being akin to the individual accountability of the Christian conscience:

Chacun, dans le silence et le secret de sa conscience, répondra. (65)

Each person, in the silence and secrecy of their conscience, will answer.

Along with the oratorical register, therefore, there is, on the one hand, a dramatic widening of the frame of reference of the speech, implicit throughout, that in terms of world history France is entering a new cycle, and, on the other, a sharpening of focus upon the notion of individual action. The ultimate success of France, therefore, is made dependent upon voluntarist individual action. The weight of individual responsibility is therefore presented as barely tolerable (and yet as easy to assume as the act of crossing a ballot paper).

The juxtaposition of the historic and the individual is maintained by the use of metaphor. In the closing lines, patriotic feeling is likened to a message/secret that is passed down through history, by both the great and the humble (67), 'de main en main' ('from hand to hand') (67). The image used to describe this act underlines both the precious and the fragile nature of that which is transmitted, and, therefore, the responsibilities and commitment of those charged with the task. Clearly, the qualities required to perform such a task are those traditionally associated with religious faith, while historical examples given of the message carriers go from Joan of Arc to those tortured by the Nazis (67). The message is:

> Un peuple a tous les droits hormis celui de remettre aux plus jeunes de ses membres moins que ce qu'il a lui-même reçu de ses aînés. (68)

> A people has every right except that of handing on to its youngest members less than that which it has itself received from its elders.

The idea of a heritage in contemporary, peacetime France is thus given all the emotional charge of France's historic trials. In this way, the speaker, himself handing the message on, confers upon his audience the qualities of constancy and courage-in-adversity. As we pointed out above, there is a blurring of the line of demarcation at this point in the speech between the audience and the French as a whole. Here, the difference between the audience and others is strongly stressed once again:

> Vous que la volonté de servir a réunis ce soir vibrants, chaleureux, innombrables, vous porterez témoignage de ce qui s'est passé ici. (73)

> You whom the will to serve has reunited this evening, vibrant, warm-hearted, and innumerable, you will bear witness to what has happened here.

However:

> Français, Françaises, mes compatriotes, mes amis . . . (74)

> French men and women, my compatriots, my friends . . .

is repeated immediately after this, thus again conflating (in the classic Gaullist form of national address), audience and nation. In the 'vous' of the first quotation, and in the 'Français, Françaises' of the second, Chirac is either referring to the real audience and then out past it to the French people, or else the actual audience has become — and this is the discursive effect — simultaneously the *compagnons* and the French as a whole, that is to say, the political actors in both the first (the banding together of disciples) and last (acclamation by the people) phases of the witness element of the Gaullist myth. The rare shifts of identity or position of the audience underline dramatically both the exclusiveness of the audience and an eventual unity of the nation. The link between the two is, of course, the leader who lays successful claim to the Gaullist heritage and can represent the RPR to itself as a rally.

The final, traditional declaration, 'Vive la République, Vive la France' ('Long live the Republic, Long live France') (75), therefore has a more than ritually formal role. Here, the subjunctive mode of the declaration ([que] vive) takes on its full charge. The mission ahead for the Gaullist movement, under the inspired leadership of Chirac, is to reenact in political action the latter part of the Gaullist myth, (the first part being *discursively* reenacted in the speech itself), that is to say, the taking of power by the visionary leader, and, national acclaim of him, in order that France live again.

NOTES

1.   The turnout for the European elections was 60 per cent. The results in terms of shares of the total vote were as follows: *Union pour la France en Europe*, 27.52 per cent (Giscardians), *Parti socialiste/mouvement des radicaux de gauche*, 23.58 per cent, *Parti communiste français*, 20.59 per cent, *Défense des intérêts de la France en Europe*, 16.24 per cent (Gaullists), (*Le Monde*, 12 June 1979).

2.   This emphasis upon the circumstantially relative claims to political legitimacy marks Gaullism off from traditional republicanism. Chirac has always claimed to be a republican and to be defending the institutions of the Fifth Republic. However, because in Gaullism the nature of political change refers to myth and does not proceed from empirical observation, the interpretation of decline within the republic is dependent upon the visionary leader. In de Gaulle's statements, as in Chirac's, where the two terms 'Etat' and 'République' co-exist, the former always take precedence. And in moments of regime crisis defence of the republic is always seen as conditional upon its functional efficacy in strengthening the State. See, in particular, de Gaulle's press conference, 19 May 1958 (*Discours et messages: Avec le renouveau* (Paris, 1970) pp. 4-10), and his television broadcast of 23 April 1961 (1970, pp. 306-308).

The name of the Gaullist party has changed several times since the founding of the RPF in April 1947. The successive names are: *Rassemblement du peuple français* (RPF), 1947-53; *Union pour la nouvelle république* (UNR), 1958-67; *Union pour la nouvelle république-Union démocratique du travail* (UNR-UDT), 1967-68; *Union pour la défense de la république* then *Union des démocrates pour la république* (UDR), 1968-76; *Rassemblement pour la république* (RPR), 1976-. Moreover, the Gaullists have often changed the name of their organisation at election times. The point of these changes is that they signify a perpetually renewed rally.

3.   'La vertu d'une Constitution consiste en ceci qu'elle procède de la volonté du peuple et qu'elle répond aux conditions dans lesquelles doit vivre l'Etat.' Speech by de Gaulle to the Consultative Assembly, 29 July 1945 (*Discours et messages: Pendant la guerre* (Paris, 1970) p. 593). The idea of 'la

Nation' is also crucial to Gaullism. It signifies the people, self-conscious of their nationhood. As such, however, the term is not, strictly speaking, part of the hierarchy: 'France', 'Etat', 'République', but a sub-category of 'France' itself.

4.   Other specific objectives automatically derive from these principles, such as the need for a strong currency, strong political institutions, non-alignment, and military strength. For a discussion of the internal political function of de Gaulle's foreign policy, see P.G. Cerny, 'Foreign policy leadership and national integration', *British Journal of International Studies*, vol. 5 (1979) pp. 59-85.

5.   *Rassemblement pour la république: Statuts nationaux, adoptés par les assises extraordinaires du 5 décembre 1976* (no publication details). The President of the RPR is elected by the *Assises nationales* of the party. His powers are considerable. He has little to do with the administrative aspects of party life which are the function of the General Secretary, who is chosen by the President, as are the members of the Executive Commission (Titre VI. art. 23).

6.   The legitimacy of this claim was strengthened by the widespread belief that the Union of the Left would win the legislative elections of 1978.

7.   The anomaly of Chirac's position was that he, as leader of the largest party in the governing majority, and, after the 1977 municipal elections, as mayor of Paris also, remained 'within' the regime (unlike de Gaulle between 1946 and 1958). See A. Sanguinetti *J'ai mal à ma peau de gaulliste* (Paris, 1978) pp. 176-7, and article by Sanguinetti in *Paris Match*, 21 December 1979.

After the elections Chirac issued the following declaration: 'Nous avons mené un grand combat pour mettre les Français en garde contre les dangers qui menacent la liberté et les intérêts de la France. Je remercie les millions d'électeurs et d'électrices qui ont compris le sens de notre message . . . Quant à nous, nous avons la conviction d'avoir dit la vérité même si celle-ci n'est pas toujours bonne à dire, et je me rappelle la phrase du général de Gaulle: Le service de la nation ne va pa sans trouble dans l'opinion ni pertes aux élections. Nous continuerons donc, avec le même courage, notre combat pour le redressement national car nous savons que les événements justifieront demain notre action et que les Français verront alors où sont leurs vrais défenseurs et les vrais serviteurs de l'intérêt national.' (*La Lettre de la Nation,* 11 June 1979, p. 3).

8.   Cf. Chirac's remark at the Pantin meeting: 'Comme chaque fois que dans l'histoire de notre pays se sont annoncées des heures graves, des hommes d'honneur, des hommes d'enthousiasme, de coeur et d'action sortent du silence et de l'ombre. Ces hommes et ces femmes de France sont venus de tous les horizons pour être ici, pour crier 'présent', face à nos adversaires qui les voudraient muets. Pour affirmer leur fierté d'être debout face à ceux qui, déjà, rêvent de les voir à genoux.' (*Rassemblement Actualité*, no. 23, February, 1978).

The notion of 'fatalité' is intrinsic to Gaullism. De Gaulle himself uses the term infrequently (see, for example, *Discours et messages*, vol. 2, *Dans l'attente, 1946-58* (Paris, 1970) pp. 30, 113, 169, 389, 404, 461, 536). Gaullist voluntarism, however, is dependent upon it. In de Gaulle's writing the idea of 'fatalité' serves two related functions. First, it dramatises opposition. Second, it highlights personal judgement by suggesting that there is a real, though not apparent, distinction between the inevitable, on the one hand, and the avoidable — or the possible — on the other. 'Fatalité' as a concept, therefore, is central to Gaullism from 18 June 1940 onwards. Moreover, its use has become more mannered and self-conscious in the rhetoric of Gaullism (see, for example, M. Debré *Ces princes qui nous gouvernent* (Paris, 1957) pp. 185-6 and 188) and is a central discursive device in contemporary Gaullism: 'Hier encore, Jacques Chirac devant la presse économique et financière a récusé la politique de l'inévitable et développé de nouveau ses propositions pour une politique de croissance économique, en démontrant que la France avait les moyens de ne pas s'en remettre à la fatalité'. (P. Charpy, *La Lettre de la Nation,* 1 June 1979). And again after the European elections: 'Aujourd'hui comme il y a trente neuf ans, des voix, et même de grandes voix, nous disent: Acceptez la fatalité. Mais nous savons, précisément depuis le 18 juin 1940, qu'il suffit d'une seule voix pour que la fatalité ne soit plus fatale et que la France reste la France.' (Charpy, *La Lettre de la Nation,* 18 June 1979). This last quotation is also a good illustration of the contemporary personalist use of myth. Chirac is being likened to de Gaulle, not only through circumstantial comparison, but also through the implication that Chirac's 'voice' is identical in purpose and power to de Gaulle's.

9. 'Because strait is the gate, and narrow is the way, which leadeth unto life, and few there be that find it. Beware of false prophets, which come to you in sheep's clothing but inwardly they are ravening wolves.' Matthew, 8, 14-15.

10. A good illustration of the metaphysical, and therefore eternal, nature of the struggle between Good and Evil and the concomitant voluntarism it calls into being in Gaullism is the following quotation from a speech by de Gaulle of 18 April 1942: 'La guerre que nous faisons n'est pas seulement une bataille entre les armées. Elle est la lutte du mensonge contre la vérité, de l'ombre contre la lumière, du mal contre le bien. Nous ne la gagnerons qu'à la condition d'attaquer le mal, de percer l'ombre, de poursuivre le mensonge. L'archange même sera vaincu s'il se laisse prendre aux artifices de Lucifer'. (*Discours et messages*, vol.1 *Pendant la guerre, 1940-46* (Paris, 1970), p. 182).

11. It is significant that Chirac refers to West Germany simply as 'L'Allemagne' (39 and 40).

12. See also J. Chirac, 'France: illusions, temptations, ambitions,' *Foreign Affairs*, vol. 56 (April 1978) pp. 489-99, where he argues that Gaullist French foreign policy is necessarily difficult to understand and needs enlightened judgement in order that it be properly explained.

13. Cf. de Gaulle's speech when receiving Adenauer in July 1962: 'S'il est vrai qu'une politique ne vaut qu'en vertu des circonstances, il l'est aussi qu'elle ne procède que des hommes.' Quoted in P. de Saint Robert, 'De Gaulle et la tradition historique de la France', Institut Charles de Gaulle. *Approches de la philosophie politique du Général de Gaulle* (Paris, 1983) p. 47.

APPENDIX: DISCOURS DE JACQUES CHIRAC

Bagatelle, Bois de Boulogne, Paris, 2 juin 1979

(1)   Amis venus de toutes les régions de France pour communier dans la même ferveur, je vous adresse mon salut!

(2)   A vous, compagnons d'Ile de France et du Centre, d'Auvergne et du Limousin. A vous Normands et Bretons, gens de Loire, du Poitou et des Charentes, d'Aquitaine et du Midi. A vous du Languedoc, du Roussillon, de la Provence des Alpes, de la Corse. A vous venus de Bourgogne, d'Alsace, de Lorraine. A vous mes compatriotes des départements et territoires lointains d'outre les océans qui êtes aussi présents au Rassemblement de la patrie française. A vous tous enfin, Français et Françaises de l'étranger qui portez en tant de pays le témoinage de la France, j'adresse mon salut!

(3)   Aujourd'hui réunis à Paris, dans la joie du printemps, comme nous étions l'an dernier dans la rigueur de l'hiver, nous sommes venus faire entendre la voix forte de l'espoir et de la confiance. Souvenez-vous de Pantin. Souvenez-vous du temps ou nous étions les seuls à croire encore à la victoire de la liberté. Souvenez-vous de la surprise d'abord, puis du sursaut national que provoqua notre Rassemblement.

(4)   Une fois encore, il nous appartient de changer le cours d'une apparente fatalité. Une fois encore, il nous faut montrer la porte étroite qui ouvre sur le seul avenir digne de la France.

(5)   Voilà mes amis, voilà, chers compagnons, pourquoi, au milieu de la fête et de l'enthousiasme populaire que vous avez su créer depuis ce matin, nous devons maintenant marquer un moment de réflexion et de gravité. Si votre choix est fait, songez à tous ceux qui cherchent encore et qui demain vous diront: 'Vous étiez à Bagatelle. Et alors?'

(6)   Alors, mes amis, il vous faudra déchirer devant leurs yeux le voile qui, une semaine encore avant le jour de l'élection, continue à masquer l'enjeu, pour la France et pour l'Europe, du choix que nous allons faire.

(7)   Paradoxalement, depuis des mois, on nous a beaucoup parlé de l'Europe. Mais nos concitoyens s'y reconnaissent de moins en moins. Il est vrai que certains brouillent les pistes! On prétend parfois que cette élection est une simple formalité qui n'aura pas vraiment d'incidences nouvelles. Mais on laisse entendre aussi qu'il s'agit d'une étape décisive dans la construction européene! On nous parle de même d'une convergence entre les Français, sur l'Europe, en s'efforçant de gommer les différences qui séparent les formations politiques de notre pays. Et les électrices et les électeurs se demandent alors: 'Mais si tout le monde est d'accord, pourquoi plusieurs listes, et pourquoi tant de débats?' En fait, Amis et Compagnons — C'est la première vérité qu'il nous faut rétablir — Tout le monde n'est pas d'accord. M. Marchais dresse un absurde constat de faillite du Marché Commun et ne se prive pas d'expliquer que moins on fera d'Europe, mieux les Français s'en trouveront. Quel point commun pourrions-nous avoir avec cette vision rabougrie de la France? M. Mitterrand prône l'Europe socialiste. Personne ne sait très bien ce qui signifierait une Europe socialiste ni comment pourraient bien la construire ensemble les travaillistes de M. Callaghan — qui sont britanniques avant d'être socialistes et européens — les sociaux-démocrates de MM. Schmidt et Brandt — qui n'ont pas du tout

envie de renoncer aux délices du capitalisme ni à la puissance des cartels allemands — et puis les socialistes du cher M. Mitterrand qui veut rompre, lui, avec l'économie libérale et en découdre avec le capitalisme . . . Tout en ayant à se garder sur sa droite du supra-national Mauroy, Ee sur sa gauche de l'anti-européen Chevènement.

(8)   Quel embrouillamini! Mais que nous importe, à nous? Ce que nous savons, c'est que nous ne voulons ni d'une Europe socialiste, ni d'une France socialiste! Nous nous sommes suffisamment battus pour cela en 1978. La vérité consiste aussi à dire ce qui nous sépare de la liste UDF.

(9)   Depuis plusieurs semaines, nous assistons à une extraordinaire entreprise de mystification de la part des responsables de la liste officielle conduite par Mme. Simone Veil et parrainée par M. Barre. Il s'agit pour eux de capter une partie de l'électorat gaulliste et, pour ce faire, d'accréditer l'idée que la politique européenne du Gouvernement actuel se situe dans la ligne de celle que, pendant plus de 15 ans, ont conduite le Général de Gaulle et Georges Pompidou.

(10)   Cela est faux, et je voudrais le prouver en rétablissant du même coup une vérité historique qui tient en une phrase: sur l'Europe, ce qui nous sépare de l'UDF est incomparablement plus profond que ce qui nous unit. La vérité historique, c'est que, depuis trente ans au moins, s'opposent deux idées nettement tranchées de l'organisation européene.

(11)   Il y a d'abord l'idée supra-nationale qui consiste à croire qu'on peut, progressivement mais assez vite, priver de leurs prérogatives essentielles les parlements et les gouvernements nationaux pour transférer l'exercice de la souveraineté à un super-Etat conçu sur le modèle des Etats-Unis d'Amerique, en oubliant que la situation de l'Europe composée de vieilles nations n'a rien à voir avec celle d'une Amérique qui s'est constituée sur des territoires vierges avec des hommes déracinés de leurs attaches. Il y aurait alors un super-gouvernement européen statuant à la majorité, un super-parlement européen dans lequel la majorité consitueée, par exemple, par le groupe socialiste, imposerait sa loi à la minorité — souvenons-nous que la France n'aura que 81 représentants sur un total de 410 — une super-justice enfin dont les arrêts s'imposeraient aux tribunaux nationaux.

(12)   La deuxième idée de l'Europe, c'est-à-dire la nôtre, est tout à fait différente. Elle repose sur le respect de l'identité et de la souveraineté des Etats membres qui ne doivent recevoir d'obligation qu'après y avoir consenti librement. Dans cette conception, les progrès de la construction européenne et la mise en place de politiques ou de projets communs résultent de la coopération et de la négociation inter-gouvernementale. C'était naturellement la vision que le Général de Gaulle avait de l'Europe. Par une action patiente — qui n'excluait toutefois pas les coups d'éclat — il a obtenu que le Traité de Rome soit interprété et appliqué dans ce sens, et non pas dans le sens supra-national. En 1965 la Commission de Bruxelles, cette instance de hauts fonctionnaires, servie par une armée de plusieurs milliers de bureaucrates, a voulu s'ériger en gouvernement européen. Le Général de Gaulle y mit le holà: la Commission redevint ce qu'elle ne doit pas cesser d'être, c'est-à-dire l'organe d'exécution des décisions du Conseil des Ministres ou chaque Etat-membre peut exprimer, à égalité, le point de vue de son gouvernement légitime.

(13)   Il est clair que cette idée de l'Europe est la seule qui soit compatible avec l'idée que le Général de Gaulle et, à sa suite, le Président Pompidou, se faisaient de la France, de son indépendance, de sa grandeur et de sa

puissance.

(14) Mais si l'on y réfléchit bien, c'est aussi la seule approche européene réaliste; c'est la seule manière d'obtenir des progrès réels sur la voie d'une unité européenne qui ne sortira pas du chapeau d'un pseudo-parlement communautaire ou d'une commission apatride, mais résultera des efforts de longue haleine que chacun de nos pays consentira pour renforcer les solidarités concrètes entre partenaires nationaux.

(15) Croyez-vous que la paix en Europe, et la réconciliation franco-allemande qui en constitue la clef de voûte sont nées par décret de la Commission de Bruxelles ou de l'Assemblée de Strasbourg? En vérité, elles résultent de l'accord et de la coopération entre deux gouvernements souverains et leurs chefs: la Chancelier Adenauer et le Général de Gaulle!

(16) Croyez-vous que la politique agricole commune soit l'oeuvre des experts de la Communauté qui pululent à Bruxelles, à Luxembourg ou à Strasbourg? En vérité, elle a été arrachée par le Gouvernement français comme contre-partie au désarmement douanier que visaient en priorité l'Allemagne et les pays du Bénélux.

(17) Croyez-vous que l'Airbus soit le fruit d'une politique industrielle enfin sortie des tiroirs communautaires? En vérité, c'est le produit de la coopération franco-allemande, d'Etat à Etat et de firme à firme, la Grande Bretagne n'ayant pris sa part de l'aventure qu'au terme d'une négociation âpre et longue.

(18) Tout ce qui privilégie les mécanismes supra-nationaux au détriment de la coopération intergouvernementale affaiblit en réalité non seulement la France, mais aussi l'Europe elle-même, dont le progrès ne peut venir que de la compétition des volontés nationales. C'est pourquoi je n'hésite pas à affirmer que nous sommes de meilleurs européens que tous les inventeurs d'institutions artificielles ou fragiles, d'autant plus artificielles et fragiles que les mêmes apprentis sorciers veulent à tout prix, au nom du sacro-saint élargissement de la Communauté, les faire fonctionner à douze et non plus à neuf.

(19) Je redoute — et je le dis ici solennellement — qu'à trop vouloir en faire, on n'arrive tout simplement à bloquer, puis à casser ce qui a été si difficilement construit depuis 20 ans. Or, la vérité historique, c'est aussi que la plupart des ténors de la liste Veil ont toujours été des adversaires de la politique du Général de Gaulle et restent plus que jamais opposés à la conception de l'Europe qu'il a fait prévaloir.

(20) Qu'on ne vienne pas me raconter que M. Pintat a été, est, ou sera gaulliste, lui qui déclarait à un grand journal de province, il y a moins de deux mois: 'Il va falloir donner plus d'ampleur à la règle du vote à la majorité au détriment de l'unanimité au sein du Conseil des Ministres. Pour aller de l'avant, il faudrait que l'Assemblée européenne ait un véritable pouvoir législatif'!

(21) Qu'on ne vienne pas me raconter que M. Diligent a été, est ou sera gaulliste, lui qui, en janvier, après avoir entendu M. Poniatowski revendiquer la filiation gaulliste, avait au moins le mérite de poser cette bonne question: 'Mais enfin, si cette ligne, de Charles de Gaulle à Valéry Giscard d'Estaing en passant par Pompidou, n'a pas varié, peut-elle être celle que défendent les démocrates sociaux?'

(22) Qu'on ne vienne pas me raconter que M. Lecanuet a été, est ou sera gaulliste, lui qui préside le CDS et adhére au parti populaire européen dont la plate-forme électorale, publiée le 14 février 1979, explique qu'il faut 'construire une Europe à finalité fédérale . . . renforcer le pouvoir exécutif de la Communauté et étendre les compétences du Parlement Européen'.

(23) Et qu'on ne me dise pas non plus que ces hommes ont changé. J'ai pris mes citations en 1979, et non pas en 1965, époque héroïque ou M. Lecanuet se faisait un honneur d'avoir mis le Général de Gaulle en ballottage avec le soutien d'un comité ou siégeait d'ailleurs M. Barre, et ou M. Pflimlin réclamait un changement radical dans l'orientation de la politique étrangère de la Vème République. La vérité historique, c'est qu'après s'être mis en sommeil le temps d'une campagne électorale, pour ne pas effaroucher notre électorat et se prêter à une odieuse entreprise de récupération, les co-listiers de Mme. Veil qui se répartiront à Strasbourg entre divers groupes politiques, espèrent bien prendre leur revanche.

(24) Ce serait, si nous les laissions faire, la revanche sur la thése gaulliste.

(25) Ce serait la revanche de l'Europe de l'impuissance, du bavardage et du désordre sur l'Europe de l'efficacité dans le respect de l'identité des nations.

(26) Ce serait enfin la revanche sur la Vème République d'une coalition hétéroclite de centristes et de radicaux appelant à la rescousse tous ceux qui, à l'étranger, veulent une Europe à l'américaine, les uns parce qu'ils n'ont pas de rôle international à jouer, les autres parce qu'ils savent qu'ils y seront les plus forts.

(27) Une chose au moins sera claire désormais dans l'esprit des Françaises et des Français: ni le passé des gaullistes que nous sommes, ni les convictions politiques, ni notre vision de l'avenir ne sont en convergence, sur l'Europe, avec les thèses centristes, qui inspirent la quasi-totalité des co-listiers de Mme. Veil. Ce n'est pas un problème de rivalité partisane ou personnelle. C'est un probléme de fond. Tout nous sépare d'eux: nous voulons, nous, faire l'Europe de la France, pas l'Europe des autres. Telle est la première vérité qu'il faut rétablir!

(28) Telle est la vérité que tous ceux qui, ici ou autour de vous, ont un rôle à jouer dans l'information des Français se doivent de rapporter scrupuleusement. Mais une fois la vérité rétablie, notre tâche n'est pas finie pour autant. 'Car, va-t-on nous dire, en fin de compte, cette Europe dont on nous rebat les oreilles, faut-il être pour? Faut-il être contre? Les communistes sont contre, et vous n'êtes pas d'accord avec eux. Les socialistes et l'UDF, semble-t-il sont pour, et vous n'êtes pas d'accord avec eux. Que voulez-vous donc ?'

(29) Je songe aussi aux jeunes gens et aux jeunes filles qui n'ont pas connu la IVème République, qui n'étaient pas éveillés à la raison politique lorsque le Général de Gaulle a quitté le pouvoir, et qui pourtant, le 10 juin, devront voter. Que se dit aujourd'hui la jeunesse de France? Que se dit la jeunesse d'Europe? Je n'aurai pas l'impudence de parler en son nom. C'est elle-même qui doit choisir l'avenir qu'elle veut vivre. Mais, par moment, je me demande si notre grand débat historique, tout nécessaire qu'il soit au rétablissement de la vérité, ne lui apparait pas irréel et bien étranger à ses préoccupations véritables, faites de générosité et d'enthousiasme.

(30) L'Europe, oui l'Europe. Mais l'Europe pour quoi faire? Que changera-t-elle au monde tel qu'il va, aux souffrances des humbles chez nous et plus

encore dans les pays de la misère, à l'injustice que perpétue l'egoïsme des forts, à l'oppression qu'étendent chaque jour tant de régimes barbares, qu'ils soient fascistes ou communistes? L'Europe est-elle seulement ce grand oiseau malhabile, à vague forme humaine, que cherche à nous vendre, à coup de millions, la propagande bruxelloise? L'Europe n'est-elle pas plutôt une réponse concrète à notre attente, pour nous-mêmes, pour notre travail, pour notre liberté, pour l'amour que nous devons au monde? Et, après tout, cette interrogation inquiète, jeunes gens et jeunes filles de France, n'est sans doute pas votre privilège. Vous aussi, Gaullistes de la première heure, recrus d'épreuves, nous aussi hommes et femmes de l'âge mur, nous la posons parfois lorsque nous lassent les joutes politiques trop bien huilées et les débats trop ronronnants.

(31) Mes amis, dans l'immense rassemblement de ce 2 juin ou se mêlent toutes les régions de France, tous les métiers de France, tous les niveaux de la société française, oublions pour un temps les listes et les sièges, les pourcentages, les partis et leurs états majors. Songeons à la route qu'il nous faut faire ensemble, demain et chaque jour. Sur ce chemin, je voudrais placer quelques repères, en forme d'avertissements que je vous demande d'entendre, pour agir et, s'il fallait, pour témoigner.

(32) Je voudrais d'abord vous dire qu'il ne faut pas croire les marchands d'illusions qui cherchent à vous vendre l'Europe comme je ne sais quel remède miracle à tous vos maux. Soyons sérieux! Quelques innovations institutionnelles dans les Communautés, l'adhésion de quelques pays nouveaux ne suffiront pas à relever le défi que la jeunesse du monde lance à la vieille Europe.

(33) Ce n'est pas parce qu'on fera l'Europe qu'on pourra du jour au lendemain travailler 35 heures par semaine, sans craindre pour notre compétitivité vis-à-vis de l'Amérique, de l'Asie, ou du Japon, bien au contraire.

(34) Ce n'est pas parce qu'on fera l'Europe, surtout si on devait l'élargir à l'Espagne et au Portugal, qu'on fera reculer le chômage — bien au contraire.

(35) Ce n'est pas parce qu'on fera l'Europe que les jeunes médecins, les jeunes avocats, les jeunes agriculteurs français trouveront à s'installer plus facilement, bien au contraire!

(36) Tout cela est un leurre, comme cette étoffe rouge qu'on met devant les yeux du taureau pour le faire baisser la tête et foncer sans prudence. Vous savez tous, et vous les jeunes mieux encore que les autres, qu'il faut d'abord compter sur ses propres forces. C'est une question de dignité; c'est une question d'efficacité. Ce que nous ne ferons pas pour nous-mêmes, les sacrifices que nous ne consentirons pas pour remettre de l'ordre dans nos affaires et pour rester dans la course mondiale au développement — personne d'autre ne le fera à notre place.

(37) Tel est mon premier avertissement: il ne faut pas vouloir faire l'Europe à tout prix en pensant que, du seul fait de son unité, elle nous permettra de résoudre nos difficultés à notre place. Le rêve européen est l'alibi de ceux qui renâclent ou renoncent au redressement français.

(38) Mon deuxième avertissement, c'est que, pour bien faire l'Europe, il faut que la France soit forte.

(39) Notre pays ne pourra se maintenir à la tête de la construction européenne,

que s'il en a les moyens, sur le plan de la démographie, de l'économie, de la défense, de la diplomatie, de la paix sociale. Or, force est de constater que la France qui, au début des années 70, était bien partie pour rattraper l'Allemagne et tenir son rang en Europe, ne cesse, depuis quelques années, de s'en éloigner. C'est particulièrement vrai dans le domaine économique et la raison en est simple: la politique que le Gouvernement conduit depuis 1976 et qui devait déboucher sur le redressement de notre pays, a échoué. Je le dis sans aucune intention polémique, je le dis comme on constate un fait qui attriste parce qu'il y va des intérêts de la France. On s'en rend compte aisément si l'on compare l'état de la France aujourd'hui et l'état de la France il y a trois ans: l'inflation n'a pas été maîtrisée et tend au contraire à s'aggraver; la sécurité sociale qui était équilibrée ne fait ses fins de mois que grâce aux avances de la caisse des dépôts; le franc s'est dévalué sensiblement par rapport au mark; le fragile équilibre du commerce extérieur n'est dû qu'à la stagnation de l'activité générale — et encore la structure de nos échanges est-elle fort mauvaise. Mais surtout le chômage a pris des proportions inconnues jusqu'alors: en moins de trois ans, il a augmenté de plus de 40 pour-cent.

(40) La même conclusion s'impose si l'on compare l'état de la France à celui de ses principaux partenaires. Dans plusieurs pays européens — notamment en Allemagne — ainsi qu'aux Etats-Unis, le chômage a décru en 1978; la hausse des prix a été presque partout inférieure à la nôtre l'an dernier, jusqu'à plus de trois fois en Allemagne.

(41) Je crois que les raisons de l'échec français sont assez simples à percer. En vérité si le discours de nos gouvernants est musclé, voire hautain et morigénateur, la réalité est molle et velléitaire; qu'il s'agisse de l'énergie, des économies à faire, de la remise en ordre des dépenses administratives, de la politique sociale. Les vraies réformes sont dans les tiroirs.

(42) Nous savons que les problèmes ne sont pas simples et qu'on ne manie pas cette discipline complexe qu'est l'économie aussi facilement que les sondages! Les courbes du chômage résistent mieux aux efforts gouvernmentaux que celles des intentions de vote recueillies par certains instituts de sondage. Mais si nous reconnaissons le droit à l'erreur aux spécialistes les plus éminents — ou les plus patentés — de l'économie, nous connaissons, avant tout, le droit des Français à la vérité.

(43) Or la vérité, que l'on cache au pays, la voici. Elle tient en deux constatations.

(44) Première constatation: il est urgent de changer de politique économique:

(45) Les Français, par leur calme dans l'épreuve, ont montré jusqu'à présent une grande dignité, un sens aigu du respect de la démocratie. Mais lorsque, mois après mois, année par année, discours officiel après discours officiel, les promesses ne sont pas tenues; lorsque le pays s'enlise dans le chômage, que l'on tente de justifier par la lutte contre l'inflation, alors que celle-ci n'est pas elle-même jugulée; lorsque tant de jeunes au sortir des écoles ne se voient offrir qu'un numéro de demandeur d'emploi, alors, mes amis, un danger réel guette. Celui que l'humiliation ressentie brise l'élan d'un peuple et son ambition. Celui aussi que, dans le desarroi éprouvé, fermentent les germes d'une explosion sociale.

(46) La seconde raison qui commande d'agir vite est la forte poussée de la gauche. Celle-ci, victime des idées de mars 78, a repris vie et espoir. Malgré ses divisions, à chaque élection depuis un an, elle a gagné du terrain.

Avez-vous dit non au collectivisme il y a un an pour qu'il renaisse demain, riche de la déception de tous ces citoyens auxquels on s'obstine à dire qu'il n'y a pas d'autre politique que celle qui leur a fait perdre leur emploi. Le danger est d'autant plus grand que, demain, l'Europe va constituer une plateforme de premier plan pour l'eurosocialisme. Déjà M. Mitterrand a déclaré samedi dernier, devant ses admirateurs français et européens, que le groupe socialiste serait le plus nombreux et le plus fort à l'Assemblée européenne. C'est assez dire ses choix et que l'internationalisme socialiste est au premier plan de ses préoccupations, bien avant les avantages ou les inconvénients que la France peut tirer de l'Europe.

(47) La troisième raison qui appelle un changement de notre politique économique est la place de la France en Europe. Une France diminuée, une France rongée du dedans et doutant d'elle-même est une France qui ne pourra tenir son rang et imposer à des partenaires réticents une véritable volonté européenne. Nous risquons d'être l'homme malade de l'Europe. Pour défendre les intérêts des Français à Bruxelles, il faut que la France soit en état de le faire. Voilà pourquoi, contrairement à ce que l'on peut dire, ici ou là, notre situation intérieure et notre situation en Europe sont très étroitement liées.

(48) Le deuxième constat que l'on doit faire lorsque l'on veut dire la vérité aux français, c'est que contrairement à ce qu'affirme M. Barre qu'il existe une alternative. Une autre politique est possible et nous la proposons depuis trois ans. Il ne faut pas le cacher aux Français. On vous dit: la France traverse la crise, comme si cela expliquait quelque chose. Les Allemands aussi ont des problèmes énergétiques; eux aussi subissent les fluctuations du dollar; eux aussi sont sous le coup de la concurrence internationale; et pourtant leur situation économique est singulièrement plus prospère que la nôtre. Oui, la crise actuelle de la France est un jugement porté sur la politique économique qui est menée! Car notre pays ne subit aucune fatalité. Il éprouve des difficultés importantes, c'est vrai. Mais il a aussi des atouts majeurs: une agriculture puissante, des industries qui, depuis des années déjà, ont fait un fantastique effort de productivité, des travailleurs parmi les plus efficaces du monde industriel, une technologie poussée dans des secteurs de pointe. Tout cela doit être mis en valeur au lieu d'être freiné par un taux d'expansion médiocre. Les moyens d'une autre politique de l'économie existent. Ils sont à notre portée. Saisissons-les. Je les ai si souvent exposées que je me bornerai ici à en retracer les lignes de forces.

(49) La priorité absolue, l'obsession fondamentale doit être la lutte contre le chômage. Ceci suppose de développer une politique audacieuse de l'investissement de l'épargne et du crédit. Il faut encourager massivement nos industries de pointe et celles pour lesquelles la France bénéficie d'un bon créneau international. Il convient également de miser délibérément sur les petites et moyennes entreprises, les artisans, les commerçants en les libérant de ce carcan de réglementations et de contrôles tatillons qui les emprisonnent trop souvent en stérilisant l'esprit de création et l'initiative. Il faut restaurer un plan véritable — car on ne pilote pas un pays sans gouvernail — et contraindre l'Etat à remettre de l'ordre dans sa propre maison, en allégeant sa gestion et en renouant avec une politique contractuelle et de concertation indispensable à un pays démocratique.

(50) Plus les gaullistes sortiront renforcés du scrutin du 10 juin et plus la France aura de chances de prendre enfin le chemin du redressement, grâce à cette nouvelle politique économique et sociale, fondée sur la priorité absolue donnée à la lutte contre le chômage et le sous-emploi de toutes nos forces de production.

(51) Reconstruire la France, voilà l'ambition que doit s'assigner notre jeunesse pour mieux préparer l'avenir européen.

(52) Et je lance maintenant aux Françaises et aux Français mon troisième avertissement: le rôle de nos représentants à Strasbourg ne doit pas être de se prêter au jeu du régime de l'impuissance et de technocratie, mais d'agir en défenseurs intransigeants des intérêts de la France dans une Europe en marche. Car n'en déplaise à M. Barre ou à M. Mitterrand, pour nous, candidats de la liste 'Défense des Intérêts de la France en Europe', l'Europe est une belle et grande idée; mais c'est une chose sérieuse; c'est une grande affaire pour les Français. Nous ne nous contentons pas, comme d'autres, de baigner dans un romantisme béat ou un verbalisme claironnant; nous ne pensons pas que l'Europe est une sorte de poudre de perlimpimpin venant au secours des gouvernements à court d'idée; nous ne voulons pas que l'Europe se dilue dans un magma informe sous domination américaine.

(53) Nous sommes, nous, beaucoup plus ambitieux pour l'Europe. Nous sommes, nous, les véritables européens. Nous disons: chaque fois qu'un choix se présente, comme jadis dans la détestable affaire du marché aéronautique du siècle, choisissons la solution européenne. Trop souvent nos partenaires ne se comportent pas en partisans de l'Europe. L'organisation européenne est, pour eux, une succursale du pacte atlantique. Ils acceptent de payer de concessions politiques mais aussi économiques la protection nucléaire américaine et souhaiteraient nous y faire consentir également. En attendant, ils ont défait, bloqué le développement de la communauté économique européenne ou privé ses mécanismes d'efficacité.

(54) J'en citerai deux exemples. Le tarif douanier de la communauté vis à vis des autres pays, qui devait être le véritable ciment entre les Etats membres, a été démantelé sous la pression des Etats-Unis et du Japon. Il n'est plus, en moyenne, que de cinq pour-cent avant d'être encore diminué, livrant nos industries à la concurrence sauvage de pays à bas taux de salaires ou à celle de pays industrialisés, qui se gardent bien, eux les champions du libéralisme à sens unique, de supprimer les protections non tarifaires dont ils se sont dotés contre les produits européens. Depuis la politique agricole, imposée par le Général de Gaulle, aucune politique commune n'a été mise en place, ni pour l'énergie, ni pour la sidérurgie, ni pour les transports, ni pour le textile, ni pour rien. Cette Europe, bardée de technocrates, est une Europe qui ne construit rien de solide entre ses membres, si ce n'est pas une réglementation souvent paralysante.

(55) C'est pourquoi nous disons qu'il faut exiger de nos partenaires que soient définies des politiques communes dans les secteurs capitaux que nous avons évoqués. Il faut revenir à la lettre et à l'esprit du traité en restaurant une véritable préférence communautaire pour la défense des industries européennes frappées durement par des concurrences extérieures déloyales. Exigeons notamment la disparition globale et immédiate de tous les obstacles non tarifaires mis par les Etats-Unis et le Japon à l'entrée des produits européens. En un mot: partout, dans tous les domaines couverts par le traité, montrons-nous européens, faisons prévaloir l'intérêt de l'Europe au lieu de se réfugier dans l'attentisme ou dans l'atlantisme.

(56) Voilà, mes amis, ce nous appelons avoir une politique européenne. Mais, pour la mener, il ne faut pas avoir honte d'affirmer la volonté de son pays, même si elle est tout à fait différente de celle de nos partenaires. Il faut aussi que ce pays sache être fort et respecté. Or, depuis des mois, les intérêts de la France sont défendus avec mollesse et notre gouvernement a cédé

progressivement du terrain, sans contre partie, ni garantie véritable. Qu'on en juge!

(57) On pourra bien nous dire que les montants compensatoires monétaires sont affaire de spécialistes, la réalité est bien claire: Le Gouvernement français s'était engagé à n'entrer dans le système monétaire européen qu'après le démantèlement des dits montants compensatoires. Et bien! Nous sommes dans le système monétaire européen et les montants compensatoires n'ont pas disparu. On pourra bien nous expliquer que la création d'une zone de stabilité monétaire en Europe est propice au développement des échanges commerciaux et à la réunification des prix agricoles, il n'en reste pas moins que nous avons mis le franc français et notre politique économique à la remorque d'un ECU dans lequel le mark pèse 33 pour-cent et pèsera sans doute 40 à 45 pour-cent demain si l'évolution actuelle continue!

(58) On pourra bien nous démontrer que l'adhésion prochaine de l'Espagne et du Portugal va dans le sens de l'Histoire, nous prendrons avec l'élargissement à douze, un risque mal calculé pour l'agriculture et la viticulture du Midi, pour le marché de l'emploi national, pour le fonctionnement même de la communauté. Je pourrais multiplier les exemples de situations dans lesquelles nous avons cédé, sans doute pour ne pas apparaître incommodes mais au détriment des intérêts de la France. Eh bien! je l'affirme à nouveau: ce n'est pas en cédant toujours que nous servirons nos intérêts; mais ce n'est pas davantage en cédant que nous servirons la construction européenne. Car l'Europe qui se prépare, dépourvue de véritable protection douanière et de politique commerciale commune, menacée de remise en cause de la seule politique réellement commune que les six aient pu construire, cette Europe-là ce n'est pas autre chose que l'Europe impuissante et l'Europe vassale que les fanatiques de l'atlantisme ont toujours rêvée.

(59) Nous, Gaullistes, nous voulons prendre un autre chemin. Ce n'est pas celui de l'Europe à tout prix mais de l'Europe du donnant-donnant. Ce n'est pas celui de l'Europe des vaticinations bruxelloises; c'est celui de l'Europe de la coopération préservant l'identité de la France. Ce n'est pas celui de l'Europe soumise mais de l'Europe européenne et indépendante. Ce combat pour la France et pour l'Europe est en réalité le même. Nous sommes exigeants pour l'Europe comme nous sommes exigeants pour la France. Nous voulons une Europe qui en soit une, qui préserve sa liberté de manoeuvre non seulement dans le commerce mais aussi dans la politique mondiale, qui cultive ses valeurs propres, c'est-à-dire ses langues, ses paysages, son héritage historique, son architecture d'hier et de demain, sa médecine, sa science.

(60) Dans une telle Europe, chaque Nation doit évidemment garder son identité. Pour ce qui nous concerne, nous voulons que la France y demeure elle-même. Ouverte au Monde, certes! Mais non pas dissoute, dispersée, détruite.

(61) La France, ce n'est pas un Etat européen comme les autres.

(62) La France est aussi la référence de tous ces hommes dans le monde qui attendent de notre pays qu'il fasse encore entendre sa voix, par dessus l'opposition des blocs. Une France étiolée, une France satellisée faillirait à la mission qu'elle a elle-même tracée, il y a près de deux siècles déjà, lorsque, par la déclaration des droits de l'homme, elle a présenté à tant de nations étonnées ces idéaux de justice et de liberté dont l'écho n'est pas près de mourir.

(63) La France, demain encore, peut étonner le monde. Non, certes, parce qu'elle regarderait en arrière ou se replierait sur son passé. Non certes, parce qu'oublieuse des limites que lui assigne la géographie, elle prétendrait égaler les super-puissances et se partager le monde avec elles. Mais parce que, dix fois au cours de son histoire, elle a su explorer des voies nouvelles et retrouver force et audace quand certains la voyaient prostrée.

(64) Français, Françaises, mes Amis, le 10 juin, tout le peuple de France sera interrogé, pour la première fois dans sa longue histoire, sur la place qu'il entend donner à son pays dans le concert des peuples. On ne vous questionnera pas, comme dans d'autres élections, sur le point de savoir si vous êtes de gauche, de droite ou du centre. Non, on vous demandera: 'Comme Français, quelle France voulez-vous face au monde de demain?'

(65) Chacun, dans le silence et le secret de sa conscience, répondra.

(66) Fasse seulement que lui revienne alors en mémoire l'incessante cohorte des hommes et des femmes de ce pays, qui, au travers de tant de siècles d'efforts, nous ont remis le pays libre qui est le nôtre.

(67) Hommes et femmes illustres dont retentissent les noms dans nos écoles, hommes et femmes inconnus dans leur humilité; tous et toutes nous ont, de main en main, transmis le message. De la chevauchée de Vaucouleurs, à la marche de Valmy, du combattant de Champagne au partisan torturé du Mont Valérien.

(68) Ce message, avec respect, avec pudeur, lisons le ensemble. Il nous dit: un peuple a tous les droits hormis celui de remettre aux plus jeunes de ses membres moins que ce qu'il a lui-même reçu des ses aînés.

(69) Mes Amis, nous qui avons assez vécu pour garder le souvenir d'une France abaissée, meurtrie, divisée, trahie, savons ce qu'il faut de peine, de temps, d'endurance pour qu'elle offre le visage qui est le sien. La France est notre bien et nous n'en aurons jamais d'autre.

(70) Mes Amis, vous qui ne rougissez pas au noble mot de patrie.

(71) Mes Amis, souvenez-vous que, déjà entre les deux guerres, on a endormi la vigilance des Français au nom d'un optimisme béat dans la société des nations. On leur expliquait déjà que l'on pouvait s'en remettre sur d'autres du poids de son destin.

(72) Nos villes dévastées, toutes ces familles meurtries, tout le sang versé sur tant de terres disent assez ce qu'il advient des peuples qui ne savent pas garder les yeux ouverts sur la tempête du monde.

(73) Vous que la volonté de servir a réunis ce soir vibrants, chaleureux, innombrables, vous porterez témoinage de ce qui s'est passé ici. Vous porterez témoignage de ces dizaines de milliers d'hommes et de femmes, de ces dizaines de milliers de jeunes qui savent que la France mérite et justifie notre ferveur à la vouloir garder intacte. En ne baissant pas les bras devant la pression étrangère; en les ouvrant à la coopération entre les peuples; en voulant un pays moderne, entreprenant, fort et capable de défendre les intérêts de ces citoyens, vous offrirez au monde le visage d'une France qui ne veut pas mourir, qui ne veut pas non plus tolérer de vivre diminuée ou menacée.

(74) Français, Françaises, mes Compatriotes, mes Amis, vous êtes l'opposé de

la tiédeur, de la molesse, ou de l'abandon. Vous montrerez demain, par vos votes, quelle foi en l'avenir vous anime. Vous montrerez que vous n'êtes pas la France vieillie, la France étriquée, la France qui dort.

(75) Vous êtes la Jeunesse de la France! Vous êtes la générosité de la France! Vous êtes l'audace de la France! Vive la République! Vive la France!

5

Celebrities in Politics:
Simone Signoret and Yves Montand

Pamela M. Moores

Political culture, defined as the relationship between civil society and political practice, focuses in a democracy on the interaction between the electorate and their political representatives, and hence on political parties, which rally and organise individuals into collective groups to achieve common aims. Yet there are also single individuals, notable figures, who play a significant part in the shaping of political activity, whilst standing deliberately outside the party system, voicing their views independently. In the context of modern France, one thinks of influential politically committed intellectuals on both the Right and Left, like Barrès, Drieu la Rochelle, Malraux, Nizan, Sartre, Beauvoir, and many others. Since the Dreyfus Affair of 1898, when the term 'intellectuel' was first brought into common use as an independent noun to refer to the writers, artists, students and teachers petitioning in favour of Captain Dreyfus against the establishment (Ory and Sirinelli, 1986), the word has carried controversial connotations, whether used perjoratively, or else to evoke the notion of an elevated vocation or mission. Figures like Sartre and Beauvoir made political protests, and in doing so, raised their voices above party political debate, speaking in the name of superior values, as if symbols of the people's moral conscience, guardians of Truth.

From the number of French intellectuals seduced and disillusioned in turn by fascism or, more commonly, by Stalinism, it is evident that the intellectual has no monopoly of truth. Nonetheless, the audience he or she reaches through publication of writings, through essays, letters, petitions, and press coverage of diverse activities, enables him or her to exercise influence on social, moral and political issues, from outside the bounds of political parties, and have an independent personal impact on the political process.

Where such an influence is perceived, this is not necessarily due to superior intellect or political acumen *per se*, but may simply be an extension of the prominence and visibility which the individual has achieved through success in his or her own specialist sphere. The novelist, Milan Kundera, has observed that man's lifelong preoccupation is nothing but a struggle to get other people to listen to him: 'Toute la vie de l'homme parmi ses semblables n'est pas autre chose qu'un combat pour s'emparer de l'oreille d'autrui'.[1] A famous writer has a head start, but he is not alone in this today. With the growth of the mass media and the cult of star personalities, celebrities who may be much less distinguished intellectually, but have other talents, notably communication skills and personal charisma, also have the opportunity to influence opinion, not necessarily by joining a party or standing as an election candidate, but simply by making public statements on political matters. The famous are more likely to be heeded. Success in one sphere, therefore, facilitates access to and success in another, irrespective of specific credentials. It is in this light that we shall examine the political activities of the film stars Simone Signoret and Yves Montand, her husband from 1951 until her death in 1985. A few years younger than Sartre and Beauvoir, they nonetheless shared many political experiences with them, but as media celebrities they represent a different professional environment, straddling the entertainment world and political life. To this extent their careers foreshadow a trend which has become particularly marked over the last 20 years, namely the growing confluence and interpenetration of showbiz and politics (Schwartzenberg, 1977).

With the rise of the cinema, the illustrated popular press and, above all, advertising and television, western societies are increasingly dominated by images, and the preoccupation with personal or party image has accordingly grown in politics. In France today, candidates and parties employ publicity agencies to devise eye-catching slogans and symbols, and seek the assistance of communications counsellors to advise them on how to project their image, and improve their performance in front of the camera (Benoit and Lech, 1986; Cayrol, 1986; Cotteret and Mermet, 1986; Gourevitch, 1986). While politicians are coached as actors, it is not surprising that professional actors and film stars, who have long since perfected these particular skills, should be tempted by the role of politicians. Vanessa Redgrave, Ronald Reagan, Melina Mercouri, and recently Clint Eastwood, are but a few amongst many examples in western democracies. In France, Schwartzenberg cites the early case of the actor Roger Hanin, who stood as a candidate (albeit unsuccessfully) in the legislative elections in 1968 (Schwartzenberg, 1977: 187). Celebrities from other spheres too, who have enjoyed public prominence and thrived on the attendant publicity, have profited from their reputations to enter politics. In March 1986 the former Olympic hurdles champion Guy Drut entered the Assembly as an RPR deputy, whilst in the May 1987 elections to the central committee of the RPR, the most successful candidates were the singer Line Renaud and the former Olympic runner, Alain Mimoun. Athletics in itself is evidently not a training for politics, but international success and media attention open doors. By far the most notable example of a French celebrity moving into the political sphere is that of the popular comedian, film and radio personality, Coluche (who died in tragic circumstances in 1986). In his bid for the French presidency in 1981, Coluche secured a 16 per cent popularity rating in the polls (mid-December 1980), thus outstripping the Communist candidate Georges Marchais, and lagging not far behind Jacques Chirac and François Mitterrand at this stage. Although this wave of enthusiasm for Coluche was short-lived, his brief success demonstrates the apparent readiness of some sections of the French electorate to conceive of the possibility of a film star or actor in the presidential role, even though Coluche had no experience of public office, and no detailed policies to propose.

Other film stars meanwhile, rather than choosing to put themselves forward as candidates in their own right, have lent their support increasingly to election campaigns. At the 1974 presidential elections Valéry Giscard d'Estaing could count on Brigitte Bardot, Sylvie Vartan, Johnny Hallyday and Michel Sardou, whilst Mitterrand was supported by Dalida, Jean Ferrat, Juliette Gréco, and Michel Piccoli. By 1988 the campaign organisers for the main presidential candidates were actively enlisting the support of showbiz personalities, with Renaud, Gérard Depardieu, Daniel Auteuil, Emanuelle Béart, Pierre Arditi, Barbara and others rallying to the Mitterrand cause, while Isabelle Adjani, Johnny Hallyday, Sacha Distel, Pierre Dux and others were to be found in the Chirac camp. The phenomenon has now become so widespread that it has inevitably given rise to facetious and satirical articles in the press. Writing about showbiz in politics in *L'événement du Jeudi* (31 January and 6 February 1985), the journalist Patrick Sery presented a detailed diagram of an imaginary government of showbiz celebrities, attributing personalities to their respective parties, and distributing portfolios. Signoret and Montand are to be found on the Socialist benches, the latter charged with responsibility for Foreign Affairs. However, the case of Signoret and Montand is interesting, precisely because, although they have a longstanding reputation as politically committed stars, they attempted for the most part to avoid party alignment in this manner, following rather the path of very many intellectuals in retaining their independent status as critics and protesters.

Signoret is probably best known to the Anglo-Saxon public as Marie in Jacques Becker's *Casque d'or* (1952) or Alice in Jack Clayton's *Room at the Top* (1958), Montand perhaps as the lorry-driver Mario in *Le salaire de la peur* (1952) or the political opposition leader in Costa-Gavras' film *Z* (1968). Montand is also known in France as a popular music-hall singer who has maintained his considerable success over many years. This was his original claim to fame, although today it is his cinema roles which largely account for his reputation. The couple are extraordinarily famous; they are two of France's major film stars. It was as a film star that Signoret made her name, but she came to be known also as a best-selling writer in the later years of her life (she died on 30 September 1985). Her first autobiographical volume *La nostalgie n'est plus ce qu'elle était* (1976) and her novel *Adieu Volodia* (1985) both figure on the list of bestsellers, the former having sold a million copies, the latter already well over a million. *Adieu Volodia* won such immediate acclaim that translation rights were sold very rapidly throughout Europe and North America.

Both stars, however, also gained a reputation with the French public as political animals. What inspired this passion for politics, and why did they never join a political party? How are their political commitment and professional careers related? Finally, and above all, how have their various activities been perceived by the French public, and do the couple represent a broader phenomenon in French political culture?

The explanations for their interest in politics are broadly similar. Both came from immigrant families, and were subject to political pressures in their early years. They themselves were so directly affected by the crises and upheavals of twentieth century European history that, as Signoret relates in her autobiography, detachment from politics seemed inconceivable (Signoret, 1976: 228).

This was particularly true for the young Montand, originally Ivo Livi, born in Montsumano Alto, Tuscany, 13 October 1921. His father Giovanni, an ambitious idealist, was known in the local community for his socialist aspirations, and fell victim to fascist thugs, who burned down his workshop, destroying the family's livelihood (Rémond, 1983). Giovanni fled on foot to Marseilles, in the hope of emigrating to the USA, but immigration had become difficult, and he got no further. He found work, and his wife and children joined him in 1923. Times were difficult, and when Giovanni's new business went bankrupt in 1932, all five members of the family had to work to pay off the debts, even eleven year old Ivo, who was taken on in a pasta factory. Sacked two years later, he found what work he could, whether in the docks, in his sister's makeshift hairdressing salon, or as a metalworker. In view of these circumstances, son of a political refugee and victim of fascism, brought up in the working-class quarters of Marseilles, it is not surprising that Montand should have shown an early commitment to socialism. His elder brother Julien became a member of the French Communist Party, and worked for the communist trade union, the Confédération Générale du Travail.

Signoret, on the other hand, came from a privileged upper middle-class background and spent much of her youth in the well-to-do Parisian suburb of Neuilly (Monserrat, 1983; Durant, 1988). It was her status as a half-Jew which made her particularly sensitive to political developments in the 1930s. Her paternal grandparents, a Polish Jew and an Austrian Jewess, had never approved her father's marriage to a French Catholic, and so although her father was assimilated into French society, she was aware from an early age of religious and cultural tensions. In *La nostalgie n'est plus ce qu'elle était*, she comments that she had never been especially conscious of her own Jewish identity, until this was brought home to her by the gut reaction she experienced on first witnessing militants of the right-wing group L'Action française demonstrating in the streets in Neuilly (Signoret, 1976: 32). During the German occupation of Paris (1940-44), she resorted to using her mother's surname, Signoret, rather than her father's family name Kaminker. She used to pretend to have forgotten her work permit, so as to conceal her origins. In her view those who claim not to have known what was going on in Germany in the 1930s must have had their eyes shut, for her school in Neuilly experienced a constant influx of German Jews, her family's flat becoming a regular staging post for Jewish refugees on their way to the USA or Palestine.

Her mother's emotional sensitivity and her father's professional activities also played their part in Signoret's political education. She herself was born in 1921 in Wiesbaden, where the family lived for the first two years of her life, as part of the French occupying forces. The prestige and privileges they consequently enjoyed were a source of personal embarassment and distress to Signoret's mother. A staunch egalitarian, she later reacted fiercely too against the rise of fascism. Signoret's autobiography recalls isolated but significant protests, as her mother made an issue, for example, of a toothbrush discovered to be 'made in Japan', indignantly refusing to purchase the products of a fascist country (Signoret, 1976: 29).

Signoret's father, meanwhile, experienced important political events at first hand. As an international conference interpreter, he frequently worked abroad. He translated Hitler's first Nuremberg speech for French radio. In 1938, he was part of the French delegation to Munich, in Signoret's words 'that famous delegation of imbeciles'. A year later he was obliged to take refuge in Britain, from where he was regularly involved in broadcasts to occupied France. After the war he worked for the United Nations in New York, and later for the Council of Europe in Strasbourg.

The family's unity and very existence were threatened by the turmoil of the war years, and circumstances forced compromise upon a young and relatively naïve Simone. Obliged to work during her father's absence, to support her mother and younger brothers, she obtained employment as a secretary for Jean Luchaire in the offices of the newspaper *Les Nouveaux Temps*. She found the job through personal contacts and had no idea at first that Luchaire was a collaborator. The family's financial difficulties impelled her to stay in the post for eight months, in a situation especially uncomfortable for a half-Jew. It was not until the summer of 1941 that she plucked up the courage to leave and finally, in a mood of revolt, symbolically crossed the Seine from the *rive droite* to the *rive gauche* to join the artists and intellectuals of the Café Flore. For the next four years, however, her non-Aryan status hampered and frustrated her attempts to establish herself as a cinema actress, for she was unable to provide documents which would satisfy the German authorities.

Despite differences in social backgound, therefore, both Montand and Signoret entered adult life strongly opposed to fascism, longing for a new era of peace and co-operation which would transcend national boundaries. It was in the euphoria and idealism following the Liberation that they met in 1949, at a time when political commitment was very much in vogue in intellectual circles. For Signoret the distressing experience of unwittingly compromising herself by working for a collaborator had taught her that it is impossible to avoid taking sides, even involuntarily. Subsequently, in her own way, she made her contribution to the Resistance movement, carrying munitions, or providing overnight refuge for friends like Claude Jaeger, who were active in the movement (Signoret, 1976: 78-79). In her memoirs she writes with great admiration of her former history teacher who became a heroine of the Resistance, Lucie Aubrac (1976: 37).

Her memoirs also specifically mention the impact that Sartre made on her generation, particularly on friends in Neuilly, who had him as philosophy teacher (1976: 32). She herself made his acquaintance in the Café Flore in the early 1940s, and he was later amongst visitors to Signoret and Montand's flat on the Ile de la Cité. Her deep respect is evident; she shared Sartre's belief that one cannot detach oneself from events, since silence and passivity themselves are tacit expressions of consent. The very language and images she uses are reminiscent of Sartre, as she argues that if she and Montand had failed to take up positions on the momentous events of modern European history, they would have deserved to be likened to inanimate, subhuman or monstrous forms ('à des légumes, à des chaises, des ectoplasmes ou des méduses'), unworthy of the title of human beings! (1976: 228). As the obituaries following Signoret's death amply illustrate, their reputation is on the contrary one of energy, passion and generosity, courage, determination and humanity.

It was through Montand, and his family and friends in Marseilles, that Signoret first came into contact with working-class people, and experienced their solidarity. Whereas she was from an educated family, had her *baccalauréat*, and was used to moving in middle-class intellectual circles, Montand had received little formal education, and had established his reputation as a popular singer, a 'man of the people'. Yet both were inspired by left-wing ideals, and, in particular, by the international appeal of socialism. Montand had been brought up by Italian-speaking parents amongst Armenians,

Arabs, Greeks and Spaniards. Signoret had come into contact with Jewish refugees from many countries, and her father's livelihood centred on co-operation and communication between nations. As for many young people of their generation, international socialism held out great hopes for the future. Along with Aragon, Vailland, Claude Roy, Merleau-Ponty, Sartre, Beauvoir and many others, their names were commonly associated with the French Communist Party in the late 1940s and the 1950s.

Yet many apparent supporters of the party in this period espoused its ideals in general terms, without wishing to submit to its dogma and discipline. They were 'compagnons de route' rather than members. This was the case for Signoret and Montand, as for Sartre and Beauvoir, for although all were long associated with the party, none of them ever joined. For existentialists like the latter, who placed great emphasis on individual freedom, choice and responsibility, party membership and collective action inevitably implied conflict and compromise, subjects which are frequently explored in Sartre's writing. In Signoret's and Montand's case the resistance was instinctive rather than being articulated in philosophical terms, but they too prized their independence preferring to use their status as celebrities in their own particular way. In characteristically amusing and paradoxical fashion, Montand explains his position as follows:

> Je n'ai jamais adhéré à un parti quelconque, parce que j'ai des raisonnements contradictoires, que je remets sans cesse tout en question, et que je ne tolère pas l'intolérance ... (Quoted by Cannavo and Quiqueré, 1981: 22)[2]

> I have never belonged to any party, because my arguments are contradictory, I am constantly calling everything into question, and I cannot tolerate intolerance ...

The Communist Party line on cultural matters was especially difficult to 'tolerate', and at the same time particularly important to Signoret and Montand, working in cinema and concert-hall. Montand objected to a simplistic propagandist view of art, to crude socialist realism and a habitually idealised representation of the working classes. He was irritated by the emphasis placed on subjects considered ideologically sound, and the disregard for creative imagination or transposition (Verdès-Leroux, 1983: 313 and 465-6). Signoret was incensed at philistine comments about Gide and Hemingway, prompted by ideological prejudice, and complained of *L'Humanité*'s distorted reporting (Signoret, 1976: 106-7). Both she and Montand were also subjected to the party's neurotic criticism of anything remotely American or decadently foreign, which is how Montand's songs *Sanguine* and *Luna Park* were branded (Verdès-Leroux, 1983: 138, 324-6).

Nonetheless it was a common assumption that Signoret and Montand were members of the Communist Party, and no effort was made by either side in the 1950s to dispell this illusion. As Verdès-Leroux argues (1983: 346), the party reputation benefited from such an association, whilst Signoret and Montand, for their part, did not want to issue categorical denials, as this would only too readily have been seized upon at the time as proof of anti-communism, whereas they were fundamentally sympathetic to communist ideals. Signoret observes in her memoirs, 'on était d'accord avec eux sur pratiquement tout' (we were in agreement with the communists on virtually everything) (Signoret, 1976: 105). Even more recently, when asked by Maurice Pons to define her relationship with the party in the mid-1970s, she responded: 'on est fiancés, mais on n'épouse pas' (we are engaged, but are not getting married) (1976: 108). It was a loose alliance which provided the opportunity to exchange ideas with like-minded people, and publicly signal where they stood in the political spectrum, whilst allowing them to retain the artist's or intellectual's much cherished liberty. Signoret thought of herself as 'le type même de l'intellectuelle de gauche' (the typical left-wing intellectual) (1976: 103), and stressed the notion of independent protest, classing herself amongst the political ranks of the 'emmerdeurs' (critics bent on making a bloody nuisance of themselves) (1976: 150). She and Montand both attributed their credibility as political observers to the fact that, as public figures in the limelight, they were free and able to attract publicity to political issues of their choosing, without becoming prisoners of a party.

However, is it justifiable to talk about Signoret and Montand in one and the same voice, as if they constituted a homogeneous inseparable unit? They were together for 36 years, and on Signoret's death, obituaries and tributes to her developed the theme of an ideal harmonious relationship. In *Paris Match* Patrick Poivre d'Arvor featured 'trente-six années de vie et de passion partagées' (36 years of shared life and passion) (18 October 1985), while *France-Soir* published a series of six photos, tracing the couple's life from their marriage until the Caesar ceremony of 1985 (1 October 1985). Political conviction is very much determined by personal experience, and, as we shall see, many of the events which marked their political evolution were shared experiences to which they reacted in unison. Indeed, Montand has commented that there would be little point in his writing his life-story, since Simone has done the job so admirably for him in *La nostalgie n'est plus ce qu'elle était* (although in an interview in early 1987 he seemed to imply that he might try his hand nonetheless (*Paris Match,* 27 March 1987)). Professionally they pursued independent careers, only occasionally appearing as a couple in films, as the Proctors in *Les sorcières de Salem* (1957), or the Ludviks in *L'aveu* (1969). In private life their roles were different but complementary. Holding traditional views on marriage, Simone stated unashamedly that she would happily have given up her career to be with her husband (Signoret, 1976: 120-1), and frequently referred to herself humorously as his 'groupie'. Whereas in their early years together, her film contracts were sporadic, Montand's concerts were much in demand. In the limelight night after night, his public profile was therefore more developed, whilst as a film actress Signoret had less direct contact with her audience. This distinction is underlined in her autobiography:

> Etre une personnalité de music-hall, c'est le contraire d'être acteur, c'est être soi, dans un costume à soi, avec l'aide d'un bon répertoire choisi par soi, de bons musiciens choisis aussi par soi, et d'éclairages réglés par soi. Prétendre amuser, émouvoir, captiver un public qui vient vous voir dans **Vous**. (Signoret, 1976: 111).

> Being a music-hall personality is the opposite of being an actor. You are yourself, in your own costume, supported by a good repertory of your own choice, good musicians you have also chosen, and lighting which you likewise determine. You seek to entertain, move and captivate an audience which comes to see you in **You**.

The public was eager to learn what the star Montand himself thought about things. Consequently, from the late 1940s onwards it was he who attracted the publicity and made the controversial decisions and statements for which he frequently found himself under fire from the press, whilst Signoret, quieter and more reflective, provided moral support and worked in the wings in the interests of common ideals. With the passage of time and growing fame, their political priorities diverged slightly, and by 1983, Signoret evidently had reservations about some of Montand's more extreme political statements. However, for many years they assumed a clear profile in the press as a politically committed left-wing couple with common views, the film star equivalents of Sartre and Beauvoir.

It was during the cold war that they first took a political stance, actively demonstrating and signing petitions as members of the peace movement, the *Mouvement de la paix*. This was an organisation generally associated with the French Communist Party, but by no means synonymous with it, as Signoret was always keen to stress (Verdès-Leroux, 1983: 162). On 14 March 1950 they signed the Stockholm Appeal, calling for a ban on nuclear arms, and immediately Montand was denounced by the press as a supporter of Stalin, on the grounds that the Soviets were supporting the peace movement in order to undermine their enemies. The couple protested against the American war in Korea, and French troops fighting in Indo-China. They sought the release of Henri Martin, a French sailor imprisoned for refusing to obey orders in the bay of Tonkin, and Raymonde Dien, who demonstrated against the transport of munitions to Vietnam. Montand's very choice of repertoire became a political act. He incensed parachutists in his audience with songs such as *Le dormeur du val, Le chemin des oliviers* and *Quand un soldat*, recorded in 1952 while the troops were fighting in Indo-China. Public reaction was so strong that these songs were banned from French radio for three years. Posters for Montand's shows were smeared with tar, smoke bombs and tear gas released during concerts, and his mail brought threatening letters. He became a regular target of the right-wing press, who sought to make capital out of the distance between his lifestyle and that of the workers whose interests he supposedly espoused. During a transport strike in 1952, for example, much was made of his riding in a superb Bentley, while the proletariat had to walk! (Cannavo and Quiqueré, 1981: 235-6). As Cannavo and Quiqueré recount, however, in Montand's eyes this was but one of life's many insoluble contradictions: Yes, he had profited from the capitalist system and risen from nothing to a position of privilege, but as far as he could see, without speculating or exploiting others. Under a different regime, his status as an artist would be different, but he had to work within the system in which he found himself, and saw no point in renouncing the benefits of success or allowing others to exploit him (1981: 236-7). He confessed that, as a Latin, he feared he had a tendency to replace God by Marx, this admission suggesting an awareness of the slightly naïve quality of his idealism. Nonetheless, he has never seemed particularly disturbed by his own internal contradictions.

Indeed, Montand's faith in communism remained firm until the crisis in Hungary in 1956. This marked a turning point in his and Signoret's political development, as it did for a whole generation of intellectuals. When the Soviets intervened to quell the unrest in Hungary, Montand was preparing for a concert tour of several Eastern bloc countries, including performances in Moscow, Leningrad, Kiev, Prague, Warsaw, Sofia, Berlin, Belgrade, Budapest . . . Preparations had been underway for a year, contracts were signed and tickets sold. Should he honour his engagements and appear to condone imperialist repression, or dissociate himself from Soviet communism by cancelling the tour? Whatever decision he made, he was bound to be criticised. After much heart searching, he decided against cancellation, whilst making available to the press his letter of explanation to his friend Obratzov, theatre director in Moscow. Here he admitted being deeply troubled by recent events, which he was not prepared to condone, but he was concerned to play his part in fostering peaceful relationships between East and West, and it was to this end that he was making his trip. With the exception of *L'Humanité* and *Libération*, the entire French press was savage in its condemnation, and Montand's final Olympia concert before leaving France had to be cancelled for fear of riots. Long after his and Signoret's departure, his controversial decision continued to be the subject of a bitter polemic in the French press (Cannavo and Quiqueré, 1981: 238-56).

The concerts themselves were a tremendous success, and Montand and Signoret had the opportunity to meet and have discussions with Krushchev, Tito, and other important political leaders, to dine with Ehrenburg, the famous Soviet novelist, journalist and propagandist, and also to experience life in a communist country for themselves. In the process they discovered the realities of Stalinism, and were deeply disillusioned. Montand felt trapped and compromised, a political pawn, used and degraded not only by Soviet propagandists, but also by French Communists like Aragon, who callously declined to rally to his support, hypocritically disowning him (Signoret, 1976: 152-3 and 157). On his return to France, his reaction was to seek temporary withdrawal from politics. It is easy to understand how such a prominent personality, with a large popular following, came to fear the way in which he was likely to be manipulated by political parties. The media too, in their desire to label and simplify, sought to identify Montand with a particular viewpoint, but he was now far too confused about his own views to allow himself to be seen as 'porte-drapeau' (or standard-bearer) for any political ideology.

His desire for independence and his 'intolerance of intolerance' were reinforced by his trip to Eastern Europe, and doubts set in. Whereas, a few years earlier, he had been critical of close friends like the poet Jacques Prévert, who had started to question Soviet communism, his own reactions now became extremely complex. East and West were locked in the cold war, and Montand and Signoret in the West were officially classed as communist sympathisers and subversives. They had campaigned for mercy for Julius and Ethel Rosenberg, executed for espionage in the United States in 1953. On four occasions they were refused visas to travel to the United States to pursue their careers in the cinema. Yet after 1956 they were equally prepared to be associated with campaigns critical of communist countries. In Signoret's words, 'Pourquoi dénoncer toujours à sens unique?' (Why always denounce one side only?) (Signoret, 1976: 332). From this point onwards they became regular demonstrators and signatories of petitions against tyranny, torture and oppression all over the world, under regimes of all colours, in Chile, Algeria, Spain, Afghanistan, Poland. France was not exempt from their criticism, and during the Algerian war they were amongst the first militants on the Maurice Audin committee founded by Sartre. In September 1960 they were party to the *Manifeste des 121*, a petition signed by 121 well-known artists and intellectuals, denouncing French torture in Algeria and encouraging conscripts in a campaign of disobedience and dissent. Over many years the couple regularly associated with eminent political intellectuals. In September 1975, Montand was one of a group of leading Frenchmen who travelled to Spain in a vain attempt to save five young Spaniards from execution by Franco, delivering a message of protest in the joint names of Sartre, Malraux, Aragon, Mendès-France and François Jacob. His travelling companions were Costa-Gavras, Régis Debray, Michel Foucault, Jean Lacouture, the Reverend Laudouze and Claude Mauriac.

Political considerations also entered into their professional decisions. They were wary of reducing their art to a mere instrument of propaganda, but chose to appear in many films exploring controversial political issues: *Les sorcières de Salem* (1957) attacking MacCarthy's witch-hunt, *La guerre est finie* (1966) focusing on the revolutionary struggle in Spain, *Z* (1968) based on the assassination of a left-wing politician in Greece, and *L'aveu* (1969) denouncing the crimes committed by Stalinists in the name of communism. The latter, in which they starred together, was particularly significant in that it inevitably attracted hostile criticism from former friends in communist circles. It was an important step for the couple politically, and Montand threw himself into the part of London, purging a sense of guilt over his communist past.

In her memoirs Signoret describes how political convictions governed her choice of parts:

> Je serais incapable de prêter ma tête, mes yeux, ma voix, enfin moi, à une entreprise qui va à l'encontre de mes convictions les plus profondes. Je peux parfaitement jouer une indicatrice de la Gestapo dans un film antifasciste. Je ne peux pas jouer une mère admirable ou une amoureuse superbe dans un film fasciste. Je ne peux pas le faire et je ne l'ai jamais fait. (Signoret, 1976: 329)

> I should not be able to take a part, devote myself, head, eyes and voice, to a venture, if it were in conflict with my deepest beliefs. I am quite capable of playing a Gestapo spy in an antifascist film. I cannot take the part of an admirable mother or a superb lover in a fascist film. I cannot do so and have never done so.

Such comments illustrate Signoret's deep concern for broad political considerations, and her relative disregard for immediate personal image. Montand appears to have been governed by similar priorities, judging by his role as the antipathetic American agent Santore-Mitrione in Costa-Gavras' film *Etat de siège* (1972), but this in the context of a film evidently intended to expose and criticise USA undercover operations in South American countries. Both stars had the good fortune of such success and enjoyed such a strong personal reputation that they were able to pick and choose professionally, whilst maintaining their political integrity. Significantly, when Montand returned to the stage as a singer in 1974, after five years' absence, it was to give a charity concert for Chilean refugees, in a spontaneous response to the crisis resulting from Pinochet's advent to power. Montand had come to know and love Chile while filming *Etat de siège,* and Signoret observes that his decision to give the concert was not merely the stereotyped act of a political militant, but a genuine impulse from the heart, a 'coup au coeur' (Signoret, 1976: 361). Their political actions generally were not predictable contributions to organised campaigns, but personal and emotional responses to particular circumstances. It is in this respect, in this independence and detachment from the system, that their role bears some similarity to that of the intellectual, representing individual moral conscience and judgement rather than a party or ideology.

Whether or not the couple themselves can be regarded as intellectuals is to some extent beside the point, although Signoret, who was cultured, well-read, and in later years a successful novelist and autobiographer, merits this description, whereas Montand, who had little formal education, at first sight qualifies less obviously. However, the profiles of both stars present many of the characteristics of the influential intellectual identified by Hamon and Rotman in their highly entertaining study of French mandarins, *Les intellocrates* (Hamon and Rotman, 1981). Living throughout their married life in the premises of a former bookshop on the Ile de la Cité, Signoret and Montand were close to the Latin Quarter, and were also well-placed in terms of essential friendships and contacts. Hamon and Rotman list three specific sources of connections as being especially significant: a past interest in communism; a reputation for protest over the Algerian War and other colonial conflicts; and, finally, participation in the events of May 1968.

Signoret and Montand clearly meet the first two criteria, but I have made no mention of May 1968 in my account of their political development, precisely because they were so little involved in events on that occasion. Signoret was at the Cannes Festival, when the 'events' of May broke out, and many colleagues rushed back to Paris. Yet, seemingly uncharacteristically, she remained in the South, a decision she feels it necessary to analyse at length in her autobiography. Surprised and irritated that so many people, who had never been moved to militant action on previous occasions, were 'jumping on the bandwagon' as she saw it, she felt weary and cynical (Signoret, 1976: 342-5). Although she had every sympathy for the students' cause, she did not see it as her battle. Nonetheless, she felt nostalgic for previous conflicts, particularly as Montand was in Paris, joining demonstrations and talking to students in the streets. Even in his case, however, this was not a conflict which was important for him personally. The repression in Prague later in the year preoccupied him much more. It was basic issues of human rights and wider international struggles which prompted the couple to action (in particular still, events in Eastern Europe), rather than internal French politics. This may be partly due not only to their traumatic experiences in 1956, but also to their family histories as

142

immigrants. What their response to May 1968 also illustrates, is the inherent individualism of most stars and their relative disinterest in mass action, for their sense of purpose and influence stems not from swelling the numbers of the rank and file, but on the contrary from lending their individual name and reputation to a cause. Hence the importance of petitions and delegations in any account of Signoret's and Montand's political history. Moreover, whether the celebrities' knowledge of politics and analytical powers are limited or extensive, and even if their opinions are on their own admission contradictory, as in Montand's case, the reputation which their name carries in their professional sphere is sufficient to attract attention and lend credence to a political stance or viewpoint.

Signoret makes this point when recalling the excellent reception she and two other filmstars of political reputation, Serge Reggiani and Michel Piccoli, met with at the Ministry of Justice on one occasion, when arriving mistakenly two days early for a political demonstration. She comments that, had they been great scholars, perhaps nobody would have taken any notice, whereas they attracted embarrassing attention and received a sympathetic hearing. The moral of the story, she concludes, is to go into cinema: 'Moralité, faites donc du cinéma!' (Signoret, 1976: 359). She and Montand had the advantage of being widely known and recognised.

In the 1980s, and particularly since early 1983, Montand appears to have become set on exploiting this advantage more directly, assuming a more prominent profile, multiplying his public statements and appearances in the media. Fascinated by Reagan's presidency, and at a time when Coluche's fleeting success in the polls as a prospective presidential candidate had captured considerable media attention, Montand began to take an interest in details of policy, and to show personal political ambitions.

Since the late 1950s, the media had made an issue of Montand's apparent U-turn politically. His repeated disappointment over the years with communist regimes has now turned him into one of the communists' most outspoken and ferocious critics, in a period when communist support in France has declined. Moreover, following 1981 and the advent of a Socialist government and President in France, instead of celebrating, Montand appears to have become deeply disillusioned with the French Left more generally. In December 1981, he criticised the Socialist government, and in particular the Socialist minister Claude Cheysson, who was reponsible for foreign affairs, for their muted reaction to Jaruzelski's dissolution of trade unions and the introduction of martial law in Poland. A year later he voiced open hostility to the French Communist Party with his much quoted exclamation : 'Marchais, je lui dis merde!' ('To hell with Marchais!').[3] In an interview in the right-wing *Figaro-Magazine* in April 1983, he congratulated the Right for contributing to the economic prosperity of the nation, whilst accusing the Left of failing to condemn Soviet imperialism. In August he signed a petition published in *Libération* (12 August 1983), openly criticising the Socialists' foreign policy in Chad. In September, when the Front National was successful in the first round of the elections in Dreux, it was not right-wing racists he attacked in an interview on *Europe 1*, but rather the efforts of the French Communist Party to silence them, on the grounds that this was a violation of freedom of expression. On 15 September 1983, as the star guest on the television news programme, *7 sur 7*, he clarified his position, saying that he was as opposed as ever to racism, and a champion of liberty, but again he took the opportunity to denounce communist hypocrisy and totalitarianism. Inevitably the communist press, incensed at betrayal by a former ally, tried its best to discredit Montand, but his outbursts have found sympathetic ears and increased his fame, as a brief survey of opinion polls during this period illustrates.

In the summer of 1983, an IFRES poll for *France-Soir Magazine* (25 June 1983) asked French women which famous personality they would like to spend their holidays with. Montand was the winner. A few months later, another IFRES poll for *Le Quotidien de Paris* (3 September 1983) revealed that 60 per cent of those questioned approved of Montand's taking a public stand on contemporary political issues. Fifty-five per cent even declared that his views were more important than those of political leaders, which, as the newspaper commented, tended to confirm what an extremely poor opinion the French public had of professional politicians. This is perhaps one of the reasons why 81 per cent of the same interviewees also felt that Montand should not attempt to become one. It is because they did not perceive him as compromised and corrupted by political in-fighting, hypocrisy and self-interest, in short, precisely because he was not a politician, that they were prepared to listen to his political views. When asked whether they believed that, after success in the cinema, Montand might move on, like Reagan, to the presidency, 65 per cent maintained that such a development would be impossible in France. Nonetheless, once this question had been put, the right-wing press seemed determined to keep the issue alive. In November 1983, a journalist from *Paris Match*, reporting on a survey indicating that Yves Montand represented the French public's ideal man, exclaimed enthusiastically what a wonderful, popular President of the Republic he would make (18 November 1983). In November Montand was man of the month in *France-Soir Magazine*. In December, in an IFRES poll for *Le Quotidien de Paris* (29 December 1983), the public singled him out from among a list of well-known personalities, as the figure whose public activities they most approved of, placing him ahead of Barre, Chirac and Mitterrand. A third of those interviewed by the *Journal de Dimanche* even maintained that they would vote for him if he put himself forward at the elections (1 January 1984). As André Bercoff observed in *Les Nouvelles littéraires* (26 January 1984 — 1 February 1984: 16), the media were proving far more successful at creating, amplifying, and institutionalising what was referred to as 'le phénomène Montand', than any carefully planned political campaign could have been.

When Montand appeared on the television show *Dossiers de l'écran* (3 January 1984), he exceeded all previous popularity ratings for the programme, and the daily newspaper *Libération* reviewing the programme, commented that it was an American-style performance, likening him to Reagan. This parallel was being drawn ever more frequently, and seemingly with ever greater justification, the more Montand voiced strongly pro-American views. Towards the end of February, he was the leading presenter of a television programme *Vive la crise* (22 February 1984), focusing on the state of the French economy, which created a great stir. The central argument was that France's problems were due to excessive state bureaucracy and public spending, restrictive employment law, and unco-operative French trade unions, compared to their supposedly more reasonable American counterparts. The solution proposed was liberal monetarism along American lines. Shortly afterwards *Le Crapouillot* published a special issue entitled 'Le Choc Montand', including light-hearted skits, like André Bercoff's '1988: Montand Président. Le Reagan de l'aïoli' (no. 74, March 1984: 25-6). The press was clearly determined to capitalise on the Reagan-Montand parallel, deriving maximum sensation from speculation on the prospect of Montand standing for election as France's own film star President. When *Paris Match* interviewed Montand, also in March 1985, his political aspirations and the presidency were once again the subject of discussion. The following month, in a television programme entitled *La Guerre en face* (18 April 1985), Montand called for a stronger defence policy to counter the Soviet threat. Later in the year, he was a leading figure in the demonstrations against Jaruzelski on his visit to Paris. The slightest political gesture on his part attracted immediate and disproportionate media coverage. His hostility to the Eastern bloc and enthusiasm for the USA were now very marked. In an interview for *Paris Match,* intentionally provoking a reassessment of political assumptions, he boldly admitted his paradoxical stance, clinging to his left-wing past, while admiring an extremely right-wing President: 'je suis de gauche, tendance Reagan!' (I am on the Left, in the Reagan faction!) (*Paris Match*, 15 November 1985).

Following Signoret's death (in late 1985), Montand retired to some extent from public life. Media coverage now consisted largely of interviews and reviews concerning, for example, his role in the highly successful films released in 1986, *Jean de Florette* and *Manon des sources*. In June 1986, however, when Montand made a trip to Israel, this attracted several pages of glossy photos in *Paris Match* (20

June 1986), accompanied by the pointed comment: 'Tous les candidats à l'Elysée, ou presque, accomplissent un voyage en Israël.' (All candidates for the presidency, or almost all, make a trip to Israel). Indeed the prospect of Montand standing for election was kept alive for some time, as an interview in *Figaro-Magazine* (17 January 1987) illustrated. The reply Montand gave when questioned about his political intentions might well be interpreted as a call for financial backing for his candidacy:

> Je ne peux aller de l'avant si je n'ai pas derrière moi les groupes industriels . . . Et si je ne suis pas soutenu sur la base d'une série d'accords précis qui me permettraient de dire aux gens la vérité.

> I cannot forge ahead if I do not have the necessary industrial backing. . . And if I am not supported on the basis of a number of specific agreements enabling me to tell people the truth.

In a SOFRES poll published by *Le Nouvel Observateur* in January 1987 (23-29 January 1987: 25), he still figured in the list of potential candidates on whose prospects public opinion was sought, and 15 per cent of those interviewed apparently thought he would make a good President. However, in fifteenth place, his prospects were very poor, even if he was still ahead of more conventional political candidates like Jean-Pierre Chevènement (14 per cent), Jean-Marie Le Pen (9 per cent) and André Lajoinie (4 per cent). His subsequent willingness to allow himself to be seen publicly with his new companion Carole, and also public denials of any aspirations to the presidency (*Paris Match*, 27 March 1987), confirmed that he could no longer be regarded as a candidate. Montand himself in fact maintained that he never sought to enter the race, but that leading questions were put to him, and he simply responded (*Figaro-Magazine,* 17 January 1987). There may be some truth in the suggestion that, as a famous star with a reputation for strong political views, he was thrust involuntarily into the position of being perceived as a potential candidate by the media, although one must say that his denials of personal political ambition have never been very convincing. If he made no effort to promote the whole 'Montand phenomenon' himself, then this simply illustrates just how easily a famous film star can enter the political arena in France today, spurred on by public admiration for popular heroes and a general thirst for excitement and innovation.

During the period of presidential speculation surrounding Montand, Signoret maintained a discreet distance. By the 1980s she was in poor health, and was leading a quieter life, devoting herself to her writing. She admitted to having been surprised sometimes by her husband's outbursts, as for example, by his reaction to the *Front National*'s success at Dreux in 1983, but confident of his underlying motivation, she appears to have been less irritated by the views he expressed, than his willingness to give interviews to the right-wing press and be exploited, in her eyes, by the media.[4] More reluctant than her husband to show open hostility to former allies in the communist camp, she nonetheless likewise found herself ultimately in this position, especially during the controversy she was involved in shortly before her death, over Mosco's film *Des terroristes à la retraite*. The film was about the deaths in 1944 of resistance members of the Manouchian group, betrayed to the Germans, possibly by communist colleagues. After some delays, the film had at last been scheduled for screening on French television on 2 June 1985, but in response to a protest campaign by the French Communist Party, and the disapproval of a jury set up to assess it by Michèle Cotta, president of the *Haute Autorité de l'Audiovisuel* (Broadcasting Authority), the film was ultimately banned. Signoret, from the moment she first read Mosco's script, had been fascinated by the subject, and therefore agreed to record the commentary for the film. While recording, she had met two of the surviving resistance fighters involved, Charles Mitzflicker and Raymond Kojitski, and it was they who inspired her with the desire to write *Adieu Volodia* (Jean-Paul Liegeois, *L'Unité*, no. 617). Moved deeply by the subject herself, she was incensed at the banning of the film, and led the protests against its censorship, on the grounds that this was an infringement of freedom of expression. Indeed, rather than taking up positions on policy debates over complex issues like the economy and defence, Signoret, the archetypal liberal, continued to devote herself to moral issues of human rights. She also remained very firmly on the Left. A typical example of her activities was her support for the anti-racist group *SOS-Racisme* which, led by Harlem Désir, refused to be identified with specific political parties, taking a fundamental stand on equal rights for all. So, while Montand was acquiring a reputation as a volatile and agressive media superstar, Signoret continued to retain the image of the traditional intellectual humanist.

The final pages of *La nostalgie n'est plus ce qu'elle était* reflect on the role of the Palais de la Justice on the Ile de la Cité, in whose shadows Signoret lived for most of her life. It stands as a symbol of a lifelong passion demonstrated in many personal crusades to prevent miscarriages of justice. On her death, several obituaries focused on this theme, with titles like 'Signoret la passion', 'La pasionaria intraitable', 'Simone Signoret, un coeur gros comme ça'. Patrick Poivre d'Arvor, for example, comments explicitly on how she distanced herself from ideologies, focusing on the causes of individuals (*Paris Match*, 25 October 1985). This may be seen partly as a typical instance of the right-wing press neutralising and integrating a sometimes troublesome personality into the nation's common memory and affection, but it is also a true reflection of Signoret's aspirations, demonstrating one of the few roles open to celebrities in politics. In 1975, she asserted that, since 1956 and over many years, she and Montand had had a consistent policy of seeking to preserve their neutrality and autonomy:

> Nous ne sommes pas allés à l'Elysée quand de Gaulle nous y a invités, nous n'y sommes pas allés quand Pompidou nous y a invités, nous n'irions pas davantage à l'Elysée si c'était Mitterrand qui nous invitait. C'est une espèce de protocole que nous avons établi entre nous depuis nos retours de voyages à l'Est et à l'Ouest. Ce n'est pas une attitude agressive, c'est une prise de distance par rapport au pouvoir. Quel que soit le pouvoir. (Signoret, 1976: 367)

> We did not go to the Elysée Palace when De Gaulle invited us, we didn't go when Pompidou invited us, we still wouldn't go to the Elysee if it were Mitterrand who invited us. It is a sort of protocol that the two of us have established ever since our return from trips to the East and the West. It is not an aggressive stance, but a conscious distancing of ourselves from power, whoever is in power.[5]

Montand, however, in so far as he subsequently allowed himself to be portrayed as a potential presidential candidate, departed from the stance of the disinterested independent observer. Yet he continued to avoid party allegiance in order to preserve his independence, whereas the party's organisation and support are clearly necessary for electoral success. In this sense, Montand was now compromised both as political commentator and candidate for office. Philippe Tesson had long since anticipated this dilemma in *Le Quotidien de Paris* (5 January 1984): 'Montand n'est utile que jusqu'au moment où on le prend pour un Président de la République.' (Montand is useful only as long as he is not thought of as a President of the Republic). In fact Montand's usefulness lay in being, as Bernard-Henri Lévy describes him, one of the last 'indignés' or indignant protestors (*Paris Match*, 1 November 1985). The expression recalls Signoret's reference to spontaneous impulses or the 'coup au coeur'. It is this uncalculating, emotional spontaneity which accounts for Montand's reputation. It is associated with the honesty and sincerity which the public often find lacking in professional politicians. Yet reason not instinct, and clarity of vision not paradoxical contradictions are necessary to become a plausible leader of a modern advanced nation. The very qualities which may be considered endearing and persuasive in Montand the critic disqualify him as a serious candidate for political office. No professional politician would dare to utter the sort of contradictory statements for which he is renowned: 'Je suis intellectuellement de gauche mais viscéralement de droite' (Intellectually I am on the Left, but deep down I am on the Right) (*Figaro-Magazine,* 17 January 1987). It is because his own professional and financial situation were secure, and he had no party or colleagues to place at risk, that he had felt free to respond and provoke in this manner. As André Glucksmann observes:

> Montand joue le rôle que devraient jouer les intellectuels: désigner du doigt les périls que la classe politique ne peut pas voir. Il assume le

> péril de dire la vérité au risque d'être mal compris, injurié. (Quoted by P. Billard, *Le Point*, 3 September 1983: 74)

> Montand fulfils the function which intellectuals ought to fulfil: pointing out the dangers which the politicians cannot see. He runs the risk of telling the truth, exposing himself to the possibility of being misunderstood, insulted.

Whereas a politician cannot afford misinterpretation and unnecessary exposure to criticism, Montand shows a disarming willingness to admit when he cannot tackle difficult questions. The public may readily identify and accept this, as long as they consider him essentially as a film star, but such candid admissions from a political leader would not inspire confidence.

Yet it is this very plain-speaking rather than confidence in Montand's political competence which account for the 'Montand phenomenon'. Television programmes such as *Vive la crise* were not Montand's own brainchild. Specialists invited him to act as spokesperson for policies to which he was known to be sympathetic, in order to capitalise on his longstanding reputation and communication skills. His language is simple, blunt, and lively, and this, as Richard Liscia explains, is fundamental to his appeal to ordinary people seeking an alternative to the technical jargon and dull, predictable routines of conventional political debate:

> Mais c'est ça justement que les gens aiment, ce langage populaire, direct, désorganisé, qui traite de la politique mais n'a aucun rapport avec ce que disent les politiciens. Et aussi cette sincérité tumultueuse, cette passion tourbillonnante qui semble s'échapper du tube cathodique pour inonder le téléspectateur. Jamais les Français ne se sont si bien identifiés à quelqu'un (un immigré italien en l'occurrence), aussi simple que la plupart d'eux, qu'ils perçoivent comme leur égal. Mais qui arrive à dire avec les mots qu'ils connaissent ce qu'ils voudraient exprimer eux-mêmes. (*VSD*, 3 January 1984)

> But it is precisely this that people like, this popular, direct, disorganised language, which deals with politics but bears no relation to what politicians are saying. And this bubbling sincerity too, this swirling passion which seems to radiate from the cathode-ray tube and engulf the television viewer. Never have the French identified so clearly with anyone (an Italian immigrant in this case), somebody as simple as most of them, and whom they regard as their equal. But who succeeds in expressing in familiar terms what they would like to say themselves.

Montand's (and also Coluche's) political following may be attributed in part to a combination of showbiz talent with ordinariness, courage and sincerity, a mixture rare amongst politicians. His bluntness merely serves to throw into relief the latter's 'langue de bois' (dull, expressionless language).

Nonetheless, temporary success in the opinion polls is a

different matter from securing votes in an election. Support for Coluche or Montand is probably more an expression of discontent and protest against the obvious options on offer, than a positive choice or a sign of things to come. Although it may be an appealing, fanciful and even glamorous notion to think of President Montand, on considered reflection few voters would seriously be prepared to take such a risk. Moreover, 'Le Reagan de l'aïoli' remains a facetious notion, in Montand's case, not least because the parallel is inappropriate. Reagan rose to power through the party system, whereas Montand remained unaffiliated, lacking the backing necessary to succeed. Election campaigns are now extraordinarily expensive ventures. Financially, the stakes are too high, even for the rich and successful Montand. Also, popularity with the masses is not a substitute for the 500 signatures from sponsors of appropriate official status required to endorse each presidential candidate.

Nonetheless, the direct challenge of showbiz celebrities to professional politicians, as opposed to their booing or cheering from the sidelines, represents a formidable threat. As the sociologist Jean Baudrillard points out:

> La classe politique n'a virtuellement plus de specificité . . . l'essentiel n'est pas d'être représentatif mais d'être branché . . . (Quoted by P. Sery, *L'Evénement du Jeudi*, 31 January 1985 — 6 February 1985: 13)

> Politicians have virtually no specific identity left . . . the main thing is not to be representative but to be 'with it' . . .

The desire to be 'with it' would seem to have inspired performances of Lionel Jospin singing, François Léotard jogging, and even the more conservative Chirac confessing a passion for Madonna. The problem is, as Baudrillard continues:

> Par là, bien sûr, les hommes politiques perdent de leur aura proprement politique et peuvent être immédiatement relayés dans l'imaginaire médiatique des foules par des hommes de showbiz . . . plus professionnalisés qu'eux dans la performance. (Quoted by P. Sery, *L'Evénement du Jeudi*, 31 January 1985 — 6 February 1985: 13)

> As a result, of course, politicians lose their specifically political aura, and showbiz personalities can at once take over from them in the media experience of the masses . . . since they are better equipped professionally in terms of performance.

Boundaries between specialisms are being constantly broken down. Sports personalities, film stars, pop stars and politicians alike publish their memoirs, give interviews to the popular press, and appear on chat shows, where they are invited, at one extreme, to divulge personal details, at the other, to make pronouncements on the complex political issues of the modern world. The chameleon promoted by the media is a feature of contemporary western culture. Montand, popular singer, film star, political actor and commentator demonstrated how easily, as a star, he was able to attract the attention of a mass audience to political issues. Even though he himself did not stand finally for the presidential race, what are the prospects of a future star from the entertainment world aspiring successfully to the French presidency?

Recent trends in French politics would appear to give distinct advantages to media celebrities. Since the inauguration in 1965 of presidential election by direct universal adult suffrage, presidential election campaigns have become highly personalised, focusing on individual candidates. This has been accompanied by an increasing tendency in French politics more generally to identify parties with personalities rather than with ideology. It is noticeable how often political commentators today have recourse to adjectives such as 'mitterrandiste', 'barriste', 'giscardien' etc. In December 1984 an IPSOS survey revealed that, whereas between 94 per cent and 99 per cent of French adults were able to recognise political leaders such as Mitterrand, Giscard d'Estaing, Marchais, Barre and Chirac from their photos, only 40 per cent knew the meaning of the initials UDF, 50 per cent the initials RPR, 55 per cent the initials FN, although the more obvious significance of PS and PC was widely recognised (97 per cent).[6] This is undoubtedly linked to the growing role of the media in politics, for as Régis Debray comments:

Les mass media marchent à la personnalité, non au collectif; à la sensation, non à l'intelligible; à la singularité et non à l'universel. (Debray, 1979: 97)

The mass media are concerned with personality, not the collective; the sensational, not the intelligible; the singular not the universal.

However, although the media may open the doors for well-known personalities to enter the political arena, the point which Montand's case illustrates is the need to define more clearly one's position in relation to the party system or resign oneself to little prospect of high office.

It is not surprising, therefore, that Montand now appears to have reverted to his more traditional stance. Following the rapturous reception of *Jean de Florette* and *Manon des sources* in the United States during the summer of 1987, and an official invitation for both films to be shown at the Moscow Film Festival, journalists questioned Montand eagerly as to whether he too would also be travelling to the Soviet Union. His response recalls the stand against oppression which he and Signoret made together so often in the past:

. . . je n'irai qu'à la condition expresse que la liberté de partir soit —

par écrit et de manière effective — accordée à Ida Nudel et aux Slepak, qui sont emprisonnés ou en exil depuis dix-huit ans. (Quoted by H. Behar, *Le Monde*, 27 June 1987: 20)

> . . . I shall not go, except on the express condition that written permission is granted and actually implemented for Ida Nudel and the Slepaks, who have been in prison or exile for the last 18 years, to leave the country.

Defender of the individual against the State, the human rights campaigner is again foremost. Montand's supposed bid for the presidency was a whimsical aberration, soon to be forgotten, for in choosing to stand outside the party system, as the couple had long recognised, one is distancing oneself from power, if not from influence.

The potential for media stars to lead public opinion has been amply demonstrated in recent years, not only by individual campaigns, such as Brigitte Bardot's defence of animal rights, or Coluche and his founding of the *Restaurants du Coeur* (soup-kitchens): Bob Geldof and Band Aid have demonstrated the possibility of mobilising support for the needy on a worldwide scale. Yet, although in each of these cases criticism of governments is implicit, the debate has taken place largely outside the arena of national politics, not to mention party politics. The star's role has been to actively campaign on specific issues, raising public consciousness and substituting his or her power for that of governmental agencies, side-stepping institutionalised structures. Signoret's and Montand's campaigns have always been more explicitly political in orientation. If media coverage is a reliable indicator, their influence on the French public has been considerable. Yet there is an inherent frustration in fighting essentially political battles outside established political structures, when one is not even seeking directly to reform or overthrow the latter.

A comparison of Signoret and Montand highlights the different forms which the celebrity's influence on politics may take. Signoret was cast in the traditional mould of protestor, campaigner and ultimately writer, whereas in Montand we see rather the cross-over to a new era where the showbiz personality comes into his own, as the mass media assume an increasingly powerful influence on political culture. Thoughts of political office came to Montand relatively late in life when he no longer possessed the drive to fully explore and capitalise on the potential he unearthed. Nonetheless the path has now been signposted, and the media are likely to revel in promoting any future star prepared to take up the challenge.

NOTES

1.   Quoted by Emile Malet in the conclusion of his book *Socrate et la rose. Les*

intellectuels et le pouvoir socialiste, Editions du Quotidien, Paris 1983.

2.   All translations into English are the author's own.

3.   A characteristically forceful statement of his utter contempt for the French Communist Party leader, Georges Marchais.

4.   For a fuller assessment of Signoret's reactions, see Pierre Billard, 'L'Affaire Montand', *Le Point*, 3 Oct. 1983: 73-74, and Patrick Poivre d'Arvor, 'Signoret-Montand. Au-delà de l'amour, l'histoire d'un couple', *Paris Match*, 1 November 1985.

5.   Mitterrand, apparently irritated by the couple's obstinate independence and detachment during his campaign for the 1981 presidential elections, is said to have nicknamed them 'les précieuses de la gauche' (*Le Point*, 3 October 1983: 71).

6.   This survey is cited by Jean Charlot in 'La transformation de l'image des partis politiques français', *Revue française de Science politique*, 36, 1, February 1986: pp 5-13.

REFERENCES

Some of the most useful source material for research on such a topic is to be found in the French press, both in the dailies and in weekly magazines. A wide range of newspapers was consulted in the preparation of this chapter (*France-Soir* and *Paris Match* proving particularly helpful). See also the special number of *Le Crapouillot*, entitled 'Le Choc Montand' (new series no 74, March 1984).

Benoit, J.-M., Lech, P. and Lech, J.-M. (1986) *La politique à l'affiche*, Editions du May, Paris.

Cannavo, R. and Quiqueré, H. (1981) *Yves Montand. Le chant d'un homme*, Robert Laffont, Paris.

Cayrol, R. (1986) *La nouvelle communication politique*, Larousse, Paris.

Cotteret, J.-M. and Mermet, G. (1986) *La bataille des images*, Larousse, Paris.

Debray, R. (1979) *Le pouvoir intellectuel en France*, Ramsay, Paris.

Durant, P. (1988) *Simone Signoret, une vie*, Favre, Lausanne, Paris.

Gourevitch, J.-P. (1986) *La propagande dans tous ses états*, Flammarion, Paris.

Hamon, H. and Rotman, P. (1981) *Les intellocrates. Expédition en haute intelligentsia*, Ramsay, Paris.

Monserrat, J. (1983) *Simone Signoret*, PAC, Paris.

Ory, P. and Sirinelli, J-F. (1986) *Les intellectuels en France, de l'affaire Dreyfus à nos jours*, Armand Colin, Paris.

Rémond, A. (1983) *Montand*, Henri Veyrier, Paris.

Schwartzenberg, R-G. (1977) *L'état spectacle. Essai sur et contre le star system en politique*, Flammarion, Paris.

Semprun, J. (1983) *Montand. La vie continue*, Denoël/Joseph Clims, Paris.

Signoret, S. (1976) *La nostalgie n'est plus ce qu'elle était*, Seuil, Paris.

Signoret, S. (1979) *Le lendemain, elle était souriante*, Seuil, Paris.

Signoret, S. (1985) *Adieu Volodia*, Fayard, Paris.

Verdès-Leroux, J. (1983) *Au service du parti. Le parti communiste, les intellectuels et la culture (1944-56)*, Fayard/Minuit, Paris.

6

Contemporary French cinema and French Political Culture: The 'New' Hegemony

Susan Hayward

It's the first time in human history that hatred of culture has become a culture in and of itself, in the name of the pleasure principle . . . (*Le Monde*, 27 March 1987)

. . . every state is ethical in as much as one of its most important functions is to raise the great mass of the population to a particular cultural and moral level; a level (or type) which corresponds to the needs of the productive forces for development, and hence to the interests of the ruling classes. The school as a positive educative function, and the courts as a repressive and negative educative function, are the most important state activities in this sense; but, in reality, a multitude of other so-called private initiatives and activities tend to the same end — initiatives and activities which form the apparatuses of the political and cultural hegemony of the ruling classes (Antonio Gramsci, quoted in Hall, 1986: 22).

Whether we like it or not, it is the movies that mould, more than any other single force, the opinions, the taste, the language, the dress, the behaviour, and even the physical appearance of a public comprising more than 60 per cent of the population of the earth (Erwin Panofsky, in Chambers, 1986: 77).

Within these three quotations lies the definition of cinema as a political cultural production and too the contemporary problematic which surrounds current film production in the Western world. In this chapter, I would like first of all to establish what I mean here by 'political culture' and 'cinema as a political cultural production' and then, with this general framework in mind, to focus on the specific example of contemporary French cinema.

Throughout history there has been a constant interaction between social organisation and culture. By definition culture is a term which refers both to material production (artefacts) and to symbolic production (the aesthetic) and in both instances culture functions as the record and reflection of social history and the social process. This synergy between social organisation and culture, which is at the basis of political culture, receives useful definition in Raymond Williams' list of the five keywords which delimit the map of modern political culture: industry, democracy, class, art, culture (1963: 13). Clearly, these terms change in their signification in relation to the changes in our social, economic and political life. Thus, today's industry has created a new society: 'hi-tech', which, in turn, has created a new iconography, that is to say, new words and images which in turn forge a new cultural representation (in the contemporary dress code, for example, 'hi-tech sneakers' replaces the term 'trainers' and, prior to that, 'gym-shoes' or 'pumps'). Put in Marxist terms, the productive base will find reflection in the non-productive superstructure. Political culture is, then, a signifying process which unceasingly reflects socio-political change.

Political culture is also the process whereby myths are created about a nation's various and particular institutions (Barthes, 1957). And once again, the notion of cultural reflexiveness is in evidence here because those same institutions must sustain and perpetuate those myths which have been created to explain them. Television news will serve admirably as an illustration of this phenomenon. Take, for example, the ubiquity of the Royals as an end-item on both the BBC's 'Nine O'Clock News' and ITN's 'News at Ten'. The spectator, for that is what he or she is, receives — almost daily — images explaining what it is that Royals do (they visit hospitals, open buildings, launch ships, have babies etc.) and in relation to whom (the loyal subjects). Thus, this particular item reflects the Monarch-subject relationship, and, at the same time, activates the myth by which the Royals as a political institution can be apprehended by the spectator. Political culture in this respect is uni-directional in its reflexiveness (i.e. it affirms what it reflects).

Marxist theory on culture to date has predominantly stressed this uni-directional relationship between base and superstructure — i.e. that culture reflects society. Viewed in this light, culture becomes a series of discourses which have been solidified into truth (culture affirms the social and therefore the political and economic relations). However, certain neo-Marxists (Gramsci, Althusser and Marcuse in particular) have argued that the superstructure can react back onto its determining base and that art can function to subvert these discourses by opposing the affirmative character of culture (Wolff, 1981: 80). By refusing the Marxist notion of transparence, art displays its radical potential effectivity to innovate artistic forms. This negative culture — through the subversion of codes (aesthetic conventions) — can react back, thus creating a two-directional relationship between base and superstructure. According to this view, art, when subverting aesthetic conventions, brings into question the ideological nature of cultural signs and renders institutional mythologies unstable (think for a moment of Manet's *Olympia* (1863) or again, in a different medium, of Godard's 1960s films which assailed all the capitalistic mythologies imaginable). Conversely, when upholding the affirmative character of culture, art serves to reinforce and even naturalise (through representation of the dominant ideology) those same institutional mythologies (Lebrun's glorification of Louis XIV, David's of Napoleon or the many monuments contemporary politicians in France are ascribing to themselves — albeit through refurbishment, take for instance François Mitterrand's ambitious scheme for the Louvre — are just a few immediate examples that spring to mind).

Within every art movement and every art form there are two apparently codifiable trends: mainstream and avant-garde. Mainstream art is either heavily reliant on its immediate predecessors (which leads to academicism or in its most dire form to mannerism), or else harks back to earlier art forms (classicism). In this respect, mainstream art opposes change and as such serves to preserve the hegemony of the ruling class. Avant-garde art, as its name suggests, is art before its time — art looking forward not backwards and attempting to break new terrain with its implicit subversion of the old codes and conventions. The first is reactionary and guilty of semiotic reductionism, the second is oppositional and redolent with semiotic expansionism (Wollen, 1976). However, as the dominant ideology becomes more swift and adept in recuperating subversive art trends and neutralising them, avant-garde increasingly runs out of steam. Take as an illustrative example the punk movement in Britain which was at its most visible from 1976 to 1978. At first a subcultural movement pertaining to the youthful unemployed working-class with its anti-music and anti-clothing codes signifying a revolt. An opposition to the sanitised image projected by the government and the culture industry, it was quite swiftly normalised into London-Chelsea chic fashion. Iconoclasm rendered iconic. This legitimation through fetishisation is certainly not what Sid Vicious had in mind one suspects — nor indeed those whom he was purported to represent.

As a cultural production, cinema presents no exception to the aforementioned aesthetic dualism of mainstream versus avant-garde. And, at this point, it would seem appropriate to locate cinema — specifically French cinema — in all of the above considerations. Since the advent of sound, French cinema has known three epochs: Classical (1930-58), Modernist (1958-68) and Postmodern (1968-). Curiously, the Modernist movement only lasted a decade, whereas the Classical and Postmodern epochs together account for almost the totality of sound cinema history (83 per cent). In relation to her older sister, painting, the brevity of this middle period is in stark contrast to the length of Modernism in art history (100 years — equal in time to the Renaissance) — the reasons for this will become clear as I briefly detail these particular periods.

Classical cinema is in essence realistic. Here the narrative codes create the illusion of reality and rest upon the canonic story line of order-disorder-order (i.e. the natural order of things, established at the beginning, gets disrupted and then finally resolved — though not necessarily put to rights; a classic example being the love triangle). The visual codes assist the narrative line and are highly communicative; they supply the visual information which facilitates the safe placing of the narrative in time and space. In this respect, the spectator is provided with a very readable text in much the same way as classical discursive painting presents itself to a reading by the viewer (for example David's *The Oath of the Horatii* 1785). Classicism not only offers a readable text, it also projects a representation of present ideologies through a representation of those of the past. Thus, the might of Louis XIV is represented, by Lebrun (the Louvre) and Le Vau (Versailles) amongst others, through a reconstruction of the classical antiquity of ancient Rome (be it painting, sculpture or architecture). So whilst classical art did indeed tell a story, it also functioned as the medium for hegemonic transparence (i.e., culture reflects the dominant ideology).

Although Classical cinema (1930-58) did not, of course, have the same visual cinematographic heritage to call upon, nonetheless, similar practices of discursivity and transparence can be found. Thus, mainstream Classical cinema (both pre- and post-Second World War) remained essentially readable: literary adaptations abounded, the narrative canons went unchallenged and the visual codes were remorselessly uninventive; simultaneously this cinema reflected the dominant discourses of that epoch — the most famous of which was the 'discours nataliste' (Garçon, 1984; Bertin-Maghit, 1980). With regard to this particular discourse, demographic and economic necessities were given unprecedented transparence in the cinema of that period. Many of the pre-war films legitimised the marriage of young women to father figures (all that was left after the devastation of the First World War). The older man outwits the juvenile and — most importantly — inexperienced suitor in their pursuit of the locus of fecundity. Post-war films, in the main, valorised the nuclear and also the extended family. The young woman now became wife, mother and dutiful daughter all rolled into one and safely placed on the hearth.

During this same epoch, avant-garde cinema was in evidence, though on a small scale. For the sake of illustration, let me just take the pre-war years. Here, Jean Vigo and Jean Renoir stand as the major, though very different, representative directors of this oppositional aesthetic. Vigo's poetic surrealism challenges narrative continuity and the visual representation of time and space. His first feature film, *Zéro de conduite* (1933), aims a beautifully constructed oneiric broad-side swipe at all representatives of authority from the 'petit' to the 'haut fonctionnaire' (the lowly and elevated civil servant). The film was banned by the board of censors as seditious. His second and only other feature film (he died prematurely of rheumatic septicaemia), *L'Atalante* (1934), sensitively portrays — from the subjective point of view of the female protagonist — the strictures and compromises that marriage entails. Renoir's films of the 1930s, while certainly far more within the camp of realism, nonetheless take that realism and push it to the farthest limits. For example, *Toni* (1935), was shot on location, in natural lighting, with natural synchronised sound recording and with non-professional actors — all of which was unheard of at the time, but which was to become canonised in the Italian Neo-realism movement of the 1940s. Renoir's realism also played a central role in the discourses narrated by the film, the most important of which were the vertical and horizontal relationships between and within social classes (essentially exposing the myth of a homogeneous society as in *La règle du jeu*, 1939), the futility of war and the importance of modest humanism (as, for example, in *La grande illusion*, 1937). Finally, in terms of cinematographic language, Renoir revolutionised film shooting through the use of depth of focus and the long take. The importance of this style of filming is that essentially it creates a greater visual realism, and this for the following reason: depth of focus shots permit foreground and background to be in focus simultaneously; this means that the camera no longer needs to keep changing its position in relation to foreground and background and, as a consequence, a sequence can be shot as one long take (the point of view is not constantly manipulated) rather than as a series of takes punctuated by cuts or other editing techniques.

Renoir and Vigo, both with very distinct and different styles of filming, and yet both equally radical, created new dimensions to — and thus enhanced — film language, and at the same time challenged the myths of their contemporary institutions and culture. Cinema as a political cultural product, then, does one of two things. Either it reflects a given image or series of discourses and, as such, is politicised from without. Co-opted as it is into the dominant ideology it contributes to a dominant matrix of social and political perceptions. Or, it refuses that role of reflection and the secure iconography that goes with that reflection and, by so doing, subverts the political and aesthetic hegemonies — in which case it is politicised from within.

Modernist cinema in France (1958-68) was born of a group of critics and theorists — the only time in sound cinema history that such a phenomenon has occurred. Exceptional also to this movement was its position of prominence over mainstream cinema (which continued to be produced): for a very brief decade, negative, avant-garde culture was at the forefront of cinematic production. This movement manifested its avant-gardisme through its virulent attacks on the mainstream cinema of its predecessors — 'le cinéma de papa' — and through its complete rupture of and with classical cinematic codes, both narrative and visual. There is no *récit*, no realistic story as such (i.e. no 'beginning', 'middle' and 'end'), no literary adaptations, no positive reflection of the dominant ideology. The time became the 'NOW-EVER-PRESENT' of the 1950s and 1960s and the discourses were contemporary: the consumer boom, nuclear war, Vietnam, student politics, adolescence. Mercilessly, bourgeois myths were taken to bits and denormalised. For example, according to Modernist cinema, the consumer boom was not about comfort and a better way of life but about prostituting the self in order to be better able to consume; the most important consumer durable of that time, the car, was exposed as the machine of violence and death which our covetousness had transformed it into: a minotaur of our age ('la déesse') the consumer durable that consumes us (Godard, 1980).

In terms of the visual, the institutional iconography, with its easy readability and comforting visual logic, was unceremoniously deconstructed before the spectators' eyes. The establishing shots (shots which safely orientate the spectator in terms of time and space) were excised. A fast editing style (achieved by jump cuts and unmatched shots) replaced the seamless editing style of before. The camera abandoned the studio and went out into the streets and suburbs of Paris. Modernist cinema was as much about the process of film making as it was about desanitising the sacred cows of the bourgeois mythology.

This last point is quite important because had this movement focused purely on form (the process of film making), on what could be termed the gesture of representation, then the implicit self-reflexiveness would have led to the unyielding formalism (almost one might say to a necro-cinephilia) so prevalent in much of today's cinema.

I have explained elsewhere (Hayward, 1987) why this Modernist movement was so short-lived. Suffice it to say that, lodged as it was between the Algerian crisis and the events of *mai '68*, this cinema of the New Wave, as it was called, was kept alive by the instability of France's institutions at a time of great political upheaval within the nation — a new Republic, a new constitution, the disastrous policy of 'involvement' in South East Asia, the bloody decolonising of Algeria, being but a few of the contributing extemporaneous factors. However, the June 1968 legitimation of de Gaulle's presidency, thanks to the landslide victory of the Gaullists at the polls, meant that the huge 'crisis' had been weathered. And just as the myths-in-the-making during that decade in the general political culture arena could now become institutionalised (de Gaulle, the Fifth Republic, Françoise Hardy etc, all could now becomes icons in their own right), so too the moment had arrived to recuperate the subversiveness of the Modernist cinema movement: the age of the Postmodern was born.

The very term, Postmodern, raises two immediate comments. First, it is consistent with the way in which contemporary Western society defines itself — that is, in relation to the past, to what has been and what is no longer (compare post-industrial society). Second, the deliberate omission (by the French at least) of the 'ism' suggests that postmodernity is not a style, cannot be labelled as an historical style in the way that Modernism or Classicism are. In the first case, the Postmodern looks back, is retrospective; in the second, it rejects history because it has none of its own — only that of others, stands eternally fixed in a series of presents (Jameson, 1983; Willeman, 1985; Zurbrug, 1986). Mannerism and stylisation become, therefore, the manifest hallmarks of the contemporary cultural aesthetic. Fixity triumphs over disruption (Hebdige, 1979), formalism and retro-discourses over film-making practices and meaning construction.

The Postmodern phenomenon is more akin to a cult than to a movement. The very absence of the 'ism' warns us that this is a non-collective movement and by implication the cult of the individual. Curiously, today's hedonism recalls the aesthetic culture of the Symbolists at the end of the nineteenth century — a neo-romantic nihilism wherein the individual artist became a cult figure (the life of the artist was turned into a work of art, a way of life marked by uselessness and superfluousness). The 'fin de siècle' mood of that time was a reaction to the political, intellectual and moral crises taking place at the national level, and the art was oppositional. Bourgeois values were rejected and art turned in on itself. The death of ideology as represented by the end of the Second Empire and the crushing of the Commune (1870-71) left the artist in the presence of a spiritual void. The concern for the artist became a question of how to fill the nothingness of the abyss. The response was aestheticism, art as an end in and of itself, a contemplative art which led to a self-sufficient formalism. In other words, only form — not meaning or content — could fill the void (Cobban, 1984).

The 'fin de siècle' mood of this, the twentieth, century is, once again, conditioned by a death of ideology, this time engendered by the apocalyptic events of the Holocaust and the dropping of the Bomb. How to go on, knowing what we now know? Such is the wailing cry of Beckett's characters. How to invent when invention can lead to such self-destruction? Such is the morose message of Kiefer's canvasses. In answer to these daunting, perhaps unanswerable questions Postmodern culture bifurcates. The majority tendency is unoppositional, symptomatic Postmodernity (uni-directional reflection) providing a conservative culture production — in other words, mainstream. The minority is avant-garde and oppositional. The similarity with Classical art of this division into affirmative and negative cultures will not have escaped the reader (a point to which I shall inevitably return).

Whether symptomatic or oppositional, the Postmodern aesthetic relies on four tightly inter-related sets of concepts: 'parody and pastiche', 'prefabrication', 'bricolage', 'intertextuality'. What separates the two tendencies is that the oppositional Postmodern aesthetic experiments with these concepts and innovates through subverting their codes, whereas the symptomatic merely replicates them. Hence the need for two distinguishing terms for the first concept — 'parody and pastiche' — and for the following reason. Pastiche pertains to the symptomatic in that it imitates previous genres and styles and in that, unlike parody, its imitation is not ironic and therefore not subversive. In its uninventiveness, pastiche is but a shadow of the former thing. Take, for example, the advert for Classic Nouveau clothes (Fig. 1). Every article, down to the skates and the telephone and its cable refer back to America of the 1950s. In their posturing, the images are retro-nostalgic and recall icons from the 1950s genre of teenage movies (more precisely, they closely reduplicate the preppie look of the teenage movie star Troy Donahue). Even the label itself is a pastiche: Classic Nouveau! Or regurgitating the past.

Postmodern art culls from already existing images and objects. In cinema, images, or parts of sequences, which were fabricated before are re-selected. In much the same way that prefabricated houses are made up of complete units of pre-existing meaning, so the 'visual arts sees the past as a supermarket source that the artist raids for whatever goodies he (sic) wants' (*The Guardian*, 1 December 1986). A film could be completely constructed out of prefabricated images (and even sounds). Beineix's *37,2 degrés le matin*, 1985 (*Betty Blue* in the English version), is a case in point with images coming from directors as far apart as Huston, Cassavetes, Bergman, and Malle amongst others. But by way of simple illustration, let me point to the cover of *Blitz* (Fig. 2a) and to its supermarket source which is of course the quintessential 'Bogie' (Fig. 2b). The new is virtually a mirror-reflection of the old. The image is prefabricated, it existed before. Prefabrication and pastiche are very close in meaning, pastiche refers to earlier icons, prefabrication selects from them.

This particular illustration from *Blitz* can usefully serve to explain the term intertextuality, or *mise-en-abyme* as it is also known. The iconography refers to the film-noir genre of the 1930s and 1940s as well as to their remakes in the 1970s (*The Big Sleep* 1946 and 1978, for example). It refers also to *the* private eye par excellence, Philip Marlowe, and thus to his creator, the novelist, Raymond Chandler. In terms of the texts referred to, therefore, the intertextuality of the *Blitz* cover — in this instance — reads as follows: a film genre, remakes of the genre, the iconography of a fictional persona, the novel genre, the novelist.

Finally, bricolage. As its name suggests it is an assembling of different styles, genres or discourses, and as such is closely allied with the previous concept of intertextuality. In writing and in film of the avant-garde, innovations within one discourse have been replicated within another. For example, the use of cut-up and montage techniques (coming from painting, photography and film)

Figure 1

Figure 2a

Figure 2b

Figure 3

Figure 4

have been incorporated into the writing of Marie-Claire Ropars (1981); or again the plasticity of video and painting have been replicated into Godard's most recent films. As a simple illustration of mainstream bricolage, the Pernod advert (Fig. 3) makes its meaning clear. Here photo, print, writing, collage are all assembled into an intertextual reference to the jazz scene of the 1950s (most likely in Paris) and of course with the contemporary message to purchase the drink which presumably can transport you to or back to those times .
. .

The image, however, that takes the biscuit is that supplied by the revised look of the *Lettre de Matignon*. This new look was instituted by Jacques Chirac when he became Prime-Minister in 1986 (this format has in part been retained by the current government). Here (Fig. 4) we are confronted with the complete legitimation and institutionalisation of Postmodernity. Bricolage is present in the form of the mixture of fonts. The intertext is clear for all to see in the form of the photo of de Gaulle: Chirac means de Gaulle. Chirac was the then resident of Matignon so the *Lettre* was — to all intents and purposes — his. Thus his text refers explicitly to an earlier one, that of de Gaulle solving problems. Modelling himself on de Gaulle as he does (see Chapter 4), it is clear that the subtext of this particular iconography is that Chirac's next place of residence is to be the Elysée.

Predominantly, the culture of the 1980s is the pastiche culture. And French cinema is no exception. This is the decade of 'Le Look' in fashion as in film ('show me your look and I'll tell you who you are'); the decade of beautifully constructed images 'cinéma nouvelles-images' and visually exciting dishes 'nouvelle-cuisine'. The age of the surface image is as much a consequence of the death of ideology as it is of the growth in importance of 'la chose médiatique' par excellence, the television. Curiously, the death of ideology coincided with the launching of this new medium. With the post-war boom came greater purchasing power — firstly in America, then in Europe and, by 1960, the television in France was a household commodity (Miquel, 1972). Television is a popular cultural production but it is also political in that it serves as transparence (as an instrument of reflection) for the relevant nation's institutional mytholgies. It is then the new instrument of myth, replacing cinema as the new form of *écriture* (i.e. of meaning construction). But it is also the new medium of popular culture, displacing cinema from its original position as sole purveyor of the popular and the aesthetic. Because it is so readily available, and indeed relatively inexpensive in relation to cinema, television has been better able to fulfil the promise of cinema. Indeed, more than any other medium, television, with its endless flow of images, is primarily responsible for the dissolution of the great divide between high and low art. Placed at such a disadvantage, cinema has had to adapt its own film-making practices which has meant, in great measure, being an aesthetic Abel to an image-conscious Caïn.

There is something both paradoxical and sadly ironic about this turn of events. In its early days, French cinema, in order to secure its economic survival, called upon renowned composers (Hindemith, Honneger, Saint-Saëns, Satie, for example) to accompany the silent images. This collaboration led to the bestowal upon cinema of an aesthetic legitimacy. Almost despite itself, cinema was elevated to the dizzying heights of the seventh art. Today, cinema is again obliged to seek economic viability. This time, however, it has had to turn to television — the very medium that threatens its survival — for funding and protection. This appeal has had the converse effect to the one launched in the silent cinema days in that cinema has, by and large, shed its aesthetic aspirations and become increasingly telefilmic. For example *Subway* (Besson, 1984) has more in common with televisual genres such as pop-videos, advertising clips and designer-violence cop drama series (*Miami Vice*) than it does with film genres and diegesis (Hayward, 1987). Hence, doubtless, its enormous popularity. Who wouldn't want to see TV in 'scope and with dolby sound?

French cinema of the 1980s is then essentially non-oppositional. It displays itself as symptomatically Postmodern in that it is both retro-nostalgic and high-tech. In its nostalgic manifestation, French film gazes back to earlier styles and genres in cinema and repeats or imitates images, even sequences, from the earlier prototypes (hence the tautology: retro-nostalgic). *Dimanche à la campagne* (Tavernier, 1984) offers a good example. A central sequence to the film finds the ageing artist and his daughter arriving at a 'guinguette', café musicians are playing and young lovers dance. Almost shot for shot, Tavernier's version recalls, sometimes repeats, the famous opening sequence of Becker's *Casque d'or* (1952). And both films refer back even further to Renoir's film *Partie de campagne* (1936) and — whilst we are mentioning intertextual references — all three give a nostalgic nod back to the impressionist paintings of this, then, new form of working-class entertainment.

Hi-tech film is designer-film. The films are redolent with designer- hyphenated images: designer-violence, designer-clothes and designer-stubble. All are profoundly influenced by advertising techniques, video clips and TV designer-violence series and special effects — almost all of which have their origin in the USA. Thus, if the retro-nostalgia has France contemplating its own filmo-cultural heritage, then high-tech is nothing short of a resurgence of American cultural imperialism. In a sense, it is as if some blinded cyclop had rolled a huge rock across the mouth of Plato's cave; small wonder, therefore, that Disneyland is coming to the suburbs of Paris — the 'guinguette' of this particular 'fin de siècle'. This then is the background to the cinema of the 1980s in France. And, in this respect, one could assert that it is not hugely different from the prevailing trends in the UK. However, what distinguishes the two countries is that — under successive governments — France has had very precise policies and goals in mind for this major cultural industry.

In this respect, mention must be made of Jack Lang's policies during his first mandate as Minister of Culture (1981-86). Lang's policies were committed to a 'politique de prestige du cinéma français' ('Cinema must find once again its role as provider of great popular leisure'). Far grander than the aims of our own British Film Year (1986), his cultural goal was to reclaim France's position (France was, after all, the birthplace of cinema) as a major cinematographic centre with Paris as the European cinema capital vigorously poised to counter US cultural imperialism (Reader, 1981). Even more ambitiously, Lang wanted to regain the cinema audience of the halcyon days of the late 1950s; 'le cinéma doit retrouver sa fonction de grand loisir populaire', he declared upon the launching of his *Réforme du cinéma*.[1] In all of this, however, there are a number of paradoxes that must be pointed out. First, both of these goals, because they are directed towards the past, lack the necessary fighting innovative dynamism that one would have expected from a minister committed to modernisation (i.e. a cultural re-orientation cannot aspire only to its past). Second, all attempts to get 'bums on seats' have failed since the advent of television as a household medium. Television is the popular-cultural machine which cinema can no longer aspire to become. Finally, by a rather complex system of taxation on ticket receipts (whereby French cinematic production receives a certain percentage of the ticket sales for American movies) French cinema needs American cinema in order to finance (in part) its own films.

It is, of course, in this walking backwards to the future that the whole inability to invent and create resides. In effect, the 'fin de sièclisme' I mentioned earlier received its official sanction through Lang's reform and its impotence to inaugurate change. This begs the question: if change did not occur, then what has prevailed? I have already discussed, in general terms, the current situation of French cinema. It now seems appropriate to look at precisely what types or genres of film have been produced over the last five years and to examine their images in the light of the political culture which they reflect.

Whether retro-nostalgic or high-tech, both categories look back to earlier prototypes. I can note nine different genres of film, although clearly a film can bear more than one generic resemblance. On the nostalgia front we can list: remakes, literary adaptations, historical movies or biopics, screwball comedy mostly valorising the family, or at least paternity. At the interface between nostalgia and high-tech come the *polars* (the abbreviated term for *films policiers*, i.e. detective or private eye movies), and the film-noir genre. The high-tech films almost exclusively concern the 13-25 generation and can be categorised as follows: adolescent-teenage movies, lost generation movies (rebels with or without a cause), psychological movies.

All genres, without exception, revivify earlier institutions and myths and as such reify them. For example the family is presented in much the same favourable light as it was during the 1940s and 1950s when the need then — as now — was to procreate (*Trois hommes et un couffin, Conseil de famille,* both 1985). Literary adaptations and remakes (*Manon des sources* (1985), which is both a literary adaptation *and* a remake, or *Un amour de Swann* (1983) for instance) consolidate a variety of myths: the good old days, rural revivalism or turn of the century gentility — all that we can no longer aspire to be or possess. Historical films seem to be particularly interested in the revolutionary period at the end of the eighteenth century (*Danton,* 1982; *Adieu Bonaparte,* 1985) — hardly surprising since the bi-centenary of the Revolution is now upon us, and the naming of 'heroes' rather than events is revealing in its *passéisme* (the old fashioned approach to history which attributes events to 'great' men) yet is consistent with the Postmodern cult of the individual.

Both the *polars* and the film-noir echo the ambiguous characterisation of the American prototype of the 1930s and 1940s. Less than virtuous, even slightly corrupt, halfway between light and dark (chiaroscuro), these knights of the night are as cynical and sceptical about the world as were their forebears and as hard-bitten and rough with their women as before (*Bleu comme l'enfer,* 1985). The environment in which they move is equally ambiguous, the melting-pot of Postmodernity. On the one hand, many of the objects surrounding them — especially their cars and coats (literally: that in which they put themselves) — are of a by-gone age (*Poussière d'ange,* 1986), thus assimilating them with the earlier iconography of say Sam Spade or Philip Marlowe or even Eddie Constantine (Eddie Constantine, incidentally, is a French parody of an American parody of the private detective). Conversely, at arms' length from and beyond the "heroes' " reach are all the electronic and technological gadgets of our modern hi-tech society. Also, as a sign of moving with the times, there are some spectacular blood-curdling special effects unseen before in this genre in France — doubtless a by-product of the popularity of Clint Eastwood's *Dirty Harry* series (in *Bleu comme l'enfer,* for example, cop and fugitive fight out a duel by hurling dynamite sticks at each other). Normal, run of the mill brutality is also reassuringly in evidence: head butting and body blows (*Police, Les ripoux,* (both 1985); *La balance,* 1981). Essentially, the image of the cop or detective (a few modern devices apart) remains unchanged. Slightly seedy, a bit 'pourri' (which incidentally is where the back-slang term 'ripoux' comes from, 'pourri' meaning rotten), somewhat brutal, the detective — his rapier-like wit notwithstanding — is often portrayed as mildly ineffectual or even ambivalent in successfully bringing about justice. The current popularity of the *polar* in France (Chabrol, for example, has made three in the last four years) is most certainly ascribable to this ambiguity and ambivalence of the cop or detective. The myth perpetrated here reaffirms existing prejudices; as agents of a repressive and negative educative function (to use Gramsci's terminology) how reassuring it must be to know that the police are as susceptible to corrupt demeanours as those self-same persons they pursue in the name of justice. However — and this is the problem — in the very act of recognising that particular reflection, the status quo of the institution is once again preserved.

With regard to the last three genres, as one might expect, it is the image of youth that predominates. I say 'image' rather than 'portrayal' because, essentially, it is only a part of youth that is held up for inspection. These films most generally depict the youth generation in relation to their, normally heterosexual, sexuality. It is particularly important to point out that, in terms of this fetishisation of youth, it is most especially the nubility of young women and teenage girls which is put on display. The spectator-viewer-voyeur's gaze is transfixed upon their sexuality which is either just barely dormant and at the stage of pubescent awareness (*L'effrontée*, 1985; *Charlotte Forever*, 1986) or unremittingly voracious (*37,2 degrés le matin*, 1985; *La puritaine* 1986). In either case, sexuality is the agent of disorder, even death. Young female sexuality is, therefore, represented as the predominant cause of disruption. In terms of reactionary iconography, it is hard to imagine a more retrograde perception of woman. Virgin, she is Lilith the temptress who rejected Adam; non-virgin, she is Eve the seductress who tempted Adam into his fall from grace.

Gender representation in the psychological films is equally problematic and regressive where women are concerned. Madness and incest are two of the more favoured psychological environments into which women are plunged. In neither instance is the point of view female. The gaze is masculine, either that of the lover or that of the father. The gaze is, of course, uncomprehending since it looks at the desired one. The lack of psychological vraisemblance, therefore, is hardly surprising. For example, in both *37,2 degrés le matin* and *Péril en la demeure* (1984) a very basic equation is drawn between the woman's nymphomania and her hysterical behaviour (the fact that the male willingly indulges the woman's sexual appetite is by-passed). This simplistic proto-Freudianism is reminiscent of many American movies of the 1950s with their very rudimentary representation of psychological disorder.[2] It is as if the revisionism of the women's movement, where female representation is concerned, has been completely erased. The image of woman as sexually armed and dangerous is not merely inaccurate in a society where the quasi-totality of sexual violence is done to and not by women, it is of course highly political in its ideological reflection (women should return to their real status of nurturing wife and mother) and consistent with the cultural admonitions of a period of economic recession (take for example the advertising campaigns in Europe and the US during the early 1950s which placed the woman — who had done remunerated work in factories etc. during the war — back in the home).

Perhaps one of the greatest sexual myths is the taboo of incest. It isn't that incest is taboo, but that talking about it is prohibited. Hence the shock value of two recent films devoted in their entirety to fathers discoursing about their incestuous rapports with their daughters: *La puritaine* and *Charlotte Forever* (both 1986) — in this last film Serge Gainsbourg actually directs himself and his daughter as the incestuous pair. The similarity between the two films is quite striking. The discourses are delivered in closed hermetic spaces (the theatre for *La puritaine*, an apartment for *Charlotte*). These spaces are not — as this hermeticism might suggest — womb-like, rather they are cold and gloomy. In these spaces, the fathers recreate the bodies of their respective daughters. They narrate the body in a fragmentary fashion in the same way that a voyeur looking through a small opening would see a woman's fragmented body. This naming of the parts — because it can be endlessly replayed — is used by the fathers to enhance their sexual fantasies. The resultant fragmentation serves to delay the gratification of the total gaze and the notion of final possession. The coldness of the space and the fragmentation of the body entomb the daughter's sexuality, her body frozen by the eye of the father.

The female body as the locus of deviancy, woman as victim of her own sexuality, are age-old myths. To see them revivified and ascribed — in the main — to teenagers displays a new kind of misogyny; a misogyny which through its assault on nubility erects as its final goal the desexualisation of all women. With women restored to their former passivity, the reassertion of male virility (which the women's movement had assailed but not really repressed) can commence.

In terms of subjects and themes, the spectator of today is reviewing and reliving the whole of classical cinema (1930-58). There are no social or political films (excepting Varda's *Sans toit ni loi*, (1985); *Vagabonde* in the English version): unemployment, Aids, racism, sexism, drug addiction, nuclear policies, France's international role in the Middle East and elsewhere are all subjects which pass completely under silence. This so-called dearth of subjects treated coincides with a cinematographic mannerism which manifests itself, in the first instance, by a prurient necrophiliac fixation with images and genres of a by-gone cinema[3] and, in the second instance, by a servile simulation of TV visual discourses.[4] And it is in this sense that Postmodern directors display a disdain for culture. In their formalism and mannerism they aim purely and simply for the well-made image. They invent nothing.

French cinema of the 1980s covers its screen with images of the already-known and, as such, comforts the complacent individualistic viewer of the Postmodern age: 'I am what I see'. But cinema of the Classical epoch was equally reinforcing of dominant codes and modes of living. Cinema is *the* art medium of the twentieth century. Soon this century will end and, with it, this millenium. Historians will be able to study this most conformist of all art forms as a visual record of the cultural and political hegemony of this century.

NOTES

1. 'Cinema must reassert its important role in popular culture'. For details of his *Réforme* see *Cahiers du cinéma* (mai 1982) no. 336.

2. I am referring here to the Method acting system which aimed at psychological realism. This particular group of actors included such luminaries as James Dean, Marlon Brando, Paul Newman and Montgomery Clift.

3. See the special dossier on mannerism in the *Cahiers du cinéma* (avril 1985) no. 370.

4. In this latter respect, the introduction of telephoto montage (whereby camera zooms — because they can thrust back and forth from foreground to background thus travelling huge distances in minute parts of a second — completely fragment space and render time and motion meaningless) is largely responsible for the death of the 'mise-en-scène' a unique hallmark of French cinema.

REFERENCES

Appignanesi, L. (ed.) (1986) *ICA Documents 4 & 5: Postmodernism*, Institute of Contemporary Art, London.

Barthes, R. (1957) *Mythologies*, Seuil, Paris.

Baudrillard, J. (1983) *In the Shadow of the Silent Majorities . . . or the End of the Social — and other Essays*, Semiotext(e) Inc., New York.

Bertin-Maghit, J.-P. (1980) *Le cinéma français sous Vichy: les films français de 1940 à 1944 — signification — fonction sociale*, Albatros, Paris.

Bordwell, D. (1985) *Narration in the Fiction Film*, Methuen, London.

Bourdieu, P. (1986) 'The Aristocracy of Culture'. In: *Media Culture & Society, a Critical Reader*, Sage Publications Inc., California.

Chambers, I. (1986) *Popular Culture, the Metropolitan Experience*, Methuen,

London.

Cobban, A. (1984) *A History of Modern France, Volume 2: 1799-1871*, Penguin, Harmondsworth.

Garçon, F. (1984) *De Blum à Pétain: cinéma et société française (1936-1944)*, Editions du Cerf, Paris.

Godard, J.-L. (1980) *Introduction à une véritable histoire du cinéma*, Albatros, Paris.

Hall, S. (1986) 'Popular Culture and the State'. In: T. Bennett, C. Mercer and J. Woollacott (eds) *Popular Culture and Social Relations*, Open University Press, Milton Keynes.

Hauser, A. (1983) *The Social History of Art, Volume 4: Naturalism, Impressionism, The Film Age*, Routledge and Kegan Paul, London.

Hayward, S. (1987) 'France avance-détour-retour: French Cinema of the 1980s'. In: J. Howorth (ed.) *Contemporary France*, Frances Pinter, London, pp. 157-67.

Hebdige, D. (1979) *Subculture, the Meaning of Style*, Methuen, London.

Jameson, F. (1983) 'Postmodernism and Consumer Society'. In: H. Foster (ed.) *Postmodern Culture*, Pluto Press, London.

Lyotard, J.-F. (1979) *La condition postmoderne*, Minuit, Paris.

McMillan, J.F. (1985) *Dreyfus to De Gaulle: Politics and Society in France 1898-1969*, Edward Arnold, London.

Miquel, P. (1972) *Histoire de la radio et de la télévision — culture ou politique?*, Richelieu, Paris.

Polan, D. (1984) ' "Desire shifts the difference": Figural Poetics and Figural Politics in the Film Theory of Marie-Claire Ropars', *Camera Obscura*, 12, pp. 67-83.

Reader, K. (1981) *Cultures on Celluloid*, Quartet Books, London.

Turim, M. (1984) 'Desire in Art and Politics: the Theories of Jean-François Lyotard', *Camera Obscura*, 12, pp. 91-109.

Willemen, P. (1985) 'An Avant-garde for the Eighties', *Framework*, 24.

Williams, R. (1963) *Culture and Society, 1780-1950*, Penguin Books, London.

Wolff, J. (1975) 'Hermeneutics and the Critique of Ideology', *Sociological Review*, 23, 4, pp. 811-28.

Wolff, J. (1981) *The Social Production of Art*, Methuen, London.

Wollen, P. (1976) 'The Two Avant-gardes', *Edinburgh '76 Magazine*, Edinburgh Film Festival, Edinburgh, pp. 77-85.

Zurbrugg, N. (1986) 'Postmodernity: métaphore manquée and the Myth of the Trans-avant-garde', *SubStance 48*, xiv, 3, pp. 68-90.

FILMS CITED

A nous la liberté, René Clair (1931)
Zéro de conduite, Jean Vigo (1933)
L'Atalante, Jean Vigo (1934)
Toni, Jean Renoir (1935)
Partie de campagne, Jean Renoir (1936)
La grande illusion, Jean Renoir (1937)
La règle du jeu, Jean Renoir (1939)
Casque d'or, Jacques Becker (1952)
The Big Sleep, Howard Hawks (1946)
The Big Sleep, Michael Winner (1978)
La balance, Bob Swaim (1981)
Danton, Andrej Wajda (1982)
Un amour de Swann, Volker Schöndorff (1983)
Péril en la demeure, Michel Deville (1984)
Subway, Luc Besson (1984)
Dimanche à la campagne, Bertrand Tavernier (1984)
Adieu Bonaparte, Youssef Chahine (1985)
Bleu comme l'enfer, Yves Boisset (1985)
Conseil de famille, Costa-Gravas (1985)
L'éffrontée, Claude Miller (1985)
Manon des sources, Claude Berri (1985)
Police, Maurice Pialat (1985)
Les ripoux, Claude Zidi (1985)
Sans toit ni loi, Agnès Varda (1985)
37,2 degrés le matin, Jean-Jacques Beineix (1985)
Trois hommes et un couffin, Coline Serreau (1985)
Charlotte Forever, Serge Gainsbourg (1986)
Poussière d'ange, Edouard Niermans (1986)
La puritaine, Jacques Doillon (1986)

7

Political Allegiance and Social Change: The Case of Workers in the Ruhr

Mark Roseman

In 1928, the famous 'red count', Alexander Stenbock-Fermor, published his description of a year spent living and working in the Ruhr. He portrayed a powerful and brutal environment, '. . . a forest of factory chimneys, mines, machine rooms, coke furnaces, blast furnaces and tenement blocks which stood out, ghost-like, against the dirty-grey, damp and cloudy sky' (Stenbock-Fermor, 1928: 7). The inhabitants of this world, the proletarians, appeared as weary figures of indeterminate age, with sunken faces and tired eyes, whose dress and manners made them instantly distinguishable from the bourgeoisie. On Sundays, the working-class neighbourhoods were filled with drunken figures, hopeless and angry, lurching through the streets. Yet just a tram journey away, in the middle-class centre of Duisburg, polite society met and chatted in prosperous cafés. The middle class, made up of shopkeepers, clerks and, higher up still, the tiny haute bourgeoisie composed almost exclusively of entrepreneurs and senior management, were viewed by the workers almost as beings from another planet. Class hatred was strong, the police were perceived as arch-enemies and, in 1923, the air was full of rumours that a red army would come and wipe out the capitalists. Many of the Ruhr workers were communists and anarchists, there were lively political discussions at the end of each shift and strikes and lock-outs were frequent (1928: *passim*).

Exactly 30 years later, in 1958, the sociologists Helmuth Croon and Carl Jantke published a study of a Ruhr mining town based on more than a year's interviewing and participant observation. Theirs was a world of small houses and private gardens, shaped but not dominated by the local pit. The social landscape had become blurred with locals unable clearly to distinguish social groups. The miners had become more integrated, quite a few had become clerks or small tradesmen, and the rest were much more accepted than in earlier times. Where once there had been inns reserved for the local middle class, now there were almost no no-go areas for the miner. The miners' own social behaviour was different; gone was the clearly recognisable proletarian dress, gone the drunkenness and the easy sociability. The miner of the 1950s was a brief-case toting family man who rarely went straight to the pub after work. Conscious of their superior earning power, many miners felt almost sorry for the clerks and lower white-collar employees and in general there was little class antagonism. The language of class conflict was never heard outside the few formal political meetings. The Communists' following in local elections had disappeared well before the national ban on the party in 1956; strikes and stoppages were a rarity (Croon and Utermann, 1958: *passim*).

The differences between the two accounts, both written by men whose quality of observation is uncontestable, are, to say the least, dramatic. Confronting each other across the passage of 30 years are two different worlds: in one, we find dark, satanic factories, a miserable, poverty-stricken, angry proletariat, and class distinctions and class antagonism running like a fault line through every aspect of daily experience; in the other, we discover a peaceful world of mutual respect and sizeable interaction between social groups whose boundaries are increasingly hard to define. In one world, we see a working class that spends much of its life together, on the streets, in numerous clubs, a working class that is highly political and often militant; in the other, quiet, family-oriented men for whom politics is largely a matter of Sunday voting.

Part of the power of these accounts, or rather of the juxtaposition of the two, lies in the symmetry between changes in social relationships and perceptions, on the one hand, and the weakening of radicalism and militancy on the other. The political content of everyday experience has apparently changed. The bourgeoisie and the workers no longer hate and fear each other, no longer avoid and despise each other, and this new social reality, so the texts seem to tell us, provides the foundation for a different kind of politics. If this is correct, one needs only a smattering of German history to appreciate its significance. After all, from the very beginning of its short life the Weimar Republic was undermined, eventually fatally so, by political polarisation. The Federal Republic, by contrast, has enjoyed long years of stability with very little support for either political extreme.

This view that dramatic social change had taken place was certainly shared by most educated Germans in the 1950s and also by many German sociologists of the time. Theodor Geiger, for example, entitled his 1949 study 'Klassengesellschaft im Schmelztiegel' (class society in the melting pot), while his colleague Helmut Schelsky believed that the 'equalised, petit-bourgeois society' (nivellierte Mittelstandsgesellschaft) was in the making (Geiger, 1949; Schelsky, 1964). According to Schelsky the collective rise of the working class, the high level of individual mobility and the loss of middle-class privileges together meant that, for analysing German society, class had lost its function as an explanatory category. Both Geiger and Schelsky believed that Marxist thinking was outdated and Schelsky castigated left-wing leaders for still holding on to outdated class rhetoric (though he was later to acknowledge that such rhetoric could still have a bargaining function) (Schelsky, 1964).

Was this all just wishful thinking by representatives of a nervous and unsettled post-war bourgeoisie? *Had* the workers' world really changed so dramatically and *was* there an inexorable logic linking changing social conditions and perceptions on the one hand and the decline of radical politics on the other? And if so, what forces could have been powerful enough to have effected such changes in just 30 years?

The problem is that a lot of the more general 1950s sociology turns out to have a very slim empirical basis. Moreover, not all of those empirical studies that *were* carried out matched the conclusions of Schelsky or Geiger (e.g. Popitz and Bahrdt, 1961). In addition, comparison of texts like those by Stenbock-Fermor with Croon and Utermann reveals the very different intentions of the authors, good observers though they were. Stenbock-Fermor wanted to bring home to a bourgeoisie that was for the large part militantly anti-labour the conditions under which workers were living and labouring. Croon and Utermann, on the other hand, were writing for an anxious society that was desperately hoping for political stability and were keen to stress those tendencies pointing towards integration and social harmony. The contrasts between their findings, therefore, may have been dictated as much by their different purposes as by objective social change.

In short, we need to find independent sources and, moreover, ones which will take us into the intervening period — into the years of fascism, war and occupation — if we are really to understand the scope and impact of social change on West German, and specifically working-class, politics. And at last the historical studies are appearing which will enable us to do this. They have been very slow in coming, above all because of the difficulty of finding trustworthy sources for the Nazi era and of making continuous observations across the very different regimes of Weimar, Nazism, occupation and the Federal Republic. The first major social-historical survey to cross the boundaries of 1933 and 1945, for example, did not appear until 1983 (Conze and Lepsius, 1983). Gradually, however, the growing body of work covering *either* fascism *or* war *or* occupation has enabled more ambitious, long-term surveys to be made. In addition, innovative work in the field of oral history, in particular by Lutz Niethammer has compensated for some of the deficiencies in sources. After all, despite its drawbacks as a historical tool, popular memory is a 'source' which survived when almost all formal types of recorded information had collapsed. The result of all this work is that we are now able to make some, albeit tentative, hypotheses about the social roots of post-war politics.

THE RUHR IN WEIMAR

Even a cursory glance at the Ruhr's election results during the Weimar period indicates that political allegiance was much more varied, and the link between it and social conditions much more complex, than the stereotype of the radical Ruhr worker would suggest. Certainly, radicalism was a powerful force in the Ruhr. Yet for much of the 1920s the moderate Catholic Centre Party commanded the biggest following. Indeed, a significant minority of workers continued to vote for right-wing 'national-protestant' parties such as the German People's Party (DVP) and the Nationalists (DNVP).

For the Ruhr as a whole (Rohe, 1987: 533), around 40 per cent of votes cast went to the two main working-class parties, the SPD and KPD. Taking working-class voters on their own, we will not go far wrong if we assume that roughly half their votes went to the socialist parties. The KPD was strongest in the Catholic areas and in the newer towns of the northern Ruhr while the SPD enjoyed its strongest following in the Protestant eastern Ruhr. Within the socialist camp, the KPD was well ahead of the SPD, taking between three-fifths and two-thirds of the socialist vote. For its part, the Catholic Centre drew a little over a quarter of the vote, putting it well ahead of the SPD and often of the KPD. The remaining votes were shared out between the various protestant-national parties (DVP, DNVP etc.) and the considerable number of splinter parties thrown up in the course of the Weimar era (Rohe, 1987; Wagner, 1983: 439 ff).

This general pattern remained fairly constant throughout the 1920s and early 1930s. From 1930 onwards, the Nazis made considerable inroads into the vote of the other bourgeois nationalist parties. By dint of mobilising new voters it increased the nationalist share of the vote, reaching a high of a little over 30 per cent of votes cast in 1932. The Nazis failed, however, to make much of a dent on the vote of the three main parties, and on the eve of the Nazis' accession to power it was the KPD which enjoyed the biggest following in the region (Rohe, 1987: 533).

If the impression of a uniformly radical working class is therefore illusory, it remains true that a considerable minority of Ruhr workers were politically extremely active, particularly in the early 1920s, and the region was scene to some of the biggest popular uprisings in the history of modern Germany. In 1919, tens of thousands of miners took part in strikes and marches in favour of socialisation of the mining industry. In 1920, in response to a right-wing putsch, there was an armed uprising in the Ruhr on a scale which made it the biggest armed insurrection in the history of the German labour movement. It is clear from the numbers involved that these protest movements were able to draw on support that went well beyond the radical vote. Within the mining industry, militant anarcho-syndicalist unions sprang up in the mid-1920s and for a while rivalled the established socialist union in strength (Lucas, 1976; Brüggemeier, 1983: 243 ff; Tschirbs, 1986: 227).

Class conditions and class consciousness in the Ruhr

What was the link between social experience in the Ruhr and voting behaviour? Should we regard the Communist vote as the authentic response to prevailing social conditions and the rest as the result of some sort of manipulation? Or was the non-socialist vote a sign that the Ruhr was not such a class society as has often been assumed?

The answer to the second proposition is that it would have been hard for even the blindest advocate of social harmony to deny the Ruhr the appellation of an almost archetypal class society, or to fail to see in the Ruhr working class many features of a classical proletariat. For all Ruhr workers in the 1920s, life, as Stenbock-Fermor knew, was hard, and this was visibly their collective fate. In 1921, inflation began to erode living standards and during the Ruhr occupation of 1923 there was real hunger. After a few years of relative calm, the mining industry, at that time by far the biggest employer in the region, entered a crisis and from 1929 onwards many miners experienced long years of unemployment. Even in the good years real wages were often below 1914 levels. Apart from the general economic conditions, there was for all underground workers in the mining industry the constant risk of death or permanent injury and consequent family poverty. By the time they had reached their early forties, most workers had passed their earning peak and were forced to move to less and less demanding jobs as their health became frailer (Brüggemeier, 1983: 162 ff).

Everyday life was full of class experiences of exploitation and solidarity. For the miners, the most important experience binding them together was work. At work, the men were not subject to the disciplines normally characteristic of industrial employment. Until the late 1920s they worked in small groups at isolated faces, spending most of the shift free from any supervision or directives. It was here, in this underground world in which physical intimacy and shared physical exertion contributed to the experience of solidarity, that the miners created their own sphere, their own semi-public domain. Of course, the independence of the miner was far from absolute; the (often arbitrary) authority of the employers continually made itself felt. Conflicts over wages were never-ending since the changing face conditions meant that piece-rates had continually to be renegotiated. Precisely because they enjoyed so little day-to-day control over the work process, employers felt obliged to be particularly hard in their approach to the men. The experience of work was therefore characterised by independence and solidarity on the one hand and, on the other, by recurrent conflicts with a rigid and inflexible authority. It was a combination designed to create a strong sense of group identity amongst the miners (Hickey, 1985: 109 ff; Brüggemeier, 1983: 75 ff).

Outside work, too, powerful, informal 'structures' of solidarity and co-operation evolved despite the many factors (such as the enormous mobility) threatening the cohesion and unity of Ruhr workers. Indeed, it was destabilising influences such as high mobility which initially provided the raison d'être for many of these informal structures. What made them doubly strong and important was the quite extraordinary degree to which the citizens of the Ruhr towns were dependent on their own resources. The shortage of housing and services, for example, forced them to resort to self-help and improvisation, thereby experiencing mutual solidarity and support. Until the early 1920s most young workers lodged as *Schlafgänger* with families. This, in turn, created bonds of attatchment and shared experience, with the tenant often becoming part of the 'half-open' family. And in many other ways the Ruhr workers created their own support systems. An enormous number of leagues and associations grew up. In the medium sized town of Hamborn, for example, the police recorded the existence of 37 choral societies, 26 other musical groups, 62 sporting associations of one sort or another, 21 social clubs, nine societies for animal fanciers, seven societies for people from different German regions (*landsmannschaftliche Vereine*), a free-thinker group, nine union branches with 16 further union-affiliated associations, four political associations and many others (Brüggemeier and Niethammer, 1978: *passim*; Lucas, 1976: 94-5; Zimmermann, 1987: 152 ff).

At the same time, segregation between the working-class communities and other social groups remained absolute. Here too, there is no doubt that Stenbock-Femor's picture is accurate. Living often within a few streets of each other were social groups who inhabited entirely different worlds, with their own rules, their own sense of identity and almost total separation (*Hochlarmarker Lesebuch*, 1981: 98; Stenbock-Femor, 1928).

Looking at the way Ruhr workers transposed these experiences into political views, it becomes apparent that the notion of 'class consciousness' is misleading. There is plenty of evidence that *all* Ruhr workers were very aware of class. How could they not be when the disparities in power and wealth and the barriers to upward mobility or free social interchange were so great? No political party could be attractive if it presented an image of society at variance with this experience. Yet the range of compatible social images proved to be considerable. Many parties managed to present political choices that, at one level or another, were meaningful to the workers in the

Ruhr. The desirability of class struggle was by no means the only political conclusion compatible with the experience of class society, as the success of the nationalist parties demonstrates. They were able to offer images of a hierarchical society in which everyone had their place — images that could be particularly convincing for workers in companies with strongly patriarchal employers. The classic example of the patriarchal employer is Krupp and it is well known that many of Krupp's employees voted in the 'national' camp (Herbert,1983b: 233 ff; Kühr, 1973: 96).

The fact remains that in the Ruhr as a whole the most successful parties were highly critical of the existing social order. This applied not only to the socialist parties but also to the Catholic Centre, particularly in the Ruhr sections which were consistently further to the left than the national party. True, the Centre party shared with its more conservative counterparts the notion of an organic, hierarchically structured society, but it added to this a strong emphasis on the social obligations of the powerful (Kühr, 1973: *passim*; Hickey, 1985: 84 ff). Evidence that Centre voting was not incompatible with support for militant, at times radical, working-class politics was provided by the groundswell of support for the strike and socialisation movement in 1919. As Franz Brüggemeier has argued, participation in the socialisation movement went far beyond the limits of socialist voting (Brüggemeier, 1983: 243 ff). By and large, therefore, the class experience of the Ruhr *did* give rise to strongly socially critical politics even though a lot of the voting was very far from where classical Marxist interpretations would expect it to be.

Churches, clubs and working-class culture

It would, however, be nonsense to assert that the Centre Party's success was due merely to the party's ability to articulate similar grievances and protests as the socialists. To explain the appeal of both Centre Party and Protestant nationalism, we have to look first of all at the conditions under which Ruhr society had been constituted. For, as the Weimar era began, the Ruhr was still a relatively new society, its character still strongly influenced by the manner in which it had been created. After all, it was only with the expansion of mining and steel-making in the mid-nineteenth century that the area transformed from a largely agricultural region to one of the biggest industrial centres in Europe. In the 40 years leading up to the First World War, the mining workforce, for instance, increased eightfold. The newcomers, both Catholic and Protestant, came from rural backgrounds in which the church had played an important part in everyday life. When they arrived in the Ruhr, it was only natural or them to seek out the familiar environment of the church, a tendency both Catholic and Protestant churches exploited by setting up whole networks of workers' organisations in the region. The denominational division within the workforce was thus reinforced by an organisational one (Hickey, 1985: 70 ff).

The size of the Centre's following throughout the 1920s indicated that a substantial number of workers continued to find in their religion an important source of social identity. This was not a sign primarily of great religiosity, although many Catholic workers in the 1920s were church goers of varying intensity (Rohe, 1987: 519). Rather, it indicated the substantial role that the church and other Catholic organisations played in communal life. The Catholics were particularly effective at providing clubs and groups for workers and it was these, along with the Catholic-dominated Christian trade union, that cemented and sustained the link between the party and its following. The Protestant church was much less effective at creating such cultural and social networks, a fact which goes a long way to explaining why it was that the socialists were able invade the Protestant-nationalist camp long before they made any inroads on the Centre's following (Hickey, 1985: 70 ff; Rohe, 1986: 121).

The Catholic Church was most successful at involving women in its various organisations. Every Catholic neighbourhood had its women's and mothers' league, its groups for younger women, choirs — which often had the added attraction of being mixed, charitable societies and so forth. Because of the preponderance of heavy industry in the region, female employment was very limited and most wives stayed at home. For such women, only indirectly involved in the experiences and struggles at the workplace, the relationships formed in the neighbourhood had all the more significance for forming their political outlook. It is thus no surprise to find that Catholic women were even more prone than their husbands to vote for the Centre (Zimmermann, 1987: 156).

Like the Centre, the Socialists too relied on a large variety of supporting groups and institutions to sustain the link between party and voter. In Bochum alone there were some 62 clubs and leagues associated with the socialist parties (Wagner, 1983: 284 ff and 452 ff). In some instances, the link between the parties and the cultural organisations was fairly thin; their political impact was presumably limited to creating a certain measure of identification with the controlling party and possibly a forum where members could occasionally talk about politics. Other groups, however, be they Esperanto societies, Communist choirs, wireless clubs or members of the International Workers' Aid organisation were far more self-consciously political (Zimmermann, 1987: 162 ff).

Communists and Social Democrats

One key political phenomenon of the early 1920s was the defection of a lot of the SPD's following to the newly created KPD. The outlook and wishes of many workers had long been at odds with the sober gradualism characteristic both of the SPD leadership and of the senior men in the SPD-affiliated free trade unions. The bulk of the labour force was, at least until the late 1920s, still in the process of adjusting to Ruhr conditions. At least until the early 1920s, Ruhr industrial workers formed an enormously mobile and unstable group, composed largely of young and unmarried men. Even those with families showed a great propensity to change dwelling and occupation (Brüggemeier, 1983: 52 ff; Hickey, 1985: 36 ff). The future was always very uncertain. Against this background, the emphasis of the free unions and SPD on discipline and organisational strength to achieve long-term goals had little appeal, whereas strikes and actions for immediate gain could often receive remarkable support. In the mining industry, for example, despite the workforce's willingness to engage in some of the most powerful strikes in the Kaiserreich, membership of the free trade union was limited prior to 1914 and declined during the 1920s to a low of about 15 per cent of the workforce (Tschirbs, 1986: *passim*). The unwillingness of Ruhr workers to join organisations was also manifest in the SPD's very low membership levels. At the end of the Kaiserreich only about 12 per cent of party voters were also members — little more than half the national average (Hickey, 1985: 253-5).

By contrast, the KPD emphasised militant industrial confrontation and locally-based action. Its demands for immediate workers' control over production, which found expression in the socialisation movement of 1919, enjoyed an enormous response in the Ruhr. Its simple slogans of 'class against class' and 'for the candidates of the poor against the candidates of the rich' found greater resonance in the social perceptions of Ruhr workers than the more moderate and cautious line of the SPD (Zimmermann, 1987: 164). The appeal of confrontational politics, particularly to the miners, was evident also in the success of the Allgemeine Bergarbeiter-Union, a union created in 1919 to offer a more radical alternative to the SPD-linked Alter Verband. Within four years, the Union was attracting more votes in works council elections than the Verband (Tschirbs, 1986: 227).

Thus, the Communists *were* in many ways a more authentic voice for Ruhr militancy than the Social Democrats, reflecting more accurately the strengths and perceptions of the militant elements within the Ruhr working class. Nevertheless the suddenness and extent of the KPD's success was as much the result of the specific national and international situation as it was of workers' outlook in the Ruhr. The collapse of established authority in November 1918 created a power vacuum which the Ruhr workers tried to exploit. In this situation the differences between the rank and file, on the one hand, and the SPD and unions, on the other, were accentuated. The former demanded socialisation; the latter, impressed by employers' concessions and nervous of disorder, opposed the demand. Even then, the SPD might have held on to its following had it not, in the absence of an effective police force or army, felt obliged to use undisciplined bands of former soldiers, the *Freikorps*, to help suppress the movement. The SPD's involvement in the bloody suppression of the Ruhr uprisings made it far more enemies than had been actively involved in the protest and reform movement itself. To make matters worse, another national political event, the Kapp Putsch of 1920, triggered renewed demands in the Ruhr for major social and economic reforms. Once again, the SPD rejected the demands and resorted to armed force to quell the protest movement. The result of these confrontations was a dramatic loss of support within just a couple of years. In the little mining suburb of Hochlarmark, for example, the SPD had won over 70 per cent of the vote in 1919 but received just 13 per cent in 1920. Years after the dead had been buried, Ruhr workers still spoke bitterly of the 'traitor' Severing (the Social Democratic figure most closely associated with the repression). In many parts of the Ruhr it was to be decades before the SPD could free itself from the taint of betrayal (Zimmermann, 1987: 154 ff).

Rationalisation and the depression

Until 1924, the Ruhr was a hotbed of industrial and political conflict, justifying the region its radical reputation. After 1924, however, protests and strikes were far more limited. Though the Communists retained their appeal at the ballot box, indeed their support grew further in the early 1930s, the great protest movements disappeared. What had happened?

Traditionally, the Ruhr had been characterised by an unusually sharp imbalance of power between labour and capital. A divided, disorganised and inexperienced workforce confronted employers who were blessed not only with enormous reserves of capital, self-confidence and coordination but also the active support of the Prussian bureaucracy and police. This unequal relationship was temporarily reversed after the First World War. For a short while, labour had the upper hand as the employers reeled from the combined impact of the revolutionary mood of 1918, the state's loss of authority and a shortage of labour. However, when inflation came to an end in November 1923 and demand temporarily collapsed in the economy, the Ruhr employers saw this as a signal to reassert their authority. Many of the concessions made in the heady days of 1918-19 were reversed in 1924. To increase control over the labour process and reduce costs, the middle years of the 1920s were characterised in Germany generally by an intense rationalisation movement. Production in the mining industry, for example, became mechanised, with the pneumatic pick replacing hand-cutting. Hundreds of thousands of jobs were lost in the Ruhr alone and by 1931 the workforce was little more than half the size it had been seven years earlier. At the same time, those still in employment found their work much more tightly controlled. The individual work teams lost both freedom and cohesion. Similar changes were experienced in other industries (Tschirbs, 1986: *passim;* Schöck, 1977; Stolle, 1980).

For all workers, the so-called 'golden twenties' were thus in reality characterised by considerable uncertainty, with the threat of job losses hanging over miners and metalworkers alike (Herbert 1983a: 84 ff). The unions found themselves on the defensive and the Ruhr working class became more passive. The workforce's vulnerability in the face of rationalisation was all the greater because of the low levels of unionisation and the divisions in the union movement. The spontaneity and locally-based character of Ruhr activism, so evident in the early 1920s, now showed its weakness. Only a highly organised union with a loyal workforce could have resisted the shift in power that took place in the 1920s.

With the onset of the slump, the vulnerability and resignation of the labour force attained a new dimension. Unemployment rose, benefits were repeatedly cut and the proportion of the unemployed who no longer qualified for unemployment benefit grew steadily. Bitter conflicts grew between the unemployed and those who still enjoyed the luxury of a job. Following a disastrous strike in January 1931, many Communist works councillors were dismissed from the mines. In other industries too, employers took advantage of the economic situation to clear the works of unwelcome militants. When the Nazis came to power in 1933, they therefore found a workforce that had already been significantly demoralised by the experiences of rationalisation and recession.

THE IMPACT OF FASCISM AND TOTAL WAR

The first thing the National Socialists brought to the Ruhr was terror. Previously, the various socialist defence groups had been able to keep the Nazi Sturmabteilung (SA) out of the working-class areas. In Wuppertal, an anti-fascist group even managed to break up an SA rally on the day Hitler came to power. The following day, however, the SA, now under police protection, marched through the working-class neighbourhoods. Over the next few days, known political opponents of the Nazis were picked up by SA and police, were beaten up, imprisoned and sometimes murdered. In succeeding weeks, the SA was able to operate relatively unimpeded all across the Ruhr. Whole streets would be cordoned off, apartments searched and the hapless suspects carted off, to the nearest police cell if they lucky, to one of the many impromptu concentration camps set up by the SA if they were not. In just three months, Hochlarmark, for example, endured seven such actions (Klein, 1981: 45 ff; Zimmermann, 1987: 178 ff; Buchloh, 1980).

From 1934 onwards, the rabid, unpredictable street violence of the SA abated but systematic terror did not. Without the protection of the unions, workers had to toe the line at work. The Gestapo and state 'labour correction camps' were increasingly used as instruments of labour discipline. Outside work too, workers had to watch what they said. There were always individuals willing to pass on some unfortunate remark. Even in an environment as traditionally ill-disposed to the Nazis as the Ruhr, the chief source of Gestapo information was denunciations from members of the public (Kunz, 1987: 184).

These individual acts of terror were complemented by the dissolution first of the workers' movement and then the other established parties. The first party to be affected were the Communists. In the Ruhr, the national action against the KPD in February and the dissolution of the unions in May were the occasion for murder and imprisonment of working-class activists on a large scale. For a short period the KPD maintained a fairly open resistance but the Gestapo's success in winding up the illegal groups soon impressed on the party the need for a more cautious strategy. The SPD's approach to resistance was, from the start, more restrained and most of the leading party activists either went abroad or into the 'innere Emigration', retaining contact with a few close friends but not engaging in any direct political activity. Not only direct political activities but also the large number of cultural and sport organisations affiliated to the working-class movement and the other political parties were dissolved within months of the Nazi takeover. Workers who had been politically active often found themselves losing their jobs as well, to be replaced by 'deserving' Nazis on the dole (Peukert, 1980a).

Thus within a few months, many of the most important links between population and parties were removed. Those local activists who had previously sustained or created party loyalty were now in prison, abroad or had fallen silent. One of the crucial consequences of this was the loss of *interpreters*. (Herbert, 1985: 28 ff). That is, a variety of contradictory, sometimes worrying, sometimes attractive new experiences were to hit the labour force over the following years and there was no one to offer an interpretation. This was especially significant for young labour which entered the labour-force during or just before the Nazi era. There was no longer anyone prepared to say publicly, to take one example, that the economic upturn was directly linked to rearmament and that the modest prosperity of the 1930s was predicated on future war. Furthermore, it is important to recognise that the destruction of established communication networks went much further than the removal of formal political and affiliated organisations. Except in the most homogeneous of areas, the openness, solidarity and informal sociability that had characterised the working-class neighbourhoods disappeared. Most workers kept their remarks to themselves and their family. Even in the family it was often not safe to speak openly. A gap opened up between parents and children. Many young workers were members of the Hitler Youth and, for a while at least, the Nazi party was often successful in mobilising their support. Even where the youngsters had not been attracted by the National Socialists, parents might well be cautious in their conversations with or in front of their children out of fear that the youngsters might inadvertently expose them (Zimmermann, 1983a: 97ff; Herbert, 1985: 20 ff).

The result of these restrictions on communication was that in the post-war period a generation of young adults would be called upon to exercise their vote and take part in political life without any sense of political traditions at all. In addition, it meant that the new experience of the Nazi era could not be placed in a traditional framework of interpretation. Those individuals who *were* capable of seeing at least part of the reality of National Socialism were not only frightened of communicating their views but often felt very isolated, unsure of what their neighbours thought. If Nazi propaganda had a great success, it was in conveying the notion that the vast majority of the population were strong supporters of Hitler (Franz, 1981: 79).

This indicates too that the individual's relationship to the community changed. Community and neighbourhood ceased to offer the psychological and emotional protection they had previously provided. It was in part because of this that patterns of sociability were altered for good and that many workers developed a more private, family-based life — a lifestyle which was to survive into the Federal Republic (Zimmermann, 1987: 178 ff; Peukert, 1980b: 24 ff).

Ruhr workers and the Nazis

Under these conditions, it is easy to see why an organised resistance movement failed to emerge on anything more than a minute scale after 1934-35. But even if they had no chance to engage in open opposition, what did the Ruhr workers think of the Nazis in private?

Many observers both then and later assumed that Germany's workers were very hostile to the Nazis. Certainly the NSDAP itself was very worried about the worker's sentiment. An enormous amount of energy was expended on collecting information about the mood on the shop floor and the street corner. There are also a number of instances, particularly as war approached, of Nazi social and labour policy being modified by anxiety about how the workers would react (Werner, 1983: 34 ff). Since then, historians have frequently echoed the National Socialists' perception. Particularly in the 1960s and early 1970s, many studies portrayed the workers as having been overwhelmingly hostile to the Nazis. Tim Mason, for example, was to argue that many workers were engaged, by such means as informal wage bargaining or absenteeism, in covert opposition to the Nazi movement (Mason, 1977; Peukert, 1976; *Hochlarmarker Lesebuch*, 1981: 133 ff).

Given the conditions outlined above, one could readily understand it if this were so. Yet it is far from the truth, almost as far, in fact, as the view arrived at by the Allies on the basis of Nazi propaganda material that 99 per cent of the German population were enthusiastic Nazi supporters. In fact, most Ruhr workers' recollections of peacetime under the Nazis are very far from being simply chronicles of terror and fear. On the contrary, the years between 1933 and 1941 are recalled as being in many respects relatively normal, in stark contrast to what was seen as the abnormality of the later war period and the first three years of allied occupation (Herbert, 1983a: 85 ff; Herbert, 1985: 28-9). This explains why, after the war, Ruhr workers did not behave towards the employers as though they had just emerged from twelve years slavery on the shopfloor. Instead, the British occupation forces were struck by the workers' willingness to co-operate with management (Ebsworth, 1960).

What made it possible to ignore or suppress awareness of the very real loss of freedom were the modest but palpable improvements in the quality of life that were taking place at the same time. Unemployment in the iron and steel industry began to fall within a year of the Nazis taking power. Mining took rather longer to benefit from the upturn in the economy but by the end of 1935 improvements were obvious here too. For the first time since before the First World War, Ruhr workers entered a period characterised by several years of stable incomes. Their wives were freed from the unenviable burden of keeping the family going on too little income. The chances of real or symbolic social mobility increased too, as we shall see, with new types of employment opening up and upward mobility within the Nazi organisations also possible. Even for those who initially benefited little or not at all from these changes, there was at least now hope of future prosperity. That feeling of being on the brink of disaster that had haunted much of the 1920s and early

186

1930s was replaced by growing confidence in the economic order (Zimmermann, 1987: 184 ff).

In addition to such real or apparent improvements in the quality of their own lives, workers responded positively to a number of more general features of Nazi rule. In some vague and indefinable way, German society seemed to be working again. After the war, even left-wingers and liberals felt bound to acknowledge that the Nazis had appeared capable and purposeful, harnessing social energies in a productive way. The Nazis drew respect from almost all sections of the population for the skill and finesse with which they organised public spectacles and for their success in getting the economy to work. Even such ruthless actions as the night of the long knives, when former SA leaders and other opponents of Hitler were cold-bloodedly murdered, were met with considerable admiration. The Ruhr working class was also not immune to the patriotic excitement generated by Hitler's foreign policy successes of the 1930s (Kershaw, 1983; Pirker, 1952; Peukert, 1982: 71-93).

Initially, the Nazis were particularly successful at appealing to younger workers and to the generation still at school. 'Die Jugend, die hatten sie voll', a then 30-year-old miner's wife later recalled:

> Wenn man einen Aufmarsch sah, alles bloß Jugend. Und dann in der Schule, da gab's nichts anderes mehr . . . da durfte noch nicht mal in der Familie jemand was sagen. (Zimmermann, 1987: 184)

> The youngsters, the Nazis had them all. When you saw them marching past, nothing but young faces. And in school nothing else was allowed, anot even family members could say anything against it.

The Nazis' appeal had a lot to do with their ability to capitalise on existing generation conflicts. In the shape of the Hitler Youth, they provided youngsters with a welcome means of challenging parents, school and church. The many trips and camps provided a sense of adventure and freedom, whilst the Nazi's exploitation of modern technology found resonance in the technical enthusiasm of most younger Germans (Zimmermann, 1983b: 97 ff; Peukert, 1982: 172 ff).

None of this is intended to suggest that most workers were particularly ardent followers of National Socialism. Far from it. Prior to 1933, the Nazis had made very few inroads into the working class and they continued to have the greatest difficult in mobilising worker's support. Even those few successes achieved by the party were often of only limited duration. The accelerated rearmaments programme, though it initially benefited from the way the Nazis had disciplined and terrorised the labour movement, actually began to undermine the Nazis' control and integration strategy. The increasing demands placed on the labour force and the awareness of their own power in the tight labour market led to growing criticism of the regime and a new aggressiveness in wage and other demands. There is also no doubt that Ruhr youngsters' initial enthusiasm for the Nazis often flagged (Peukert, 1988: 163). For those in work, and even more so those who were studying after hours for the *Abitur* or the mining school, the demands on time and energy made by the Hitler Youth were a burden indeed. The fact remains, however, that enough social and economic changes pointed in a positive direction for the workers to endure, indeed often to suppress awareness of, the curtailment of their liberty.

The erosion of social and cultural barriers in the Nazi era

One of the most important features of the 1930s was the rapid growth of alternative, well-paid employment in the Ruhr mining areas. Since the turn of the century mining had enjoyed a fairly low status but for most miners' sons, the chance of finding other work had been negligible. Mining was, after all, by far the biggest employer, the steel mills employed by preference the sons of steelworkers, and apprentices' wages in other trades were so low that financial support from the parents was necessary, which a miner could ill afford. The armaments boom of the 1930s, which involved a rapid expansion of steel, metallurgical and construction industries, altered this situation substantially. A survey of miners' sons in Oberhausen Sterkrade, for example, established that whereas 89 per cent of those born between 1900 and 1909 and almost 70 per cent of those born in the following decade became miners, less than 50 per cent of the miners' sons born 1920-1929 followed their fathers into the industry. It became impossible for the mining industry to get the apprentices it needed. Mining work, from seeming a predetermined fate, became a sign of not having made the grade. Now that they had a choice, the young women of the neighbourhood gave those in the higher prestige and often better paid metal industries their preference — as many young miners of the time ruefully recall. For many youngsters in the mining communities, the world seemed more open and the chances of a minor piece of upward mobility seemed real and tangible (Lange-Kothe, 1958; Zimmermann, 1983a: 101 ff).

The rapid disappearance of unemployment in the 1936-37 period gave the workers ample opportunity to improve their earnings through job-changing or individually renegotiating their contract. As labour scarcities increased, employers caught up in the rearmaments boom were ever more willing to pay over the odds for the so vitally needed labour. It is true that, as Tim Mason has pointed out, German labour generally was still unable to attain the share of national income that it would probably have been able to had a powerful union movement still been in existence. But this was counterbalanced for the men by evidence of the way personal effort could improve their social and material situation. The gains made were individual rather than collective (Peukert, 1980b: 24 ff).

Though changes in class composition were far from dramatic, there is evidence in Germany as a whole that mobility from manual to white-collar positions increased considerably in the 1930s. In addition quite a number of workers, particularly youngsters in the Hitler Youth, experienced a sort of informal upward mobility outside work by taking on positions of responsibility in Nazi organisations. In the Hitler Youth, for example, it was to be a not infrequent experience of resourceful working-class youngsters that they would be put in charge of boys from higher social origins. Similar experiences were to be had in the *Reichsarbeitsdienst* and, during the war, in the army (Mooser, 1984: 113 ff; Zimmermann, 1983a: 97 ff).

An even broader and more thoroughgoing change than the expansion of such individual opportunities was the erosion of the communicative and cultural barriers separating the working-class neighbourhoods of the Ruhr from the outside world. This was not due solely to the Nazis. Even without them, the growth of mass culture, particularly the cinema, which gave the youngsters of the mining community tantalising glimpses of the outside world and accentuated their desire for freedom, would have been enough to widen the division between the generations. But the Third Reich accelerated the process considerably (Franz, 1981: 80 ff).

The enforced interaction between the classes was one example. Through the Hitler Youth, young workers met social groups and entered neighbourhoods which had formerly been a closed book to them. Everywhere there was the characteristic and peculiar mixture of *Führer-Prinzip* and egalitarianism. Former no-go areas for the workers, such as the *Stammkneipe* of the local bourgeoisie, could not close their doors to the worker in SA uniform. Another source of new experience were the enhanced opportunities for travel. Hitler Youth, the League of German Girls and the Nazi People's Welfare organisation all offered camping trips and hikes, trips to the North Sea and to the Alps to youngsters from working-class families. Many adult workers took advantage of the Sunday outings organised by the DAF. The Nazis' encouragement of radio and of national sport events also helped to focus local interests beyond the local community (Zimmermann, 1987: 184 ff; Mason, 1977: 175 ff).

The changing experience of society on the part of the younger generation was accompanied by changes in their self-perception and this in turn found expression in new forms of dress. The characteristic Sunday dress in the working class neighbourhoods of a cap and open neck shirt without a collar was replaced by the collar and tie. It might seem strange to modern eyes that the very generation whose desire for freedom had led it to the Hitler Youth should be the one to introduce collar and tie. But freedom was not seen as being in opposition to organised society; freedom meant discovering the wider society beyond the narrow social and geographical limits of the neighbourhood. The collar and tie was a sign of belonging to that wider society. And even after confidence in or sympathy with the Third Reich had been lost and, indeed, after the fall of the Nazi regime, these new perceptions of self and society, and the values and patterns of behaviour that developed from them remained (Croon and Utermann, 1958: 107 ff).

If the 'proletarian milieu' was on the wane, so was the religious observance of the Ruhr population. True, we know that Catholicism in the Ruhr (and elsewhere) was to benefit somewhat from the pathos of being a 'beleaguered citadel'. Between 1929 and 1935 the number of Catholics celebrating Easter Mass increased in numerical terms and as a percentage of the population. But amongst the younger generation the secularisation process already underway before the arrival of the Nazis was accelerated considerably and between 1935 and 1948 the numbers attending Easter Mass fell by between a quarter and a third (Rohe, 1987: 519). This was another example of the way the incursion of national culture, in conjunction with the terroristic assault on existing organisations, eroded the specific features of the local milieus.

The impact of war

During the war, economic and military mobilisation created new job opportunities and further chances of upward mobility. Retraining programmes, for example, enabled a considerable number of unskilled or semi-skilled workers to obtain a new qualification and better rates of pay. The army itself offered substantial opportunities for advancement. Such advances were not always easily transferable to the civil sphere but in practice a good war career proved advantageous at most levels of the post-war job market. For those German workers who remained in the factory, the influx of foreign forced labour was to create a macabre form of collective upward mobility. By the end of the war foreigners made up one-quarter of the labour force and almost 50 per cent of the mines' underground workforce. Many German employees now found themselves elevated to the position of overseers and foremen. In some cases, solidarity developed but in general the Nazis were successful in actively involving an increasing number of German workers in the control and repression of the forced labour. From interviews we know that many workers did perceive their new responsibility as a sort of promotion and, just as for their counterparts in the army, the experience of authority was often a significant and lasting one (Roseman, 1987: 48-9; Herbert, 1983c: 251 ff).

For Ruhr women, the war created a different set of

opportunities. True, these were more restricted than in some other countries embroiled in total war because of the Nazis' initial unwillingness to put German women to work. Nevertheless, the limited possibilities for female advancement in wartime were almost revolutionary in the Ruhr context, where the dominance of heavy industry and the conservatism of the users of white-collar labour had traditionally resulted in very little work being available for women. Many white-collar positions were offered to women for the first time and a number of female clerks were able to take on tasks of considerable (though often not formally acknowledged) responsibility. Other jobs such as operatives in air raid crews or in the red cross also offered local women the chance of new occupational challenges (Niethammer, 1983a: 181 ff).

Apart from providing such opportunities, the war was to maintain and indeed increase the assault on local parochialism and local traditions. Many women and children had the experience of being evacuated to rural communities far removed from their own. For enlisted men, of course, there was a great deal of travel involved. Many accounts of the first years of the war sound — until they reach the Eastern Front — very much like recollections from an extended holiday, a welter of vivid scenes and impressions from strange and colourful countries; the parallel with tourism extends even to the cheap bargains that were to be had at the exchange rates imposed by the Nazis. To paraphrase Clausewitz: war as the continuation of tourism by other means. The war thus extended what had already begun in peacetime — the breaking down (via the media, tourism and social mobilisation) of the barriers of local consciousness. For many young miners in particular, the war, assuming they survived it, signalled the conclusive break with their background and their profession (Niethammer, 1983a: 163ff).

As the war progressed, however, it was the experience of shortages, destruction and terror that increasingly dominated life on the home front, while for the soldiers, particularly in the East, life was reduced to a battle for survival. At home, the Nazis introduced ever more draconian sentences for alleged acts of defeatism, for listening to foreign radio and other similar acts. The Gestapo became routinely involved in cases of underproduction or absenteeism at work. The increasingly fierce discipline reflected the authorities awareness that the workers, exhausted by the Allies' regular night-time bombing raids, were continually being called upon to work extra shifts. Food and clothing shortages and disrupted transport only exacerbated the burden of long hours (Werner, 1983: 193 ff).

Nevertheless the war did, in a curious way, serve to bring labour and employers closer together. The more disordered everyday life became, the more attractive was the dependable regularity of the work itself. Whereas in the late 1930s, discontent manifested itself in climbing rates of absenteeism, the war years saw astonishingly stable levels of productivity and absenteeism despite increasingly unfavourable conditions (Gillingham, 1985: 133 ff, 154; Werner, 1983: 356). Both employers and labour shared an interest in protecting plant from call-up and from labour transfers. Once the workers had become overseers of the foreign conscripts, both shared managerial responsibilities. And as the employers saw defeat approaching, many were at pains to mend bridges with the labour force (Mai, 1986: 232). This tentative alliance was to be reinforced during the immediate post-war years by common interests *vis-à-vis* the Allies.

In general we can say that the war undermined the Nazis' own appeal while reinforcing many of the social changes which they had initiated in the 1930s. It was the increasingly obvious hopelessness of the war that cost the Nazis what limited support they had enjoyed amongst German labour. Yet through isolation and terror, through collective and individual mobility and through the forging of new loyalties and solidarities, the war confirmed the Nazis' assault on class traditions. It also reinforced the anti-Communism which the Nazis had already succeeded in transmitting through the Hitler Youth. Interviews with Ruhr workers reveal that they experienced brutality from the Russians often without being aware of the greater wrongs being committed by their own side. In addition, many former Communists who fought in the East were deeply disillusioned by the backwardness of the Russian economy.

OCCUPATION AND RECONSTRUCTION

Perhaps more than any other development hitherto, the defeat itself broke through the narrow horizon of many workers and gave them a sense of the realities of power beyond workplace and neighbourhood. Whereas the First World War had ended without a single foreign soldier entering German soil, in 1945 every single German community witnessed the incursion of foreign soldiers and thus irrevocable proof of national defeat. Defeat and occupation penetrated, indeed burst asunder, the worker's everyday sphere even more thoroughly than the Nazis had done. For it was clear to all that everyday issues of work, remuneration, food and shelter, indeed of personal survival, were directly dependent on distant, high-level decisions (Niethammer, 1983b: 79 ff).

Though the Ruhr was part of the British Zone of Occupation, the inhabitants of the region were aware, very soon, that real power lay in the hands of the Americans. It had, in fact, been US troops who first entered the Ruhr in March and April 1945. Over the next few years, the miners were to receive various incentives that came from American resources. It was the Americans who, in 1947, prevented the British from socialising the mining industry. Above all the currency reform in 1948, where the economic and social order, from the highest level to the *Tante Emma Laden* on the corner, was reformed by foreign decree, was an unmistakeable sign of American power. Even after the occupying powers had withdrawn, the acute sense of world power realities continued to influence Ruhr labour's outlook. They were, for example, very aware of foreign industrial competition. As sociological investigations in the 1950s discovered, most workers believed that rationalisation and modernisation were essential because of the necessity of surviving against foreign competition. In the *Industriegewerkschaft Bergbau*'s annual reports during the 1950s, foreign competition was frequently used to legitimate changes in the industry at home, indicating that union functionaries felt this type of argument would make sense to the members. This awareness of global imperatives was to be crucial in shaping working-class politics in the post-war era (Industriegewerkschaft Bergbau, 1950/51: 25 ff; Neuloh and Wiedermann, 1960).

As well as roughly casting aside the parochialism of Ruhr labour, the presence and actions of the Allies in the Ruhr also had the effect of altering the nature of class relations. In the first place, they depoliticised the restoration of capitalism within Germany. As Lutz Niethammer argues, the unfair advantage given to those with goods and productive capital by the currency reform caused great bitterness amongst workers in the Ruhr, but this bitterness could not be directed against the local beneficiaries of the reform, the industrialists and the shopkeepers, because it was too obvious that not they but a higher power with which they had nothing to do had introduced the reform. Awareness of the might of the occupying powers helped therefore to defuse criticism of the restoration (Niethammer, 1983b: 79 ff; Roseman, 1987: 209-14).

The Allied presence also led to the construction of strange alliances between works councillors and employers. The employers, who were often under suspicion in denazification investigations, needed the support of the works councils both to clear their names and also to strengthen their hands in negotations with the British. The employers were also very glad to leave the vexing question of which workers should be offered scarce resources, such as company housing, to the works councils. For their part, the works councillors responded to the acute levels of destruction and shortage by recognising the need for good discipline and the highest possible production compatible with conditions. Both works councils and employers opposed Allied policies such as dismantling German factories and exporting large quantities of under-priced German coal. Both were involved in successful black-marketeering to procure resources for both production and the labour force (Industriegewerkschaft Bergbau und Energie Bezirk Ruhr Nord,

1980: *passim*; Zimmermann, 1987: 212 ff; Niethammer, 1983b: 69 ff).

Works councillors proved to be very effective suppliers and allocators of scarce resources (a fact which contributed not a little to high levels of unionisation in the period). Almost every conceivable item from company housing through blankets and bicycle inner-tubes to bacon and potatoes passed through the works council offices. Even after the currency reform, when many of these goods ceased to be in short supply, the councils continued to be essential providers of services and resources. In effect, the years of Allied rule and controlled economy marked out a role for the works councillors which they were to maintain and strengthen in the following years. The Federal Republic's works council legislation in 1952 thus served only to confirm a pattern in which the employers accorded works councils considerable authority, in return for which the works councils largely avoided strike action. To the workforce they presented a picture of functioning, institutionalised class relations, long before this was enshrined in law (Zimmermann, 1983b: 277 ff.)

New labour in the Ruhr

Just as important as the changing conditions in which the workers found themselves was the changing composition of the workforce itself. This was most dramatic in the mining industry where the loss of foreign conscript labour at the end of the war had left a workforce almost 50 per cent under strength. Between 1945 and 1957 over half a million new miners, the vast majority with no previous mining experience, signed on at the pits. The fact that so many newcomers could be found was a measure of the massive dislocations of post-war Germany, in which former soldiers and ex-Nazis, expellees and refugees, displaced persons and workers from industries prohibited by the Allies or unwanted in peacetime were all on the move in search of work and a future. In time, the steel industry, too, would draw on these reserves, as well as on the millions of former agricultural labourers who in the 1950s left the land in search of the higher wages in the cities (Roseman, 1987: *passim*).

The influx of these newcomers served only to emphasise many of the other changes taking place. For instance, they helped to weaken the cohesion of the working-class communities. In the first place, they increased the heterogeneity of neighbourhood and workforce. Formerly Catholic strongholds now had to reckon with an influx of Protestant miners and to a certain extent the reverse was true of Protestant areas. The newcomers also brought different accents, often different styles of behaviour and patterns of sociability with them (Roseman, 1988: 192-6).

194

Secondly, they contributed, particularly in the mining industry, not a little to the changing character of class relations. In the early years, quite a number of the new miners came from skilled or white-collar occupations or were youngsters from middle-class households. Often more mathematically gifted than the established workforce, more verbally confident and with a greater sense of self worth, many new miners rapidly became the spokesmen for their work group — despite their inexperience. They did not allow themselves to be outwitted or intimidated by the deputies in the negotiations over piece rates. They helped to remove the bitter feeling of powerlessness that had often characterised the workforce in the past. In its place they substituted a greater confidence in the chance of obtaining just rewards through the system. The new miners' readiness to leave the mine if not justly treated helped to force management to change its style. Whereas, for example, managers had traditionally addressed the men with the paternal 'Du', the need to adjust to the newcomers' standards prompted the Ruhr Employers Association to advocate the use of the polite form 'Sie'. Many new miners availed themselves of the opportunities for upward mobility in the mining industry during the 1950s, a development which strengthened the general awareness that the gap between men and management was not unbridgeable (Roseman, 1987: 324 ff, 347 ff).

Perhaps most important, the hundreds of thousands of newcomers who came from outside the Ruhr had their origins in quite different political and cultural traditions. Many of them were youngsters and, like the youngsters in the Ruhr itself, had grown up with no notion of democratic politics. In addition, they often had little or no background in industrial employment. This underlined the openness of the post-war political situation and the challenge facing all the established Ruhr parties.

From the 'uncontrolled' economy to the economic miracle: changing lifestyles in the late 1940s and 1950s

Within the space of a few years, the workers experienced a transformation from a situation of chaos in which flooded pits had, albeit briefly, ceased operation, food was so scarce that foraging trips to the country were necessary, and the housing shortage was so acute that whole families were perched in a single room, to a situation of burgeoning prosperity. Just after the currency reform in the summer of 1948, the real earnings of the face worker still lay at 20 per cent less than in 1929. But between the summer of 1948 and summer 1956, real wages in coal mining almost doubled (Europäische Gemeinschaft für Kohle und Stahl, 1960: 16 ff). Workers were at last able to buy household goods, clothes and other consumer articles that went beyond the bare necessities. A clear sign of this new affluence was the decline in the number of workers rearing farm animals or cultivating small plots of land. The inhabitants of a company estate belonging to the mine Friedrich der Grosse, for example, had in the pre-war era kept over 200 pigs, a couple of dozen of sheep and even a cow. By 1954 there were less than five pigs on the whole estate (Roseman, 1987: 385).

What was the impact of these changes? It is well established that simply becoming better off does not make a worker 'bourgeois' and indeed may make little difference to his outlook. In any case, until the end of the 1950s German workers received lower earnings than many of their European counterparts. And, of course, enormous disparities remained between the workers' wealth and power and that of the employers, although it is true that the gap between manual and white-collar earnings was closing.

There is no reason to suppose therefore, that the modest affluence of the 1950s was sufficient, in itself, to make any great impact on the workers' outlook. The impact of the economic miracle lay rather in its relationship to what had gone before. In the first place, the contrast between the rationing system that did not work and the free market which did could not have been sharper. The ideological impact of this contrast was all the stronger because the major theme of German socialism in the immediate post-war period had been that socialism was an economic necessity, i.e. that only strong central control of the distribution of goods could prevent the economy from collapse. For functionaries in the labour movement and for ordinary workers a good part of the traditional critique of capitalism thus lost plausibility.

Secondly, the arrival of prosperity after so much destruction had the effect of channelling the workers' energy into rebuilding house and home. Refugees, migrant workers, locals who had lost their homes through bombing, and everyone else who had been deprived for many years of essential goods and services, now saw their chance to make good these deficiencies and, indeed, to attain a living standard previously denied them. Long hours and overtime were testimony to the tremendous desire to recreate an intact and pleasing home environment (see Chapter Two in this volume). This commitment had important repercussions on other aspects of the workers' behaviour and experience. Above all, it was not compatible with frequent strike action and it did not allow many evenings to be spent at the local inn or in a club (Zimmermann, 1987: 217 ff; Schmitz, 1952; Industriegewerkschaft Bergbau und Energie Bezirk Ruhr Nord, 1980: 170).

It was in their leisure activities that the workers of the 1950s differed most from their forbears or younger selves in the 1920s. The lively informal sociability of 1920s working-class culture did not survive the combined onslaught of fascism, war, the influx of newcomers and the workers commitment to rebuilding an intact

home environment. As Croon and Utermann observed, the drink
after work was now replaced by a beer at home. Participation in
clubs and leagues was much reduced, with only the sports clubs
continuing to enjoy a vibrant existence. Many younger workers,
having once been enthusiastic members of the Hitler Youth, now
consciously eschewed any sort of political or ideological
commitment. There was a strong feeling of having done with all that
and the phrase 'mich kriegst Du in keinen Verein mehr' (You won't
get me to join anything) was a common one at the time. Moreover,
the character of those groups which did survive had changed. In part
because of the social changes effected by the Nazis, in part because of
the labour movement's decision not to revive the old cultural
organisations, the sports and cultural leagues of the post-war period
were of mixed social composition and not linked to any particular
political party. That reaffirmation of group identity, which had
previously been such an important part of club life, largely
disappeared (Beduhn, 1980: 122; Croon and Utermann, 1958;
Krüger and Wensierski, 1988: 208-9; Schelsky, 1963).

RUHR POLITICS IN THE POST-WAR PERIOD

At first sight, the similarities between the politics of two post-war
eras were considerable. After the Second World War there was, as
after the First, a period of radicalism in which hunger fused with
political demands. In the *Land* elections of 1947, for example, the
Communists gained considerable support. The demand for
socialisation was raised in the Ruhr in 1947 as it had been in 1919,
and thousands of workers turned out to demonstrate for the cause.
Then came a restoration of employers' power and deflation and the
Ruhr quietened down in 1948 just as it had done in 1924 (Maier,
1981: 327 ff; Niethammer, 1975: 339 ff).

On closer inspection, however, it is clear we are dealing with
two very different political landscapes. In the first place, the unrest
after the 1945 was tame indeed when compared with the hotbed of
discontent that the Ruhr had been after the First World War. The
strikes and demonstrations in favour of socialisation were disciplined
and limited affairs and it was only on a few spring days in 1946 and
1947 that there was any great number of local protest strikes
(Kleßmann and Friedemann, 1977). Even at their post-war peak in
1947, the Communists did not attain their earlier success (15.3 per
cent of the voters in 1947 as against 22.5 per cent in 1932). Whereas
for much of the Weimar era the SPD had trailed behind the
Communists, the relationship was now reversed and the SPD enjoyed
a comfortable margin even in the hungriest, angriest months of 1947
(Rohe, 1987: 533). After the deflation at the end of 1923, many Ruhr
workers had continued to vote for the KPD even though they now

lacked the strength to engage in direct political action. After the currency reform of 1948, the situation was the opposite. The rare, but almost universally supported, strikes of the 1950s, such as for instance the political action of 1955 ('Reusch' strike), proved that the Ruhr workers had the muscle to engage in highly successful action (Borsdorf, 1988). Unionisation was now extremely high, around 80 per cent in the mining industry, for example. Yet for the most part the workers eschewed radical protest or industrial militancy and, after 1948, support for the radicals simply collapsed. In the 1953 election (the last national election in which the KPD was allowed to participate) the party received just 3.5 per cent of the Ruhr vote (Rohe, 1987).

Apart from the demise of the radical alternative, it was the new success of the Social Democrats which constituted perhaps the single most striking difference between the two eras. Condemned in Weimar to be an also-ran behind the Communists and Catholic Centre party, the SPD emerged in the very first election for the Bonn parliament as the single largest party in the region. Its share of the vote was two and a half times the level attained in the last national election before the Nazis came to power. This success was by no means achieved solely at the cost of the KPD. As detailed studies have shown, the SPD was able to mobilise a considerable part of the electorate that had previously been in the nationalist camp. In other words, what might seem a rather unholy alliance of former Communists and National Socialists had swelled the SPD's ranks. In addition, the party was able to gain considerable support amongst the region's many newcomers, the refugees, expellees and so on. Finally, it also drew off some former Centre party voters. During the 1950s, it is true, the SPDs rise was slowed and, indeed, temporarily reversed by the very broad appeal enjoyed by Konrad Adenauer and his CDU, the successor party to the Catholic Centre. Yet in the 1961 Federal election, at the latest, the loss of Christian support to the SPD was plain for all to see. In that year, the SPD obtained almost half the Ruhr vote. Four years later over 50 per cent of votes cast in the region fell to the Social Democrats. This was a truly remarkable turnabout for a party which had traditionally faced such difficulties in the region (Rohe, 1987: 513 ff).

The new political framework in the post-war era

There is no doubt that at least some of these new features of post-1945 working-class politics had nothing to do with the changing nature of the working class and reflected instead the new political framework in which the workers found themselves. In other words, even if the Weimar workers had entered the post-war era with their social composition, their presuppositions and their way of life completely intact, they would *still* have changed their political behaviour — because the political options open to them had changed.

The contrasts between the two post-war eras in the levels of radicalism and revolutionary activity, for example, were clearly influenced by the very different situations facing Germany in 1918 and 1945. There had, after all, been a power vacuum in Germany in 1918 whereas in 1945 Western Germany was occupied by an enemy whose overwhelming military and economic superiority was never in question. The possibilities for local insurrection were very limited in the latter case. The strength of the military presence, the scale of the defeat and Military Government's control over Germany's food supply made it either impossible or undesirable to go beyond carefully controlled and limited protest actions. Secondly, the evident power of the Americans to determine Germany's future made any political option involving close links with the Soviet Union unrealistic. It is plausible that many workers rejected the KPD as a political option because an anti-American, anti-Marshall Plan strategy simply had no future.

Another important difference in the post-1945 political situation was that the Christian alternative had changed in nature. The Centre Party of Weimar times offered two things which the post-1945 CDU did not: on the one hand, as a purely Catholic party, the Centre could mobilise Catholic loyalties by employing the image of beleaguered Catholicism in a country with a Protestant establishment; on the other hand, it was steeped in the social teachings of the Catholic Church and offered potent criticism of capitalist society's ills. It was true that, after the Second World War, the Centre Party attempted to compete with the CDU; yet it was clear from a very early stage that it was not a viable alternative. Thus, voting 'Christian' meant voting for a party whose religious credentials were increasingly bland and nebulous and one which was also very evidently the establishment party (Narr, 1966: 89 ff, 160 ff).

There are other differences too between the political choices open to the workers in Weimar and Bonn, differences which there is no room to consider here. Yet even when they have all been taken into account, they leave many things unexplained. There is, for instance, the rapidity with which the SPD established itself after the war and the fact that it did not lose its following on the journey to Bad Godesberg and the political centre. Then, there is the speed with which the KPD lost support. The American presence will not suffice as an explanation for this. There are plenty of examples from other countries and periods when labour has steadfastly registered radical, protest votes though there was little prospect of their party obtaining power — why did this not happen in the Ruhr? It is time to draw some conclusions about the relationship between the workers' changing environment and experience, on the one hand, and their new political behaviour, on the other.

Social change and political allegiance in the Ruhr

Whatever changes *had* taken place to the working class, it is clear that the views of Schelsky and the like were highly exaggerated. In the first place, dramatic inequalities in power and wealth still existed and the experience of work in the 1950s was not dissimilar to that of the Weimar era. Many of the constituent elements of class society remained. Secondly, more workers than ever recognised the necessity of strong class representation. Union membership was far higher than it had ever been and far fewer workers voted for bourgeois parties, be they on Catholic or nationalist lines. It could well be argued that, in political terms, the Ruhr workers were more than ever a 'Klasse für sich'. Or, to put it another way, deradicalisation was only one of a number of parallel changes in political loyalty, changes which converged on the pragmatic, institutionalised representation of class interests offered by SPD and unions.

On the other hand, there is certainly more to Schelsky's view than his detractors in the 1960s and 1970s have allowed. It seems clear that the style and ideology of Germany's ever more pragmatic Social Democracy *did* find resonances in the experience and outlook of the Ruhr working class. The Ruhr working class had, by the 1950s, indeed changed considerably in relation to 30 years earlier. This change was not the result primarily of *material* changes, that is, of greater wealth. Far more important than individual affluence were what one might call socio-cultural changes, in particular in the relationship between the worker and society and in the interface between politics and social life.

Perhaps the single most significant fact was that for over twelve years, the everyday relationships and practices which formed the basis of Weimar politics were in abeyance. Long-established ties between parties and voters or between parties, 'pre-political' organisations and members were cast aside with a ruthlessness and a thoroughness unparalleled in modern European history. Traditions were not passed on to the younger generation, ideas and slogans remained unvoiced. Even within the family, it became too dangerous to transmit traditional ideas and loyalties. To cap it all, after 1945 a huge body of newcomers entered the Ruhr whose youth and different background allowed them in many cases no notion of the Ruhr's political traditions. This gave the political scene after 1945 an unusual degree of openness, with large chunks of the electorate 'up for grabs'. The Ruhr parties found themselves with a difficult challenge, particularly when it is born in mind that Nazi terror had cost both Communists and Socialists many of their best functionaries. On the other hand, they also gained a valuable opportunity to win over constituencies formerly bound to other parties.

This loss of tradition was particularly damaging for the Communists. No longer shielded from outside influences by the protective umbrella of working-class counter-culture, young workers in the 1930s proved far from immune to anti-Communist Nazi propaganda. And, unlike their French or Italian counterparts, the German Communists could not draw after the war on the pathos of having been involved in a successful resistance movement, even though, in reality, the KPD's heroism against the Nazis had been no less striking. The KPD thus found it extremely difficult to win over younger workers and especially to draw support from the large numbers of refugees and expellees.

Another major difference between the Ruhr workers of Weimar and Bonn lay in their perceptions of self and society. Nazism, economic growth and war had thrown up a whole bundle of social changes such as greater vertical and horizontal mobility, erosion of the social and cultural barriers between the classes and so on. There was a blurring of lines of social interaction and social conflict, a weakening of group identity and of group segregation. It is possible that, had the local political elites not lost their voice, the effects of these social changes would have been limited. As it was, in the absence of authoritative voices to interpret what was happening, the wealth of new experiences in the 1930s and 1940s helped to produce a younger generation of Ruhr workers whose self-definition was very different from that of their forbears. Many of the empirical surveys during the 1950s indicated that the workers, while being well aware of continuing interest conflicts between labour and capital, did not believe that social or economic divisions had the significance that they had had in the past. They did not understand or did not employ Marxist terminology and they did not respond to the language of the class struggle when the odd union functionary still employed it at a meeting. That is one important reason why the class antagonism of Weimar years was replaced by the gentler conflicts and tensions of Bonn. At the same time, secularisation, closer links with national culture and loss of parochialism vitiated also the appeal of those local sub-cultures that had previously bridged the classes, namely political Catholicism and Protestant nationalism.

One other critical change at the interface between society and politics was that, even before the introduction of the Federal Republic's new industrial relations legislation, the vital link between struggles at work and radical politics had been broken. The tradition of locally-based activism at the grass roots level had, as we have seen, been eroded from the mid-1920s onwards. The struggle for better earning had been further individualised and depoliticised by the removal of the unions in the Third Reich. Many of the radicals who might have reversed this after the war were eliminated by the Gestapo. During the war and in the immediate post-war era, coalitions of interest between employers and labour often emerged.

All these factors inhibited and weakened grass-roots militancy.

It is just possible that a union strategy of active confrontation after 1948 might have mobilised the workforce and have rekindled a more militant and radical spirit amongst the workers. Yet this did not happen — the social partnership ideology of the unions and the imposition of a new legal framework prevented it. Similarly, it is conceivable that active church support for a separate Christian union would have led to a revival of pre-war unionism which in turn might have inured a larger section of the Ruhr workers to the appeal of the SPD. Yet in the early years, the spirit among leading Christian figures in the working-class movement was overwhelmingly in favour of unity. There is little doubt that the SPD's strength within the unions and works councils helped to draw more workers to vote for it in regional elections. Pragmatic unionism and the appeal of the *Volkspartei* reinforced each other and, by the beginning of the 1960s, the SPD's dominance in the Ruhr was assured.

REFERENCES

Beduhn, R. (1980) *Chronik des Arbeiterradfahrerbundes 'Solidarität' 1986-1987. Zur Wiedergründung und Entwicklung des Arbeiter-Rad- und Kraftfahrerbundes 'Solidarität' nach dem 2. Weltkrieg*, Atalas, Münster.

Borsdorf, U. (1988) ' "Die Belegschaft des Hüttenwerkes scheint geschlossen in den Betten zu liegen". Ein Streik für die Montanmitbestimmung'. In: L. Niethammer, B. Hombach *et al.* (eds) *"Die Menschen machen ihre Geschichte . . ."*, 3rd edition, J.H.W. Dietz Nachf., Berlin-Bonn, pp. 196-200.

Brüggemeier, F-J. (1983) *Leben vor Ort. Ruhrbergleute und Ruhrbergbau 1889-1919*, C.H. Beck, München.

Brüggemeier, F-J. and Niethammer, L. (1978) 'Schlafgänger, Schnapskasinos und schwerindustrielle Kolonie. Aspekte der Arbeiterwohnungsfrage im Ruhrgebiet vor dem Ersten Weltkrieg'. In: J. Reulecke (ed.) *Fabrik, Familie, Feierabend. Beiträge zur Sozialgeschichte des Alltags im Industriezeitalter*, Hammer, Wuppertal.

Buchloh, I. (1980) *Die nationalsozialistische Machtergreifung in Duisburg*, Walter Braun, Duisburg.

Conze, W. and Lepsius, M.R. (eds) (1983) *Sozialgeschichte der BRD*, Klett-Cotta, Stuttgart.

Croon, H. and Utermann, K. (1958) *Zeche und Gemeinde. Untersuchungen über den Strukturwandel einer Zechengemeinde im nördlichen Ruhrgebiet*, Mohr, Tübingen.

Ebsworth, R. (1960) *Restoring Democracy in Germany. The British Contribution*, Praegar, New York.

Europäische Gemeinschaft für Kohle und Stahl (ed.) (1960) *Entwicklung der Löhne und die Lohnpolitik in den Industrien der Gemeinschaft 1945-56*,

EGKS, Luxemburg.

Franz, F. (1981) *Ich war ein Bergmannskind. Eine Zeitgeschichte aus dem Kohlenpott*, (author's own publication), Duisburg-Neumühl.

Geiger, T. (1949) *Die Klassengesellschaft im Schmelztiegel*, Kiepenheuer, Cologne/Hagen.

Gillingham, John (1985) *Industry and Politics in the Third Reich. Ruhr Coal, Hitler and Europe*, Methuen, London.

Herbert, U. (1983a) ' "Die guten und die schlechten Zeiten". Überlegungen zur diachronischen Analyse lebensgeschichtlicher Interviews'. In: L. Niethammer (ed.) *"Die Jahre merkt man nicht, wo man die heute hinsetzen soll". Faschismus-Erfahrungen im Ruhrgebiet*, J.H.W. Dietz Nachf., Berlin-Bonn, pp. 67-96.

Herbert, U. (1983b), 'Vom Kruppianer zum Arbeitnehmer'. In: L. Niethammer (ed.) *"Hinterher merkt man, daß es richtig war, daß es schiefgegangen ist". Nachkriegserfahrungen im Ruhrgebiet*, J.H.W. Dietz Nachf., Berlin-Bonn, pp. 233-76.

Herbert, U. (1983c) 'Apartheid nebenan. Erinnerungen an die Fremdarbeiter im Ruhrgebiet'. In: L. Niethammer, *"Die Jahre weiß man nicht . . ."*, J.H.W. Dietz Nachf., Berlin-Bonn, pp. 233-66.

Herbert, U. (1985), 'Zur Entwicklung der Ruhrarbeiterschaft 1930 bis 1960 aus erfahrungsgeschichtlicher Perspektive'. In: L. Niethammer and A. v. Plato (eds) *Wir kriegen jetzt andere Zeiten. Auf der Suche nach der Erfahrung des Volkes in nachfaschistischen Ländern*, J.H.W. Dietz Nachf., Berlin-Bonn, pp. 19-52.

Hickey, S. (1985) *Workers in Imperial Germany. The Miners of the Ruhr*, OUP, Oxford.

Hochlarmarker Lesebuch (1981) *Kohle war nicht alles. 100 Jahre Ruhrgebietsgeschichte*, Asso, Oberhausen.

Industriegewerkschaft Bergbau (1950/51), *Jahrbuch*, Bochum.

Industriegewerkschaft Bergbau und Energie Bezirk Ruhr Nord (ed.) (1980) *Jahre die wir nicht vergessen 1945-50. Recklinghäuser Bergbaugewerkschaftler erinnern sich*, IGBE, Recklinghausen.

Kershaw, I. (1983) *Public opinion and political dissent in the Third Reich. Bavaria 1933-45*, OUP, Oxford/New York.

Kleßmann, C. and Friedemann, P. (1977) *Streiks und Hungermärsche im Ruhrgebiet 1946-48*, Campus, Frankfurt.

Klein, U. (1981), 'SA-Terror und Bevölkerung in Wuppertal 1933-34'. In: D. Peukert and J. Reulecke (eds), *Die Reihen fast geschlossen. Beiträge zur Geschichte des Alltags unterm Nationalsozialismus*, Hammer, Wuppertal, pp. 45-64.

Krüger, H.H. and Wensierski, H.J. v. (1988) 'James Dean und die "Wilden Engel" von Borsigplatz. Die "Halbstarken" der 50er Jahre'. In: L. Niethammer, B. Hombach et al. (eds) *"Die Menschen machen ihre Geschichte . . ."*, 3rd edition, J.H.W. Dietz Nachf., Berlin-Bonn, pp.

205-9.

Kunz, C. (1987) The History of National Socialism in Herne, 1925-49, (DPhil. Oxford).

Kühr, H. (1973) *Parteien und Wahlen im Stadt- und Landkreis Essen in der Zeit der Weimarer Republik*, Droste, Düsseldorf.

Lange-Kothe, I. (1958) 'Eine Bergmannssiedlung und ihre Bewohner', *Der Anschnitt* 10, 1, pp. 12-15.

Lucas, E. (1976) *Zwei Formen von Radikalismus in der deutschen Arbeiterbewegung*, Roter Stern, Frankfurt /Main.

Mai, G. (1986) ' "Warum steht der deutsche Arbeiter zu Hitler?" Zur Rolle der Deutschen Arbeitsfront im Herrschaftssystem des Dritten Reiches', *Geschichte und Gesellschaft* 12, 2, pp. 212-34.

Maier, C.S. (1981) 'The two post-war era and the conditions for stability in twentieth century Western Europe', *American Historical Review,* 86, 2, pp. 327-52.

Mason, T. (1977) *Sozialpolitik im Dritten Reich: Arbeiterklass und Volksgemeinschaft*, Westdeutscher, Opladen.

Mooser, J. (1984) *Arbeiterleben in Deutschland 1900-70. Klassenlagen, Kultur und Politik*, Suhrkamp, Frankfurt/Main.

Narr, W-D. (1966) *CDU-SPD: Programm und Praxis seit 1945*, Stuttgart.

Neuloh, O. and Wiedermann, H. (1960) *Arbeiter und technischer Fortschritt. Untersuchungen in der nordrhein-westfälischen Metallindustrie über die Anforderungselemente technischer Neuerungen und die Reaktionen der Arbeiter*, Westdeutscher, Cologne and Opladen.

Niethammer, L. (1975) 'Strukturreform und Wachstumspakt. Westeuropäische Bedingungen der einheitsgewerkschaftlichen Bewegung nach dem Zusammenbruch des Faschismus'. In: H.O. Vetter (ed.) *Vom Sozialistengesetz zur Mitbestimmung. Zum 100. Geburtstag von Hans Böckler*, Cologne, pp. 303-58.

Niethammer, L. (1983a) 'Heimat und Front. Versuch, zehn Kriegserinnerungen aus der Arbeiterklasse des Ruhrgebietes zu verstehen'. In: L. Niethammer (ed.) *"Die Jahre weiß man nicht . . .", J.H.W. Dietz Nachf., Berlin-Bonn, pp. 163-232.

Niethammer, L. (1983b), 'Privat-Wirtschaft. Erinnerungsfragmente einer anderen Umerziehung'. In: L. Niethammer (ed.), *"Hinterher merkt man . . .",* J.H.W. Dietz Nachf., Berlin-Bonn, pp. 17-106.

Peukert, D. (1976) *Ruhrarbeiter gegen den Faschismus*, Röderberg, Frankfurt.

Peukert, D. (1980a) *Die KPD im Widerstand . . . Verfolgung und Untergrundarbeit an Rhein und Ruhr 1933 bis 1945*, Hammer,Wuppertal.

Peukert, D. (1980b) 'Kolonie und Zeche. Arbeiterradikalismus, Widerständigkeit und Anpassung der Bergarbeiter zwischen Faschismus und Wirtschaftswunder', *Sozialwissenschaftliche Informationen für Unterricht und Studium*, 8, pp. 24-30.

Peukert, D. (1982) *Volksgenossen und Gemeinschaftsfremde Anpassung, Ausmerze und Aufbegehren unter dem Nationalsozialismus*, Bund, Cologne.

Peukert, D. (1988), 'Arbeiterschaft und Nationalsozialismus'. In: L. Niethammer, B. Hombach *et al.* (eds) *"Die Menschen machen ihre Geschichte nicht aus freien Stücken, aber sie machen sie selbst." Einladung zu einer Geschichte des Volkes in NRW*, 3rd edition, J.H.W. Dietz Nachf., Berlin-Bonn, pp. 159-63.

Pirker, T. (1952) 'Die Jugend in der Struktur unserer Gesellschaft'. In: Deutscher Gewerkschaftsbund, Abteilung Jugend (ed.) *Protokoll der Arbeitstagung der Gewerkschaftsjugend 1951*, Düsseldorf, pp. 7-30.

Popitz, H. and Bahrdt, H-P. (1961) *Das Gesellschaftsbild des Arbeiters*, Mohr, Tübingen.

Rohe, Karl (1986) 'Konfession, Klasse und lokale Gesellschaft als Bestimmungsfaktoren des Wahlverhaltens — Überlegungen und Problematisierungen am Beispiel des historischen Ruhrgebiets'. In: L. Albertin and W. Link (eds) *Politische Parteien auf dem Weg zur parlamentarischen Demokratie in Deutschland. Entwicklungslinien bis zur Gegenwart*, Droste, Düsseldorf, pp. 109-26.

Rohe, K. (1987) 'Vom sozialdemokratischen Armenhaus zur Wagenburg der SPD. Politischer Strukturwandel in einer Industrieregion nach dem Zweiten Weltkrieg', *Geschichte und Gesellschaft*, 13, pp. 508-534.

Roseman, M. (1987) 'New miners in the Ruhr. Rebuilding the workforce in the Ruhr mines, 1945-58', (PhD Warwick University).

Roseman, M. (1988), 'Arbeiter in Bewegung. Neubergleute im Ruhrrevier 1945-1958'. In: L. Niethammer, B. Hombach *et al.* (eds) *"Die Menschen machen ihre Geschichte . . . "*, 3rd edition, J.H.W. Dietz Nachf., Berlin-Bonn, pp. 192-195.

Schelsky, H. (1963) *Die skeptische Generation. Eine Soziologie der deutschen Jugend*, Diederichs, Düsseldorf-Cologne.

Schelsky, H. (1964) *Auf der Suche nach Wirklichkeit*, Diederichs, Düsseldorf/Cologne.

Schelsky, H. (1963) *Die skeptische Generation. Eine Soziologie der deutschen Jugend*, Diederichs, Düsseldorf-Cologne.

Schelsky, H. (1964a) 'Die Bedeutung des Klassenbegriffes für die Analyse unserer Gesellschaft'. In: *Auf der Suche nach Wirklichkeit*, pp. 352-88.

Schmitz, R. (1952) 'Das Gedinge, seine Bedeutung und seine Wirkung auf die zwischenmenschlichen Beziehungen im Ruhrkohlenbergbau', (PhD Münster University).

Schöck, E.C. (1977) *Arbeitslosigkeit und Rationalisierung. Die Lage der Arbeiter und die kommunistische Gewerkschaftspolitik 1920-28*, Campus, Frankfurt/Main.

Stenbock-Fermor, A. (1928) *Meine Erlebnisse als Bergarbeiter*, Stuttgart (new edition Schröder, Düsseldorf, 1987).

Stolle, U. (1980) *Arbeiterpolitik im Betrieb. Frauen und Männer, Reformisten und Radikale, Fach- und Massenarbeiter bei Bayer, BASF, Bosch und in Solingen (1900-1933)*, Campus, Frankfurt/Main.

Tschirbs, R. (1986) *Tarifpolitik im Ruhrbergbau 1918-33*, Walter de Gruyter, Berlin.

Wagner, J.V. (1983) *Hakenkreuz über Bochum. Machtergreifung und nationalsozialistischer Alltag in einer Revierstadt*, Studienverlag Dr. N. Brockmeyer, Bochum.

Werner, W.F. (1983) *"Bleib übrig". Deutsche Arbeiter in der nationalsozialistischen Kriegswirtschaft*, Schwann, Düsseldorf.

Zimmermann, M. (1983a) 'Ausbruchshoffnungen. Junge Bergleute in den Dreißiger Jahren'. In: L. Niethammer (ed.) *"Die Jahre weiß man nicht . . ."*. J.H.W. Dietz Nachf., Berlin-Bonn, pp. 97-132.

Zimmermann, M. (1983b), ' "Geh zu Hermann, der macht dat schon". Bergarbeiterinteressenvertretung im nördlichen Ruhrgebiet'. In: L. Niethammer (ed.) *"Hinterher merkt man..."*, J.H.W. Dietz Nachf., Berlin-Bonn, pp. 277-310.

Zimmermann, M. (1987) *Schachtanlage und Zechenkolonie. Leben, Arbeit und Politik in einer Arbeitersiedlung 1880-1980*, Klartext, Essen.

8

Political Culture Change and Party Organisation: The SPD and the Second 'Fräuleinwunder'

Eva Kolinsky

The West German Social Democratic Party (SPD) more than its parliamentary rivals, has been challenged to adapt its policies and its organisational practices in response to a changing society. The numerical decline of the blue-collar sector in the labour market cut into the traditional SPD clientele and forced the party to modify its Marxist heritage and broaden its socio-economic base. The first landmark of the transition was the so-called Godesberg Programme of 1959. Named after the town where a special SPD congress discussed and accepted it, the Godesberg Programme replaced the basic programme of 1925 and addressed itself demonstratively to the post-war era. This meant acknowledging that in a world of increased affluence and of socio-economic mobility well-honoured demands for socialisation or for class-based politics would not find the popular support they aimed for. It also meant acknowledging that West German society was geographically and ideologically mobilised. The war and its aftermath had affected the lives, and the personal living environments of most West Germans. The cohesive networks of socialist support which had been part of traditional working-class culture, had been broken up. The SPD could no longer rely on a working-class milieu for organisational and electoral backing, but had to appeal across all groups and strata to a newly mobile, and potentially dealigned electorate. The full force of this socio-economic regrouping, and the mobilisation of political preferences, hit the party only in the 1970s when the post-war generation reached political adulthood and came into the party as members and potential voters. These were well-educated young people from new middle-class professions whose political aspirations and ideological commitments bore little semblance to those of the traditional SPD supporter (Becker and Hombach, 1983). The children of West German democracy regarded the SPD as the party of social and political innovation after two decades of CDU-led governments. For them, loyalty to the party organisation or empathy with SPD milieus and policies were superseded by the desire to make a personal and relevant contribution to West German politics (Kolinsky, 1984: 73 ff).

Among these new SPD recruits, women played an unexpectedly

prominent role. Their share of the membership rose from 17.3 per cent in 1970 to near 26 per cent in 1987. In the SPD electorate, women have outnumbered men since 1980, after a women's electoral deficit had seemed endemic throughout the party's history (Hofmann-Göttig, 1986). Women have become more important for the organisational and electoral vitality of the SPD than at any point in the past. In this chapter, I shall examine the place of women in the SPD in an historical perspective, and the party's response to the influx since the late 1960s of educated, new middle-class women with expectations to participate in the organisation and in policy formulation.

To highlight the element of unexpected change and the mismatch between the perception of women by the party and women's political orientations and economic situation in German society, I have chosen the metaphor of *'Fräuleinwunder'*. It entered the German and also the American language when soldiers of the occupying armies were surprised to discover that German women were attractive, open, companionable while they had been led to expect frumpy Nazi maidens, full of Germanic obsessions about the vices of make-up and the virtues of nation building through motherhood (Klaus, 1983). This first 'Fräuleinwunder' may be taken to indicate that German society was more mobilised and also more pragmatic than ideological precepts would suggest (Ruhl, 1985). That the currency of American cigarettes was a more potent means of persuasion than promises of socialisation, for instance, might have borne the message for the SPD that short-term economic improvements were the key to political success in the transition from National Socialism to West German democracy. This chapter is mainly concerned with the 'Second Fräuleinwunder' — the unexpected political participation of well-qualified, well-educated women whose lifestyles no longer matched conventions that women should choose between being housewives and mothers or seeking paid employment and even careers. With the focus on women, the ability of the SPD is under scrutiny to adjust to the changing socio-economic and political environment of contemporary West Germany.

WOMEN AND THE SPD BEFORE 1945

How to relate to women, and which role to envisage for them in society or allow them within the organisation, have been troublesome questions from the outset for the German Social Democratic Party. In the founding years, Lasalle and his brand of early socialism demanded that women should remain at home; if they had to seek employment, this should be carried out in their own home, and if their situation needed improving this could not be accomplished by bestowing voting rights on them, but only by bettering the situation of men in society and politics. The rival socialism of the 1860s recognised that female employment in industry could not be reversed, and that the fledgling labour movement should encourage women's groups, women's trade unions and women's enfranchisement. The two diverse camps joined forces as the Social Democratic Party at the congress in Gotha in 1875, without resolving their differences over the place of women in party and society (*Handbuch 1863-90*, 1892). Socio-economic transitions had outpaced the views and preferences of many SPD leaders and activists. In Imperial Germany, a growing number of women sought paid employment and the structure of female employment shifted from farming or domestic service towards the secondary and tertiary sectors of a fast growing economy (Albrecht *et al.*, 1979: 463). Between 1882 and 1907, the proportion of women among blue-collar workers rose from 27.5 per cent to 36 per cent, and that among white-collar workers from 3.7 per cent to 12.4 per cent; in the same period, the overall number of women in paid employment increased from about four million to nearly ten million (Müller *et al.*, 1983: 35; Wilms, 1980). Trade union membership of women rose from 4,300 in 1892 to over 200,000 in 1914. Working women had become an expanding part of the working class, and a target group which the SPD could not overlook (Neumann, 1921: 60; Albrecht *et al.*, 1979: 471-2). They had to be regarded as a potential clientele. That the Gotha Congress refused to support voting rights for women underlines the ambiguous position of early social democracy towards women. Equality and a chance at emancipation for women seemed to emanate from remaining outside the economic and political structures of capitalism. Thus paid employment for women was viewed as a sign of poverty. The party should pledge itself to create conditions in society where women could stay at home, not send them into the economic or political market place (Quarteart, 1979: 153 ff).

Despite reservations about the rightful place for women, the SPD was the first party to look towards women and offer special channels of political participation which were pioneering and also ambiguous. The party encouraged women to attend political meetings, when their attendance of public rallies was still against the German law at the time, and women had to wear men's clothes as disguise. Since the ban did not extend to meetings called by individuals, many SPD functions adopted this format. After the repeal of the Anti-Socialist Legislation in 1890 the SPD seemed set to grant women equality in the party organisation. Female membership rose from 1 per cent in 1890 to around 16 per cent in 1914. From the outset, the party designed bonuses to ensure the representation of women. The 1890 SPD Congress, for example, decided that localities should normally elect a woman among their delegates. If this proved impossible, a woman should attend the party congress in addition to the official delegation (Quarteart, 1979: 141). This preferential treatment meant that in the early years the proportion of women delegates at SPD congresses was higher than their share of the party membership (Albrecht *et al.*, 1979: 474t). Since many of these women had been co-opted and were not, in fact, party members, their presence at SPD congresses was not indicative of existing political influence. In 1908, German legislation was revised to grant women full rights of assembly and political participation. At this point, women became full members to the SPD and special protective measures to ensure women's representation at congress were abolished. Immediately, it plummeted. Before 1908, the proportion of women among congress delegates had been higher than among party members; since then, it has remained well below membership levels. The full membership status of women also brought an important organisational recognition: after 1908 the head of the SPD women's bureau, which had co-ordinated activities since 1899, was co-opted into the party executive as an ex-officio member. Women's affairs were recognised as a concern of the party but were confined to a separate track outside mainstream SPD activities. This pattern was to remain in force until the late 1960s, and substantive change has only been attempted in the mid-1980s.

The early commitment of the SPD to the enfranchisement of women is a further example of SPD ambiguities, i.e. a blend of goodwill and reservations about the political role women should play. Since 1895, the SPD had called in the *Reichstag* for equal voting rights for all adults over the age of 20. That women would support the SPD if and when they would win the right to vote, was to be expected. Thus, an election leaflet of 1903 stated 'women, and especially women workers who have hitherto been prevented from an unrestricted use of their human rights, have in the big question of our time which is being prepared by the election results, every reason to support the Social Democratic candidates. If they cannot vote, they can agitate' (*Vorwärts*, 1 May 1903: 1). Enfranchisement itself was regarded as the beginning of mass support: 'the unfree woman adheres to the clergy, the free woman will be a socialist' (Clara Zetkin quoted in Hofmann-Göttig, 1986: 23).

Women's activities remained under strict control. Since they were held to 'conduct agitation' only with the consent of the party executive, the women's bureau was reduced to following the party rather than initiating issues or policies (Neumann, 1921: 18 ff). For instance, when it made franchise the core theme of a first International Women's Day in 1911 and brought over 45,000 women into the streets in Berlin alone, the executive feared that the women's activities would rival the traditional May Day rallies, and curbed the momentum by moving the date from March to mid-May (*Die Zukunft ist weiblich*, 1986: 13 ff; *Handbuch der SPD 1910-13*, Bd. II: 135 ff).

Despite its vanguard role in matters of franchise, the leadership and the rank and file remained unsure whether women could and should be politically equal to men. They were, above all, considered an educational challenge. Instructions to party speakers in 1922 warned that the political awareness of women was at about the same level as that of workers had been in the 1870s (*Zur Agitation*). At the 1913 party congress, demands for 'full citizens' rights for women' elicited the much applauded cautioning by a male comrade that the party should not back a special women's campaign as 'it was well-known that women would take the whole hand as soon as one offered them a little finger' (*Die Zukunft ist weiblich*: 17).

The Weimar experience

In Germany, women won full voting rights in November 1918, after the SPD had become one of the governing parties in the Council of People's Representatives, which monitored the transition to political democracy after the First World War and after socialist, bourgeois, denominational and other women's organisations had joined forces and demanded the vote (Thönnessen, 1976: 85 ff). The Weimar years disappointed the hopes placed in politically equal women. The SPD could never break the electoral preferences of women for the Catholic Centre Party and for parties of the right, and fared worse among women voters than among men. For the 1920 parliamentary elections, an analysis of 18 electoral districts where male and female votes had been counted separately suggested that the parties of the left did less well among women because the wives of their male voters frequently abstained (*Statistische Berichte*, 1921: 150-1). This echoes the well-worn complaint that SPD comrades failed to interest their spouses in the party, let alone involve them as members. In the closing years of the Weimar Republic the women's deficit of the SPD nearly disappeared, a change which can be linked to the increased turnout among women voters (Hofmann-Göttig, 1986: 32t).

In the Weimar parliaments, the SPD had from the outset the strongest contingent of women members, between 11 per cent and 13 per cent of the parliamentary group. In all, 34 women represented the SPD in the *Reichstag,* many of them throughout the Weimar years. A further eight women served in the National Assembly. After 14 years of Germany's first democracy, only 42 SPD women had gained parliamentary experience at the highest level — none as a minister. The secondary levels of electoral politics seem to have been more accessible to women. In 1920 alone, 44 women were members of SPD land parliamentary groups, and 470 had been elected into local assemblies (Altmann-Gottheimer, 1920: 27, 31).

Views have been divided, whether the party and its women in parliament made a significant contribution towards the socio-economic and political equality of women. Some argued that the focus on special women's topics made no impact on the 'crucial processes in the economic and political existence of people and peoples' (Zepler, 1920: 597). Others stressed the potential and the promise of political innovation: 'The Social Democratic Party, unlike any other, has articulated steadily and consistently the interests of women in all fields and for all occupations, from the academic to the worker and housewife. May this fact be more effective and more acknowledged in the future in the fight of Social Democracy for the minds and the souls of women' (Schneider, 1933: 78; in considerable detail: *Die Frau in Politik und Beruf*, 1929). By the time this vote of confidence was published in 1933, the National Socialist seizure of power had already destroyed democratic government, abolished women's right to vote, outlawed their parliamentary participation, started on the persecution of Social Democrats and the political left, and prepared for the ban of all political parties and the contribution through them of citizens to the political process.

THE SPD IN SEARCH OF A 'FRÄULEINWUNDER', 1945-65

After National Socialism and the Second World War, the social map of Germany had changed greatly. The loss of life during the war, and the detention of former German soldiers in prisoner-of-war camps until the mid-1950s meant that post-war German society was characterised by a so-called surplus of women. The 1946 census in the three Western zones revealed that women outnumbered men by several million (Kuhn, 1984: 171). Women constituted 54 per cent of the population and nearly two in three potential voters were women. For the SPD, the numerical significance of women was politically all the more salient since the division of Germany had deprived the party of some of its strongholds in the protestant East. The political balance in the areas which were to become the Federal Republic tilted towards Catholicism and the conservative preferences among women that went with it.

Given the past difficulties of the SPD to win support among women and the new socio-political imbalances, one might have expected an updated electoral or political strategy. Despite repeated reminders from within its own ranks that women were in a majority and would decide Germany's political future, the SPD presented itself as the party whose democratic principles had been vindicated and whose policies needed no adjustments. Addressing the 'men and women of Berlin' in 1946, an electoral poster stated: 'The SPD remains your party . . . Your troubles are the troubles of the SPD. We want food and shelter, clothing and heating, and a clean administration. Our fight for freedom and socialism is aimed at your happy future'. The special appeal to women was merely practical, a promise that the shortages of the day would be alleviated by the party. 'Mother — Worries! That need, hunger and suffering will be eliminated, for this fights and works the SPD'. Women were, above all, the carers and homemakers who had to provide the day-to-day necessities for their families and children in hard times. When Kurt Schumacher blamed the women for the SPD defeat in 1949, he addressed them as misguided housewives: 'Because women were not bothered about politics, there was no heating fuel this winter and factories have been closed and unemployment has risen. Because women have stood on the sidelines of politics, or have let themselves be tempted at the eve of polling day by misleading slogans, the bread prices are soaring sky high' (Schumacher, 1949: 2). Women seemed more in need of political refinement through education than ever in the past. In a speech delivered at the First SPD Women's Congress of the post-war era, Erich Ollenhauer, Schumacher's deputy since 1946 and successor in 1952, stressed that younger women in particular had no personal experience of democratic participation and of 'the big values and qualities, which always go to the dogs in a dictatorship or in a war: comradeship, humanity and social responsiblity'. The future of democracy depended on whether or not women would absorb these values as elements of their everyday social and political behaviour (Ollenhauer, 1947: 12 ff).

Given the emphasis on the numerical imbalance between men and women in post-war society, and given the poor showing of the SPD among women in early elections, the party was surprisingly inactive. There was some talk about reaching those women who had voted SPD and recruiting them as party members, but this was not followed through. In rebuilding the SPD, the socialist women's movement was brought more firmly into the party than it had been in the Weimar years and earlier. Then, a network of milieu-centred clubs and associations had existed alongside and in support of the party. The decision not to revive this working-class subculture of choirs, sports teams, debating societies or brotherhoods of political self-defence gave more weight to the party organisation as the only arena of political participation (Klotzbach, 1982: 37 ff). Which role women should play in this organisation was less apparent. The first woman to speak at the 1946 congress pleaded for help: 'Up to now, it has been the case in the Social Democratic Party that the male element has been exceedingly predominant. It is now up to you, men, to make the women's movement strong, by doing away with your own personal comforts and involve your wives and daughters, and persuade them, to be trained in our circle' (*PT 1946*: 121). Judging by the applause at congress, the delegates in 1946 saw as the prime function of women 'to prepare socialism in the family' (*PT 1946*: 136).

Women between work and home

This vision of the 'socialist homemaker' was too much indebted to the past to respond to the new parameters of work and family life for women in the 1940s and 1950s. The impact of National Socialism has often been seen as driving women back into domesticity, after the Weimar years had brought a taste of social and economic independence and mobility. Despite the vociferous ideology of womanhood, and initial discrimination against women in the labour market, the employment of women during the National Socialist period of government remained steady — it neither fell, when the party tried to drive women out of employment, nor did it increase when attempts were made since the mid-1930s, and especially during the war to alleviate the shortage of labour and entice women into paid employment (Mason, 1977: 278 ff).

The failure to recruit female labour obscures two important processes of change: National Socialist labour policies shifted the nature of female employment back from industrial and white-collar work to farming and domestic service, i.e. into sectors which had been in decline since the late nineteenth century. The compulsory year of work experience also forced girls back into domestic or agricultural service (Stephenson, 1981). The second process of change concerns qualifications for women: since a quota system decreed that only 10 per cent of the student population in National Socialist Germany could be female, academic qualifications among women declined; on the lower levels of training, girls were squeezed out of vocational training with the exception of so-called women's careers. During National Socialism the type and quality of female employment deteriorated (This is not seen by Schönbaum, 1966). In the closing years of the war, more women were recruited into armament and other core industries to work on the shop floor or as administrators. Industry regarded these women as stop-gap labour; their contribution at the various levels of employment in the wake of war appeared temporary to the employers and often to the women themselves. Many experienced their jobs as a welcome extension of their social and economic opportunities, but the majority worked because they had been compelled to do so (Wiggershaus, 1984: 27 ff) or to make ends meet. This is also true for the so-called *Trümmerfrauen*. While popular myth has it that they sorted the bricks and cleaned up the ruined cities for love of their country or a similarly elated reason, young, single women were in fact conscripted, and others enlisted to qualify for the preferential food rations. Again, this work was temporary, a job rather than a career. At the end of the war, the liberation of the eight million foreigners who had been forced and conscripted to work in German war industries and in agriculture under slave-like conditions, (Homze,

1967; Milward, 1966) created an unprecedented number of vacancies and labour was short despite restrictive industrial plans and dismantling of plant. To alleviate the labour shortage, women who had been drafted into the war industries were kept on. By 1947, the situation turned full circle when the influx of refugees and the return of former soldiers generated a peak demand for employment; at this point, many women lost their jobs and were replaced by men. Some protested against the dismissals and saw their role as working and career women, but many wished their economic situation would allow them to be only housewives and mothers (Schubert, 1984). That women's work tended to be low-skilled, temporary and badly paid reinforced the secondary position of employment in women's lives. This began to change in the 1950s, when many women came to see working as a positive dimension of their lives. The main difference concerned married women who remained in the labour market or who returned to the labour market although their husbands were in paid employment and able to support them (Müller *et al.*, 1983: 82 ff). In the context of our discussion, we can only point to some of the factors which facilitated the new place of women in the labour market. After the deprivations of the post-war years, many women worked to help with purchases to equip their home and family with the material possessions deemed desirable; others had improved educational and vocational qualifications, and began to regard work as one dimension of self-fulfilment. The 1950s also felt the effects of a drop in the marital age and the child-bearing age of women. By the time they were 40, their children had often left home, and a core task of homemaker was no longer required. The shifts towards the nuclear family had separated generations, with the old living in their own homes, or in geriatric institutions, again reducing the needs for a homemaker role of women.

These social and economic changes triggered changes in the political culture. In West Germany, the modern adaptation of the bourgeois ideal of the homemaker who does not have to seek paid employment, gradually gave way to notions that work could enhance the social and personal experiences of women. Work for women came to mean, above all, paid employment in the service and administrative sectors of the economy, often part-time (*Frau und Gesellschaft* 1/77; 1/81; *Frauen in der Bundesrepublik*, 1986). Women's employment increased in the very areas where the SPD had yet to gain a foothold. In the founding decade of the Federal Republic working women were not a ready clientele for the SPD; nor were their homemaker sisters.

The representation and organisation of women in the SPD, 1945-65

The SPD had difficulties relating to this duality. Although the party claimed that 50 per cent of its women members and 80 per cent of members' wives were housewives, (*PT 1950*: 192-204) and although the notion of women as socialist homemakers had not yet been abandoned, housewives were an elusive target. They were mentioned as day-to-day consumers whom the SPD could instruct on the shortcomings of the CDU-led economy. To give one example: under the heading 'Troubles of the Housewife in Parliament' the SPD women's journal *Gleichheit* reported how the party fought overpricing of staple foods — potatoes, low fat milk, butter — to improve the plight of the hard pressed housewife (*Gleichheit*, 1, 1950: 34). The SPD, we learn was the only party that articulated the everyday grievances of the housewife at parliamentary level (*Gleichheit*, 1, 1950: 2).

To change society and improve the living standards of women, however, the SPD concentrated on the working conditions, wages, welfare provisions of working women. In the women's question and in general, the SPD viewed work as the pivotal point of societal reform. The target woman was the working woman, not the housewife. The focus on the 'right to work' would also, it was assumed, 'reach women who are otherwise not interested in politics and convince them of the necessity of party political decisions, and of party political participation' (*Genossin*, 2, 1949: 39).

Throughout the 1950s, the SPD remained uncertain whether it should target working or non-working women, and how this could best be done. At the 1946 party congress, it was suggested that women should run the party press to reach the women inside and outside the party. That the proposal was turned down meant, in the first instance, that women had no special control over the communication process intended in and through the party's own media. It also meant that these media ignored women as a group, and the issues which were deemed of particular interest to women. The whole realm of women's affairs was confined to the SPD women's press which was written by women for women, and virtually ignored by the mainstream party. Until 1949, a monthly paper, *Genossin*, was published to provide women functionaries with the necessary background knowledge for their day-to-day politics. Contributions were packed with statistical data on the structure of female employment, on women's vocational training or university education, and on wage inequalities in the immediate post-war years. They are mines of information, but hardly inspiring reading. In 1950, the most famous title of the Socialist Women's Movement, *Gleichheit*, was revived. The new *Gleichheit* intended to reach the politically undecided reader and wanted to do so without 'lowering a certain standard' (*SPD Jahrbuch 1950-51*: 199). This meant the contents should remain as they had been for the party functionaries, but spiced up by a title photograph, a few women's themes, household hints or cookery recipes. The paper did not have the intended success, remained unknown to most women even within the SPD and was closed down in 1964. The uncertainty of focus seems to be the main reason for its poor resonance. The SPD wanted to keep options open; it aimed for the working women while it hoped to appear as if it spoke for the ordinary housewife. It targeted working women at a time when work was not widely accepted as a positive goal in women's lives and it targeted blue-collar women while the growth of female employment occurred elsewhere. SPD women's policies at the time were out of phase with trends in the political culture.

In the organisational reconstruction after 1945, the SPD made a more affirmative statement about the place of women in politics. Compared with other parties, women were well-represented in the executive, the party committee, at congress and at local level. When Mechthild Fülles surveyed the representation of women in 1969, she observed a converse development for the SPD: while women's membership had declined as a part of the total membership and stagnated numerically, (Fülles, 1969: 40-1; 121,000 in 1951; 123,000 in 1960, i.e. 20 per cent and 17 per cent respectively of the overall membership) the representation of women at executive level increased. In 1946, one woman was elected to the party executive as an honorary member; in 1947, four women were elected, one of them a fully paid-up member; in 1949, five — four of them honorary members — gained seats on the executive; until the late 1960s, the number never fell below five, from a total executive membership between 20 (in 1946) and 34 (in 1966).

The Party Committee which became the Party Council in the organisational reforms of the late 1960s (Braunthal, 1983: 23) was a special target for women's representation. Designed to give districts a say at executive level, its composition depended on regional membership numbers. In 1947, congress accepted a resolution that districts with 5,000 or more women members should be entitled to an additional delegate, a woman. One year later, congress consented that districts with an above average female membership should also be allowed to send an additional woman delegate. By the mid-1960s, women had more than doubled their representation from eight in 1946 to 17 in 1963 on the Party Committee, although their overall membership in the party had not increased. The women's bonus did not operate for party congresses, and women's representation here declined from an early highpoint of 14 per cent until 1950 to just over 7 per cent in 1966. (See the stenographic reports for the various *Parteitage*). Appeals that districts should nominate more women delegates were heard and ignored regularly at SPD congresses.

From 1946-56, the main voice of SPD women's policies in the organisation was the women's officer (*Frauenbeauftragte*), Herta Gotthelf. As the one paid-up woman member of the executive, and holding a regular spot at party congress for a detailed report on the 'women's movement' she appeared to enjoy the kind of recognition and party integration from which political muscle might be derived. In fact, comrade Gotthelf and the women's issue had little such muscle. As an activist who made her mark in the Weimar years, Herta Gotthelf subscribed to the notion of a women's movement, parallel to the party, whose main task would be to activate members and milieu. Two organisational devices were to ensure the effectiveness and the continuity of the women's activities: a network of women's groups at district and local level, who would draw for their work on the journals — *Genossin* and *Gleichheit* — and on information materials produced at the central level for dissemination throughout the party. This plan failed on two counts. Women, as mentioned earlier, hardly knew the publications intended for them. Secondly, women's groups proved difficult to establish. At its best, the SPD had just over 2,000 women's groups. This compares with an organisational network of over 10,000 local branches (*Ortsverbände*), some 3,000 districts (*Kreisverbände*) headed by 22 regional (*Bezirks*) and eleven county (*Land*) organisations. Within the massive and interlinked organisational structure which constituted the SPD, the women's groups were an additional, voluntary facet without representation, influence or even power. The SPD had created an organisational format for women, but one with little consequence.

Prevailing ambiguities whether women should be regarded as homemakers or as a segment of the labour force, exacerbated the reluctance at party executive and lower organisational levels, to give more than verbal support to the women's branches. Herta Gotthelf saw the organisational solution in the appointment of a full-time paid women's officer in each of the Land organisations, and preferably at district or even local level. In the late 1940s, eight such officers were in post at county level; by 1950, only four counties reported that they had a full-time women's officer (*Jahrbuch* 1950: 193); that number had shrunk to three by the time Herta Gotthelf was eased out of office in 1958. In her view, the refusal of the party to create paid posts with responsibility for women was a major impediment: 'Despite all self-sacrifice of the honorary women functionaries it is impossible to work as successfully as would be necessary. The experiences of the last two years have shown, that in those localities where intensive work was possible, new members and voters have been won and we were able to generate interest among women, who have hitherto not been susceptible to Social Democratic propaganda' (*Jahrbuch 1956-57*: 270).

In 1958, the party abandoned the efforts to develop an organisational network of groups which could activate women members and win new ones. Instead of participation in the party, the SPD now concentrated on electoral mobilisation. Coinciding with the Godesberg Programme which presented the SPD as a catch-all party, which had something to offer for all groups and interest segments in society, the new approach to women's affairs aimed at highlighting general aspects — the place of women in the modern world, not that of women in the power structure and representation network of the party itself. This detachment from day to day party work was apparent in the change of leadership. Herta Gotthelf was replaced by Marta Schanzenbach, who was also a member of the Bundestag. To give visible prominence to the role of women in the SPD, Marta Schanzenbach was co-opted into the party presidency as its first woman member. The shift from internal participation to external profile generated a number of changes. The well-intentioned but ineffectual *Gleichheit* was discontinued, as the readership had dropped well below 10,000. Small-scale women's workshops and tours to Berlin were replaced by specialist seminars with leading journalist and media personalities who could project the aims of the SPD, and its women's policies outside the party. The function of the women's report at party congresses also changed. In the past it had presented the participation of women at all levels of the party's organisational and electoral spectrum; now, it focused on electoral gains among women, and on a broad appraisal of the role of women in society and politics. Even at this new electoral pitch, members remained lacklustre. At the 1962 congress, for instance, the women's speech was accompanied by so much talking and other activities to warrant a reprimand from the session chairman: 'I must ask you to show a little more respect for the work of the reporting delegate' (*PT 1962*: 450). In 1966, the women's report was abandoned altogether as the SPD geared up to join the CDU in a governing coalition.

The electoral focus further reduced the scope for women's activities to concentrate on themes which were not mainstream SPD concerns. In some matters, the SPD leadership had been at loggerheads with demands which arose from women's groups and the party rank and file. In the late 1940s, for instance, a campaign to reform the legislation governing abortion in West Germany had been stopped by the executive as too controversial. A move to make some contacts with the elusive housewife by holding coffee mornings for women who were neither interested in politics nor set to join the SPD, received no support. The 1958 reorganisation took no account of grass-root intentions and removed the elbow room for possible initiatives. As women were incorporated into top level committees, they gained prominent positions in the party, and made women publicly visible as members of the SPD leadership. There was hardly a commission in the SPD without a women member, and the late

1960s saw the graduation of some women to commission chairs.[1] The integration of women at the top also served to curtail unsolicited activities from below. To facilitate communication about women's issues across the party, and to mobilise women members, the patchy network of women's groups with their voluntary membership was replaced by statutory representation through spokeswomen in the counties and regions (*Jahrbuch 1966-67*: 185). The women's organisation in the SPD consisted only of functionaries, not members, since the women's groups were dissolved and not replaced. It was headed by a women's committee which was affiliated to the party executive. The newly centralised body could draw on regional organisations to enhance the public profile of the party and project the new tone of SPD women's policies: 'Modern democratic society is based on the partnership of groups and sexes. However, the conventions of our society are often still in conflict with this view — in particular as far as women are concerned' (*Jahrbuch 1966-67*: 183).

In 1966, Marta Schanzenbach was replaced by Annemarie Renger who had started her political career in the SPD as the private secretary of Kurt Schumacher and was to become the first women president of the Bundestag in 1972 (Huber, 1984: 121 ff). Annemarie Renger could be relied on towing the line of the executive, but that line had changed since the 1940s and 1950s. The old dichotomy of homemaker or working women had given way to a broad commitment to opportunities for women. The place of women in the party had been overshadowed as an issue of interest and practical concern with marketing the SPD as the party of emancipatory innovation. In 1968, six regional conferences were organised to enlighten the public and the membership that the SPD was pledged 'to enable women, in line with the requirement of the Basic Law, to contribute to shaping society and not just to enter a society determined and shaped by men' (*Jahrbuch 1966-67*: 186). The same emphasis on the homemaker *and* the working women was evident when Willy Brandt announced for his government in 1969 that women 'should be helped more than to date to fulfil their equal role in the family, at work, in politics and in society' (*Jahrbuch 1970-72*: 321). Publicity work and policy pledges of this nature at the threshold of the 1970s contributed to the widespread perception of the SPD as the champion of equal rights and extended opportunities for women in all walks of life. Although the promise of equality helped to attract an increasing number of women as voters and also as members, the SPD did not extend its mobilisation to the party organisation and consider new avenues of representation or participation for the new clientele. In its bid for electoral appeal after 1958, it had developed a high profile on top level representation for women, and had, at the same time, demolished the channels and groups which had allowed women to participate in the everyday organisational and political life of the party at grass-root and at intermediate level. This discrepancy between the organisational scope for women and the place they expected to occupy in the party, set the agenda of adjustment to political culture change in the SPD to the present day.

THE NEW WOMEN AND THE SPD — REPERCUSSIONS OF THE SECOND 'FRÄULEINWUNDER' SINCE THE LATE 1960S

West German women themselves, and notably the post-war generation had outgrown the dichotomy of roles which had troubled the SPD for so long. As sustained economic growth created an affluent society with the highest personal living standards Germans had yet experienced, a number of important changes took effect. Ingelhart and others have pointed to the shift in attitudes from materialism to post-materialism; studies of political culture found increases in democratic attitudes and a willingness to take an active part in politics. On the everyday level, a surplus of training places and the expansion of the educational system provided young people for the first time with a range of choices and opened avenues of social and economic mobility which had not been accessible for earlier generations.

Girls, who had in the past fallen short of their male peers in educational qualifications or vocational integration, began to catch up. In educational terms, they not only closed the gap, they reversed it with more girls qualifying at middle and higher levels of schooling than boys (Hurrelmann *et al.*, 1982). Girls have been shown to achieve better grades in school examinations, and to make extensive use of educational opportunities at tertiary level. To some extent, the educational motivation has been an attempt to compensate for the mismatch between educational qualifications and employment opportunities. Girls continue to find it harder than boys to secure vocational training places and move into employment (*Sechster Jugendbericht*, 1984). Whatever the reasons to seek education, increased access to it broke the mould of party preferences and political orientations which had characterised women in politics since they gained the vote.

In the 1970s, perceived discrepancies between the motivations and self-perceptions of women and the place women could secure in society gave rise to the women's movement. Although the movement seemed to focus on abortion as a yardstick of self-determination, the underlying theme was that of equality and the mismatch between expectations and realities. The women's movement sensitised women and men of all age cohorts to the patterns of inequality and it generated in women the expectation if not the confidence that home or work, motherhood or career need no longer be dichotomies and restrict their choice. A survey among girls between the ages of 14 and 19 found in the early 1980s, that the younger ones were sure they would wish to be both, wives/mothers and career women while the older ones were looking for modifications and compromise after they had encountered obstacles such as rejected applications for training places. Being a wife and mother for them was a retreat, not a positive goal as it had been for their mothers or grandmothers two decades earlier (Burger and Seidenspinner, 1982). At the same time, women of all orientations were more prepared than their sisters in the past to take an active role in political life (Köcher, 1986: 67 ff). The newly mobilised educational and occupational situation of women made politics an acceptable activity for them. More women than in the past talk politics in conversations, especially outside the family; more women join groups with informal action groups and citizens initiatives favoured over hierarchical structures and political parties. More women are prepared to speak out in public or in meetings. In the political culture change of the 1970s towards participation in parties and politics, women had a major stake. Younger women in particular saw the SPD as the force of innovation and social equalisation. That their expectations of equal opportunities and careers in line with educational achievements have to some extent been frustrated by endemic unemployment since the mid-1970s which hit women harder than men, has contributed to the continued salience of the women's issue as a bid for equality in all walks of life. In the SPD organisation, the pressures emanating from the new generation of women — the 'Second Fräuleinwunder' — are just beginning to bite.

Membership Patterns

The move towards a participatory political culture in the 1970s brought new members into the political parties who doubled their overall membership between 1969 and 1979 from about two million to four million. Although the SPD grew less rapidly than the CDU (Troitzsch, 1980: 81) it reached the million mark in the mid-1970s (Table 8.1) and had gained over 220,000 members since the beginning of the decade. Many of them were young, and many were women. Overall SPD membership has since fallen to about 920,000 in 1987. The rapid shift to participatory democracy seemed to grind to a halt in the mid-1970s, with losses again across all parties (Does, 1976).

Attempts to explain the membership drift have suggested that people might be 'tired of parties' — *parteiverdrossen* — or disappointed in the political participation parties could offer. If we look at women in the SPD rather than membership overall, we find that such a reversal of participation did not take place. Between 1970 and 1972, 43,549 women joined the SPD, amounting to one in four new members; by 1987, 40 per cent of the new members were women. With the exception of 1980-82, the number of women in the SPD has increased since 1960; while their percentage score remained stagnant in the 1960s when men also joined, it crept up in the 1970s from near 17 per cent to over 25 per cent. As male membership declined in real terms, female membership figures rose. Today, the SPD has just over 10,000 more male members than in 1970 but 90,000 more female members.

Table 8.1 Women in the SPD, 1965-87

Year	Total Membership	Women	Women %
1965	710,448	123,565	17.4
1967	733,004	126,978	17.3
1969	778,945	134,963	17.3
1971	847,456	150,928	17.8
1973	973,601	185,079	19.0
1975	998,471	202,226	20.2
1977	1006,316	217,881	21.7
1979	981,805	222,408	22.7
1981	956,490	223,645	23.4
1983	925,630	226,778	24.5
1985	919,457	232,371	25.3
1987	920,000	233,600	25.4

Source: EDV Membership statistics supplied by the SPD Bundesgeschäftsstelle

The newcomer women shifted the gender balance and the socio-economic balance of the SPD. Of the new members in 1970-71, 44 per cent of the men gave their occupation as workers, so did 5 per cent of the women; more than half the women in employment worked in white-collar or civil service positions; among the men, the new middle class amounted to one in three. A study of the SPD in Bremen found for 1982 that 79 per cent of the working women were white-collar employees or civil servants compared with 66 per cent of the men (Hoecker, 1986: 53). In the early 1970s, half the new women members were listed as housewives. The figure was probably lower since education or training were not recorded as separate occupations and women were counted as housewives if they were not in paid employment. The Bremen study suggests for the membership as a whole that housewives account for 17 per cent of the women members, and the proportion of housewives in the SPD is lower than in the CDU (27 per cent) or the FDP (23 per cent) (Hoecker, 1986; Roth and Wiesendahl, 1986).

As mentioned earlier, education has been a potent source of

interest and participation in politics. The educational average for members of all parties is higher than those in the population as a whole. The same is true for women. The party women of the 1970s and 1980s are significantly better educated than the average female citizen, and they are as well-educated as their male counterparts in the party. The Communication Study of the SPD showed in 1976 that one in five SPD members had been educated to A level or above; Becker and Hombach confirmed this percentage for North Rhine-Westphalia in 1982 (Becker and Hombach, 1983: 62). At that time, about 13 per cent of the population had been educated to this level. For Bremen, Roth and Wiesendahl showed that 28 per cent of the male and 25 per cent of the female SPD members were educated to A level or above; at the opposite end of the educational spectrum, more men (34.4 per cent) than women (32.6 per cent) had only basic education, although women were more likely than men to have left school without a final examination (Hoecker, 1986: 151; Roth and Wiesendahl, 1986: 115 ff).

In the context of our discussion of women in the SPD it is worth noting that recruitment from a Social Democratic or affiliated milieu such as a trade union background is less common for the women of today than recruitment from a politicised social environment. In the Bremen study, women who joined the SPD reported that political discussions had played an important part in their parental homes. Similar to men, they took up membership to make a personal contribution to the course of politics. For the 1960s, Diederichs had noted that SPD members tended to be motivated by loyalty to the organisation; (Diederichs, 1973) in the 1980s, personal expectations have become the dominant motivation for SPD membership (Hoecker, 1986: 178).

Party membership has come to reflect personal aspirations and intentions. For the SPD, the wish to demonstrate organisational loyalty had been the major reason to join. Personalised participation was less significant than institutional affiliation. The change to a more personalised pattern of party membership means that parties cannot rely on members to emerge 'automatically' from certain social settings, and they have to cater for the diverse expectations these party members bring into the organisation. The SPD which had a high proportion of passive, loyal members in the past is now particularly pressed to offer novel channels of participation and modes of communication (Paterson, 1986: 134 ff). For women, the relative dislike of hierarchical structures and the concomitant preference for non-hierarchical activities have been mentioned as possible deterrents of party involvement. The Bremen study also suggests that women's party membership may be less individual and more circumstantial than that of men. Fifteen per cent of all women who belonged to a political party stated that they had joined at the request of their husbands — 0.7 per cent of men had joined to please their wives. Similarly, 74 per cent of married women belonged to the same party as their husbands, 31 per cent of married men to the same party as their wives (Hoecker, 1986: 178-9). Since these data are not differentiated by party, we do not know whether the husband syndrome applies evenly across parties. It can also be assumed that older women would be more likely to follow their husband's political orientations while younger women would be less likely to do so (Noelle-Neumann, 1983).

Table 8.2 SPD members in Bremen by occupation and sex (% of membership)

Occupation	Women	Men
Worker	7.5	14.9
White-collar Employee	30.9	27.6
Civil Servant	12.1	23.9
Self Employed	1.1	6.9
Professional Soldier	-	0.5
Pensioner	21.4	17.0
Housewife/man	17.1	0.4
Student/In Training	4.2	2.1
Other/n.a	5.8	6.7

Source: B. Hoecker (1986) *Frauen in der Politik*, Leske & Budrich, p. 155.

The generation of the 'Second Fräuleinwunder' were newcomers to the SPD in the last two decades. They shifted the balance between men and women in the party in favour of the latter; most joined with their own personal expectations of contributing to West German politics; most came from non-socialist milieux, with educational and professional qualifications that could match those of the average male party member. With the values of the socialist homemaker no longer relevant to this generation, traditional loyalties to the organisation were displaced by demands for an improved and equal participation inside and outside the party. The social welfare concerns which had permeated the Socialist Women's Movement have receded for a generation who had gained its first taste of political activity at the time of the student movement, at extra-parliamentary and action group level and joined the party to make their commitment more concrete and fruitful.

That younger women perceived the SPD as the party of social and political innovation is also borne out by the electoral results. Since 1969, the majority of SPD voters have been women; in 1972 and 1980, the party even attracted more than half the women voters in West Germany. Although the Christian Democrats have retained their women's bonus, it has been narrowed and challenged, and women have become of unparalleled importance to the electoral future of the SPD (Klingemann, 1985). The entry of the Green party into West German parliamentary politics at regional level since 1979 and at national level since 1983 has intensified the electoral and political pressures on the SPD. Initially, the Greens followed in the footsteps of small parties and attracted more male than female voters. This gender gap has begun to narrow in the mid-1980s, with visible gains for the Greens and concomitant losses for the SPD among urban, educated women in the 25 to 45 age cohort (Kolinsky, 1987). To the left of the SPD, the Greens have emerged as a potent rival for the political support of young West German women, who expect to play an active and equal role in their social and political environment. For the SPD, the significance of women as potential voters was as persuasive an argument as any long-standing commitment to women's rights, to impress upon the party the need to come to terms with the 'Second Fräuleinwunder' and find a newly relevant place for women in the party organisation, and in West German politics.

The Association of Social Democratic Women

One of the first signs that a more assertive generation of women had joined the SPD were demands at full organisational representation inside the party and in parliamentary politics. Well-worn priorities such as trying to find ways of reaching women who were presumed to be uninformed and politically naive, were submerged by a new confidence that women's abilities and political acumen were on a par with men's and only needed organisational recognition. The initial bid for such recognition proved disappointing. In December 1971, the SPD agreed to discontinue the practice of earmarking places for women on the executive. SPD women were proud to point out they could and should be judged by their qualifications, not their sex (Braunthal, 1983: 129). When the 1972 party congress elected only two women instead of the previous five to executive positions, it was evident that the delegates and presumably the SPD membership had yet to share the commitment to women's representation in their party. [2]

The response was organisational. A special women's committee recommended that a working group (*Arbeitsgemeinschaft*) for women should be created with a parallel structure and function to those for youth, the self-employed or SPD lawyers. Since May 1973, women in the SPD have been summary members of the Association of Social Democratic Women, ASF, although active participation has been under 10 per cent. The ASF provides an organisational network from local to national level for women to gain political experience. To some extent, it revived the women's groups of the immediate post-war years with their emphasis on local activities. ASF groups would operate where and when individuals were interested to set them up. A complaint at the ASF conference in 1977 underlined that it could be difficult to project a unified image in such diversity: 'actions which have been authorised nationally or in the regions must not be scrutinised again and rejected by districts or localities' (*SPD: Protokoll*, 1977: 113). But similar to the other *Arbeitsgemeinschaften*, the ASF had a hierarchy of office holders, and representation in the executive, and combined the top heavy approach of the 1960s with the coffee morning appeal of the 1950s.

While the ASF was created to accommodate the expectations of the new generation of women to participate on equal terms, the new generation was not immediately visible at the leadership level. True to the SPD tendency to keep its women functionaries and politicians in office until they opt to retire, the first ASF convention on 23 May 1973 elected Elfriede Eilers to the chair. She had joined the SPD in 1945, had been a member of the Bundestag since 1957 and a member of the party executive since 1966. In the autumn of 1966, she took the chair in the newly created special committee for women's affairs. This committee was under the direct control of the executive, and intended as a forum for regular consultations with women's functionaries and district chairmen, to communicate the party's policies to the grass roots. She could be expected to head the new women's association in line with the party's wishes, in particular the intention to keep all associations under central control, and use them as a mouthpiece for executive priorities. From the executive's perspective, creating working groups such as the ASF or the Young Socialists was, above all, an attempt to allow restive groups in the party their say and also keep firm control from the top. In this spirit, Elfriede Eilers reminded delegates on accepting her office, that activities and aspirations had to conform to the Godesberg Programme at all times.

For the ASF membership different issues headed the agenda. Uppermost was women's representation in parliament. A booklet *Mehr Frauen in die Parlamente* stated the case, although Elfriede Eilers seemed to blame women for their poor parliamentary presence when she wrote in the preface: 'We can only accomplish the aim "more women into parliament" if more women take part in the meetings which decide over nominations' (*Mehr Frauen in die Parlamente*: 5). In 1973, the ASF conducted a survey of 220 district and subdistricts to find out where women were or had been parliamentary candidates. Replies were received from 40 of which ten reported that they had women candidates (*Frau und Gesellschaft*, 6 December 1973).

For the 1976 elections the ASF ran their own campaign, coined their own slogan — 'women know what they want' — and published their own election magazine *Frau Aktuell* in one million copies. While the newly prominent part of women during the campaign may have contributed to consolidate the electoral position of the SPD among West German women under the age of 40 — the party women made virtually no gains. In 1976, 15 women entered the Bundestag for the SPD. At first glance it may appear that women were better represented than in 1972, when their share of seats had fallen to an all-time low of 5.4 per cent (Table 8.3). In fact, the same number of women entered the Bundestag in 1976 for the SPD as had been in it at the end of the previous legislative period (Huber, 1984: 257). Not only had the focus on women failed to render tangible results; the CDU/CSU had overtaken the SPD, sending four more women in the Bundestag.

This 'depressing result' (*Jahrbuch 1975-77*: 311) called for revised strategies. Institutionalised measures were to replace the web of pleading, goodwill and disappointment which had surrounded the issue of women's representation since the founding days of the SPD itself. Since the obstacles to women's equal participation within the party were perceived as a product of unequal chances for women in society at large, the ASF resolved to intensify its campaign for equal conditions and opportunities in society (Huber, 1984: 35-6).

Table 8.3 Women and social democratic women in the Bundestag, 1949-87[3]

Year	All Women in BT	% of BT	SPD Women	% of SPD
1949	28	6.8	13	9.6
1953	45	8.8	21	13.0
1957	48	9.2	22	12.2
1961	43	8.3	21	10.3
1965	36	6.9	19	8.8
1969	34	6.6	18	7.6
1972	30	5.8	13	5.4
1976	38	7.3	15	6.7
1980	44	8.4	19	8.3
1983	51	9.8	21	10.3
1987	80	15.3	31	16.0

Sources: P. Schindler (1983) *Datenhandbuch des Deutschen Bundestages 1984*, p.188; for 1983, *Kürschners Volkshandbuch für die 10. Wahlperiode*, 1983, p. 235; for 1987, *Das Parlament*, 31 January 1987.

To underpin the determination to improve the situation of women in society as well as in the party, the 1977 ASF congress elected Elfriede Hoffmann, a former trade union organiser, to head the association. She declared the fight for shorter working hours, for lightening women's dual burden of housework and employment, and increasing partnership in all walks of life as the core of ASF policies. The shock result of the 1976 elections, however, unleashed a further topic which received at least as much attention as the concerns for working women: how to force women's equality on the SPD. Women's quotas were discussed and rejected as an unsuitable way towards true equality. In 1977, the party created an Equalisation Commission to review the situation and make recommendations. Willy Brandt, who chaired the Commission and whose support for women's issues had already been apparent during his time as chancellor (*Frau und Gesellschaft*, 4, 1974) favoured representation across the party organisation in line with women's membership while the ASF insisted on *Frauenförderpläne*, plans to help women compete for positions without earmarking a certain number in advance (*Jahrbuch 1977/79*: 311 ff). The 1979 ASF congress in Erlangen rejected a quota arrangement but referred the matter for discussion to the party congress in Berlin. In December of the same year, congress accepted a resolution on *Equal Opportunities for Women*. It was submitted by Hesse-South, a district with a left-wing reputation which had in fact been one of the last to delegate women to the party congress. The main points of resolution 326 were that by 1984, party congresses at district, land and federal level were to receive reports on the participation of women, with special emphasis on women in leading posts, in positions where they would speak for the party in public, and on access for women to training programmes for SPD functionaries. Every two years, the various party levels were to present plans how to improve and develop the participation of women (*PT 1979*: 1589). That the party showed more inertia than the ASF had expected, transpired at the 1984 SPD congress in Essen. The reports from regional and district organisations revealed little new. Women continued to be poorly represented and find access to political office difficult as regions and districts claimed that suitable women were not available for the offices under consideration (Wettig-Danielmeyer, 1984: 10 ff).

Despite the salience of the women's issue at executive level and at congress, the party was still unwilling or unable to transpose its principles about equality for women into organisational practice. Positions of influence and access routes to political power which the party could offer, were not normally open to women (Martiny, 1986). What had changed was the attitude of the women in the SPD. They were no longer prepared to follow in the footsteps of the Socialist Women's Movement and graciously accept a marginal post or engage in welfare work alongside the male career politicians. The new tone reflected the aspirations of the younger generations and was introduced by Inge Wettig-Danielmeyer who had been elected in 1981 to chair the ASF. As the first leader of the new generation, her style has to be seen as indicative of the new assertiveness among the generation of the 'Second Fräuleinwunder' in the SPD.

By the time action was demanded in the party debate on equal opportunities, women of that generation had in fact supported the

SPD as members and voters for over a decade. The West German women's movement had sensitised young West Germans of both sexes, and especially younger women to the patterns of inequality in everyday life, while groups such as the ASF had advocated change through innovative institutions and a consensus of partnership. In this socio-political climate it seemed paramount for the ASF to accomplish equality in their own party before they could hold out the hope to make an impact in the more complex world outside. In the 1970s, the ASF had intended to use persuasion and change the 'male self-awareness', only to dicover that *Genosse Hinderlich* — 'Comrade Obstruction' — had not been re-educated and remained the backbone of the SPD party machine:

> Comrade Obstruction is especially numerous at the level of the local and district executive. He administers his office in a patriarchial and authoritarian fashion and believes in hierarchies. Professionally, he came up the hard way, often via trade union and party courses, which turned the former worker into a white-collar employee, the man in the boiler suit into one wearing a clean shirt and tie. . . . Comrade Obstruction is easily offended even by rationally delivered criticism; because he serves the cause of the party for the sake of his own person he has not learned to deal with criticism in a rational manner. Comrade Obstruction likes to be the centre of attention, and sees himself as a courteous friend of the female sex. His personality only permits him to regard women as 'little women' and regard personal political expectations of women with misgivings. He is not capable of acknowledging female achievement, and he always feels threatened by it. (Martiny, 1975: 733)

From persuasion to regulation

This thumbnail sketch of Comrade Obstruction was written in 1975 but seemed equally true ten years later. By now, the ASF was determined to abandon persuasion and replace it by regulations. At the party congress in 1984, regions and districts were ordered to report in future on the specific steps they had taken to involve more women, rather than claim that none had been suitable or willing to hold office (*Frau und Gesellschaft*, May 1984: 34 ff). In September 1985, the Party Council appealed to regions and districts to nominate more women for the 1987 federal elections (Vorlage für die Sitzung des Parteirates vom 16 September 1985). With 21 of its 102 members women, and with Willy Brandt in the chair supporting the bid for equality, the party council was more forthcoming than could be expected of the party at large. Barely one month later, the ASF decided at its congress in Hanover to replace pleas for better opportunities with demands for equality by quotas. The congress slogan *Sisters, to the Sun, to Equality* echoed the revolutionary sentiments of the red anthem 'Brothers, to the Sun, to Freedom'. It wanted to signal to the party and to society what the women themselves called 'the end of modesty': 'The SPD has a large number of very highly qualified women for all functions, mandates and public offices. This means that women Social Democrats also have to be considered for the office of chancellor, and register this claim for the future. For the federal elections in 1987 we demand that the election team and the future cabinet will include an equal number of men and women' (*Dokumente*, 24, 1985: 8-9).

Throughout the party, the ASF proposed a quota system with a minimum of 30 per cent women at all levels, and a target of 50 per cent to be reached in the 1990s. The terminology of persuasion had given way to that of obligation: terms such as 'has to', 'is compelled to', or 'the aforementioned proportion of mandates for women is obligatory' (*zwingend zu verwirklichen*) accompanied a prescription of percentage adjustments at all electoral levels, and within the party organisation (*Dokumente*, 24: 6-8). The party executive was called upon to present a detailed report at congress on the selection procedures not only for parliamentary mandates, but for the parliamentary and government offices which the party could fill. Here, women also registered a bid for equal consideration, and for full and public accountability of the party and its branches (*Dokumente*, 24: 9).

Between October 1984 and June 1986, party congresses at district level passed a variety of resolutions on the subject. Only southern Bavaria suggested a fixed quota. Hamburg voted against obligatory quotas but accepted that more women should be involved in the party (Pfarr, 1985). Hesse, to give another example, recommended numbers and a time schedule. When it failed to adhere to them, its female representatives in the Equalisation Commission resigned to protest against the *Zögerlichkeit*, the reluctance to put the spirit of the resolution into organisational practice (*Bericht über die Gleichstellung der Frauen in der Partei*, 1986: 34). In May 1986, the SPD in Rhineland Palatinate decided by a 19 vote majority against writing women's quotas into its statutes (*Sozialdemokrat Magazin*, 506, 1986: 4). When the pre-election congress of the SPD in Nürnberg accepted the principle of women's quotas in August 1986, the complex nature of attempting to generate gender equality by regulations was still evident in the uneven pattern of decisions at the lower organisational tiers (Table in *Bericht*: 36-38). Nevertheless, progress towards equal representation has been visible.

From 1983 and 1987, the number of SPD women in the Bundestag has increased from 21 to 31. Taking female candidacies, the SPD reached its quota of 30 per cent in 1987, although just 15.3 per cent of the SPD parliamentary party were women. The new women's emphasis has also been reflected in nominations to constituency candidacies, i.e. the electoral position which is most evident to the voter, and through which the party would attempt to project its image and aims in a given locality. In 1972, when the new generation of women began to look for participation, the SPD entered nine women as direct candidates of whom four were elected. In 1983, the SPD fielded 19 women as constituency candidates, and had three elected; in 1987, 42 women were competing for constituency seats of which eight were elected. With the exception of 1972 when the SPD had its best ever result and electoral chances, and when it entered established women politicians as constituency candidates, the success rate has been about 15 per cent; the larger numbers in the 1980s produced a larger contingent in parliament. The shift towards women is more clearly evident in the selection of new candidates. In 1983, 47 new candidates were selected, of these four were women (8.5 per cent); in 1987, 99 newcomers sought election, 28 of them women (28 per cent). The quota appeals did not produce the expected quota of SPD women in the Bundestag but gave women a more prominent place among the contestants.

Table 8.4 SPD women in Land parliaments 1979-87 *

	Elections 1979-82			Elections 1983-87			
	SPD Total	SPD Women	%	SPD Total	SPD Women	%	+ / -
Baden-Württemberg	40	3	7.5	41	8	12.1	+
Bavaria	71	7	9.9	71	9	14.7	+
Berlin	61	6	9.8	48	9	18.7	+
Bremen	52	8	17.3	58	11	19.0	+
Hamburg	64	11	17.2	53	17	32.0	+
Hessen	49	5	10.2	51	6	11.8	+
Lower Saxony	63	6	9.5	66	9	13.6	+
North Rhine-Westphalia	106	7	6.6	125	10	8.0	+
Rhineland Palatinate	43	4	9.3	40	5	12.5	+
Saarland	24	2	8.3	26	4	15.4	+
Schleswig Holstein	31	3	9.7	34	5	14.7	+
Overall	595	59	9.9	627	84	13.4	+

* Figures at point of election; Data from *Frauen in Familie und Beruf*, p. 189; *SPD Frauenbericht*: Bericht über die Gleichstellung der Frauen in der Partei, Parteitag der SPD, 25-29 August 1986 p. 21; *Frankfurter Rundschau*, 19 May 1987.

The representation of women has also improved in SPD parliamentary parties at Land level with numerical and percentage increases in all regions since the late 1970s (Table 8.4). In Berlin and Lower Saxony teams of three men and three women led the campaigns in 1985 and 1986 respectively. In 1986 women ran six (11.5 per cent) of the 52 SPD held ministries at Land level; after losing the elections in Hesse in 1987, the party retained 44 ministerial posts, five of them (11 per cent) held by women.

At communal level, the share of women among SPD councillors has risen between 1982 and 1986 from 23 per cent to about 34 per cent in local assemblies, and from 17 per cent to 25 per cent at district level. In 1985 42 per cent of the women councillors in towns and cities with more than 20,000 inhabitants were Social Democrats holding 1,300 of the 3,100 seats occupied by women (*Der Städtetag*, 8, 1985: 567). The generation of the 'Second Fräuleinwunder' has gradually become visible in the parliamentary politics of social democracy.

The homemaker as party leader?

Within the party, the bid for equal representation has encountered obstacles and some success. The data released in 1986 by the SPD head office on gender balance in the organisation shows that women have begun to hold more functions, but progress had been patchy. As in the past, the post of chairman had remained a male preserve at national level, in the eleven Land organisations and in the 22 districts. In 1986, eleven of the 47 district deputies (23.4 per cent) were women; two years earlier, only six (13.4 per cent) women held these positions. In some districts, 30 per cent of the executive members were women (Weser Ems), in others as few as 6 per cent (Ostwestfalen-Lippe). At Land level, women's share in the executive ranged from 35 per cent in Schleswig Holstein to 6.7 per cent in Hesse. At federal level, seven of the 40 executive members (17.5 per cent) in 1984 and ten in 1986 were women; at the party congress, the proportion of women is beginning to creep up again to its pre-1908 level of 20 per cent; in the Party Council, it reached 20.5 per cent in 1984. Most party conferences, seminars and public hearings had at least one woman among the main speakers; in the parliamentary party executive, women increased their share from 11.4 per cent in 1984 to 20 per cent in 1986. With 25 per cent, women are well-represented in the SPD group of the European Parliament, and a woman, Katharina Focke, headed the SPD team for the 1984 European elections (Vallance and Davies, 1986).

Local branches have been the traditional training ground for future politicians. Here, 659 of the more than 10,000 branch organisations were headed by women in 1986. An analysis of the political careers of women candidates for the 1987 Bundestag elections showed that for women, positions at district level or in the party executive were more accessible than chairing their local branch (Unpublished ASF survey, 1986). The observation that one in four *Schriftführer* in the North Rhine-Westphalian SPD of 1982 were women underlines that women in the local executive often play a merely supportive role such as taking notes and processing information for the chairman or branch secretary (Kolinsky, 1984: 82).

There have been many attempts at explaining why women do not play a more prominent part at the grass roots of the SPD. Could it be — as has been suggested as far back as 1904 — that smoking at meetings has driven women away? Or could it be that holding meetings in backrooms of pubs has made them unattractive to women; or has the timing of meetings been unsuitable for women? Or has local party work tended to centre on a clique or personality rather than on political convictions, commitment or efficiency? It has also been mooted that SPD members harbour plenty of reservations and traditional attitudes, including a reluctance to see women step out into political leadership positions within their immediate radius of experience. While the organisation in its overt policy commitment has tended to support the bid of the new cohort of women to participate actively and hold party or electoral offices, the traditional SPD clientele of blue-collar worker or social riser appeared to cherish the familiar notion of women as homemakers. For them, leadership should emanate from men while milieu should be the realm of women. However, in September 1988, the party congress in Münster accepted a resolution that the gender balance in the SPD should be transformed by the mid-1990s. At all levels of responsibility and political office, women should hold no less than 40 per cent of all posts. These quota regulations reflect the new participatory political climate of the 1980s and will ensure in future that women are visible in the SPD and in the larger field of West German politics.

NOTES

1. In 1968-69 there were 29 possible commissions. Of these women held the chair in Unterausschuß Sowjetzonenflüchtlinge: Lisa Korpspeter; Bundesfinanzausschuß: Annemarie Renger; Jugendpolitischer Ausschuß: Irma Keilhack; Ausschuß für Kriegsopfer: Marie Schanzenbach; Ausschuß für Frauenpolitik: Elfriede Eilers see *Jahrbuch 1968-69*: 314-15; at Land or county level, there were no women in the chair.

2. For the discussion whether or not the representation of women in the SPD should rely on an institutionalised women's bonus, it is worth remembering that the removal of such a bonus in 1908 brought a similar decline of women's representation as occurred in 1972. It seems that the mere presence of women in committees etc. does not establish a practice of political equality of opportunities, especially if this representation rests on the assumption that women would organise and participate along the separate track of women's organisations.

3. The figures in Table 8.3 relate to women's representation at the beginning of a legislative period. At the end of a legislative period, the number of women is normally higher than at its beginning. In West Germany, elections are held at regular intervals of four (in some regions five) years.

Parliamentary seats which fall vacant during a legislative period are filled without a by-election from the party lists which had been compiled for the previous elections. Women often enter parliament in this way, although becoming a mid-term MP does not guarantee a higher place on the Land list, or a direct nomination in the next elections.

REFERENCES

In preparation of this chapter research was conducted with the assistance of the Alexander von Humboldt Foundation at the Archiv der Sozialen Demokratie (ASD), Bonn, and Archiv beim Parteivorstand der SPD, Bonn, where collections of party documents/ASF proceedings and posters are located.

Albrecht, W. *et al*, (1979) 'Frauenfrage und deutsche Sozialdemokratie vom Ende des 19. Jahrhunderts bis zum Beginn der zwanziger Jahre', *Archiv für Sozialgeschichte,* vol. XIX.

Altmann-Gottheimer, E. (ed.) (1920) 'Die Frau im neuen Deutschland', *Jahrbuch des Bundesverbandes deutscher Frauenvereine,* Teubner, Leipzig/Berlin.

Becker, H. and Hombach, B. (eds) (1983) *Die SPD von innen. Bestandaufnahme an der Basis der Partei,* Neue Gesellschaft, Bonn.

Bericht über die Gleichstellung der Frauen in der Partei. Vorgelegt auf dem Parteitag der SPD in Nürnberg, 25-29 September 1986 (mimeo).

Braunthal, G. (1983) *The West German Social Democrats 1969-82. Profile of a Party in Power,* Westview, Boulder, Colorado.

Burger, A. und Seidenspinner, G. (1982) *Mädchen '82,* Deutsches Jugendinstitut, Munich.

Die Frau in Politik und Beruf (ed.) (1929) Parteivorstand der SPD Berlin n.d.

Die Genossin, (ed.) Herta Gotthelf, Hanover 1947-49.

Die Gleichheit, (ed.) Herta Gotthelf, Bonn, 1950-64.

Die Zukunft ist weiblich. 75 Jahre Internationaler Frauentag (1986) (ed.) ASF Frauen in der SPD Bonn n.d.

Diederichs, N. (1973) 'Zur Mitgliederstruktur von CDU und SPD'. In: J. Dittberner and R. Ebbighausen (eds) *Das Parteiensystem in der Legitimationskrise,* Westdeutscher Verlag, Opladen.

Does, J. (1976) *Jugend und Politik 1976: Tendenzen und Perspektiven,* Sozialwissenschaftliches Forschungsinstitut der Konrad Adenauer Stiftung, Bonn/St. Augustin (mimeo).

Frau und Gesellschaft (ed.) (1971) Sozialdemokratischer Informationsdienst ASF.

Frau und Gesellschaft (ed.) (1977) Zwischenbericht der Enquête Kommission, Deutscher Bundestag, *Zur Sache,* 1 (also BT Drucksache 7/5866).

Frau und Gesellschaft II (1981) Bericht der Enquête Kommission und Aussprache im Plenum des Deutschen Bundestages, *Zur Sache,* 1.

Frauen in der Bundesrepublik Deutschland (1986) (ed.) Der Bundesminister für Jugend, Familie, Frauen und Gesundheit, Bonn.

Frauen in der SPD (1985) Dokumente Nr. 24. Sozialdemokratischer Informationsdienst, November.

Fülles, M. (1969) *Die Frau in der Politik,* Wissenschaft und Politik, Cologne.

Handbuch der Sozialdemokratischen Partei 1863-90 (1892). Bearbeitet von Wilhelm Schröder, Bick, Munich.

Handbuch der Sozialdemokratischen Partei 1910-13, n.d. Bick, Munich.

Hoecker, B. (1986) *Frauen in der Politik. Eine soziologische Studie,* Leske & Budrich, Opladen.

Hofmann-Göttig, J. (1986) *Emanzipation mit dem Stimmzettel. 70 Jahre Frauenwahlrecht in Deutschland,* Neue Gesellschaft, Bonn.

Homze, E.L. (1967) *Foreign Labour in Nazi Germany,* Princeton University Press, Princeton.

Huber, A. (ed.) (1984) *Die Sozialdemokratinnen. Verdient die Nachtigall Lob, wenn sie singt?* Seewald, Stuttgart.

Hurrelmann, K. *et al.* (1982) *Bildungsbeteiligung von Mädchen im allgemeinbildenden Schulbereich.* Special report as background material for the Sechster Jugendbericht, Universität Bielefeld (typescript).

Jahrbuch. SPD yearbooks cited with relevant year and page number.

Klaus, M. (1983) *Mädchen im Dritten Reich,* Pahl Rugenstein, Cologne.

Klingemann, H.-D. (1985) 'West Germany'. In: I. Crewe and D. Denver (eds) *Electoral Change in Western Democracies.* Croom Helm, London.

Klotzbach, K. (1982) *Der Weg zur Staatspartei. Programmatik, praktische Politik und Organisation der deutschen Sozialdemokratie 1945-1965,* Dietz, Berlin/Bonn.

Köcher, R. (1986) 'Die Frauen sind aktiver geworden'. In: H. Geißler (ed.) *Abschied von der Männergesellschaft,* Ullstein, Frankfurt/Berlin.

Kolinsky, E. (1984) *Parties, Opposition and Society in West Germany,* Croom Helm, London.

Kolinsky, E. (1987) 'The German Greens — a Women's Party?' *Parliamentary Affairs,* 4 (Winter).

Kuhn, A. (1984) 'Die vergessene Frauenarbeit in der deutschen Nachkriegszeit'. In: A. E. Freier and A. Kuhn (eds) *Frauen in der Geschichte,* Schwann-Bagel, Düsseldorf.

Martiny (Riedel-Martiny), A. (1975) 'Genosse Hinderlich und die Frauen. Die Situation weiblicher Mitglieder in der SPD', *Neue Gesellschaft*, 22.

Martiny, A. (1986) *Wer nicht kämpft hat schon verloren. Frauen und der Mut zur Macht*, Rowohlt, Reinbek.

Mason, T. W. (1977) *Sozialpolitik im Dritten Reich. Arbeiterklasse und Volksgemeinschaft*, Westdeutscher Verlag, Opladen.

Mehr Frauen in die Parlamente (1973) (ed.) ASF, Preface Elfriede Eilers, Bonn (booklet).

Milward, A.S. (1966) *Die deutsche Kriegswirtschaft 1939-45*, Deutsche Verlagsanstalt (Vierteljahreshefte für Zeitgeschichte series), Stuttgart.

Müller, W. *et al.* (1983) *Strukturwandel der Frauenarbeit 1880-1980*. Campus, Frankfurt.

Neumann, A. (1921) *Die Entwicklung der sozialistischen Frauenbewegung*, Dissertation der Friedrich Wilhelm Universität, Berlin.

Noelle-Neumann, E. *et al.* (1983) *Eine Generation später*, Allensbach.

Ollenhauer, E. (1947) *Rede auf der Ersten Reichsfrauenkonferenz in Fürth*, 24-25. 6.1947, Hanover (booklet; ASD number A28677).

Paterson, W.E. (1986) 'The German Social Democratic Party'. In: W. E. Paterson and A.H. Thomas, *The Future of Social Democracy*, Oxford University Press, Oxford.

Pfarr, H. (1985) 'Verständnis der männlichen Parteimitglieder reicht nicht', *Frankfurter Rundschau*, 29. 11.1985.

PT: proceedings of party congresses cited as PT with relevant year and page number.

Quarteart, J.H. (1979) *Reluctant Feminists in German Social Democracy 1885-1917*, Princeton University Press, Princeton.

Renger, A. 'Die Gedankenwelt Kurt Schumachers bestimmte meinen politischen Weg'. In: Huber (1984)

Roth, R. and Wiesendahl, E. (1986) *Das Handlungs- und Orientierungssystem politischer Parteien. Eine empirische Fallstudie*. Forschungsgruppe Parteiendemokratie — Analysen und Berichte 17, (mimeo), Bremen.

Ruhl, K.-J. (ed.) (1985) *Unsere verlorenen Jahre. Frauenalltag in Kriegs- und Nachkriegszeit 1939-49 in Berichten, Dokumenten und Bildern*, Luchterhand, Cologne.

Schindler, P. (1984) *Datenhandbuch zur Geschichte des Deutschen Bundestages 1949-82*, Nomos, Baden-Baden.

Schneider, M. (1933) 'Frauen an der Wahlurne', *Die Gesellschaft*.

Schönbaum, D. (1966) *Hitler's Social Revolution. Class and Status in Nazi Germany 1933-39*, Weidenfeld & Nicolson, London.

Schubert, D. (1984) Frauen in der deutschen Nachkriegsgeschichte. In: vol. I of A. Kuhn (ed.) *Frauen im Nachkriegsdeutschland*, Schwann, Düsseldorf.

Schumacher, K. (1949) *Ruft die Frauen,* Sonderdruck Hanover 1949. ASD No. 10051, A26871.

Sechster Jugendbericht: 'Verbesserung der Chancengleichheit von Mädchen in der Bundesrepublik Deutschland', Deutscher Bundestag 10. Wahlperiode Drucksache 10/1007, 15.2.1984.

Sozialdemokrat Magazin (membership journal), (ed.) Parteivorstand der SPD, Bonn; years as stated in text.

SPD: Protokoll des Parteitages 1977, SPD Bundesvorstand, Bonn.

Statistische Berichte für das Deutsche Reich (1921) 'Wie Frauen wählen'.

Statistisches Bundesamt (ed.) (1983) *Frauen in Familie, Beruf und Gesellschaft.* Ausgabe 1983, Kohlhammer, Stuttgart.

Stephenson, J. (1981) *The Nazi Organisation of Women,* Croom Helm, London.

Thönnessen, W. (1973) *The Emancipation of Women. The Rise and Decline of the Women's Movement in German Social Democracy 1863-1933*, Pluto Press.

Troitzsch, K. (1980) 'Mitgliederstrukturen der Bundestagsparteien'. In: H. Kaack and R. Roth (eds) *Handbuch des deutschen Parteiensystems,* vol. 1, Leske & Budrich, Opladen, pp. 31-100.

Vallance, E. and Davies, E. (1986) *Women of Europe. Women MEPs and Equality Policy,* Cambridge University Press, Cambridge.

Vorlage für die Sitzung des Parteirates vom 16.09.1985 in Archiv beim Parteivorstand der SPD: re TOP 1 c X-2 Kandidatenaufstellung-K.

Wettig-Danielmeyer, I. (1984) Ergebnisse des Essener Parteitages, *Frau und Gesellschaft*, Dokumente Nr. 22, Mai 1984.

Wiggershaus, R. (1984) *Frauen unterm Nationalsozialismus,* Hammer, Wuppertal.

Wilms, A. (1980) *Die Entwicklung der Frauenerwerbstätigkeit im Deutschen Reich.* Beiträge zur Arbeitsmarkt- und Berufsforschung, Beitr. AB 50, Bundesanstalt für Arbeit, Nürnberg.

Zeppler, W. (1920) Die erste Periode der politischen Mitarbeit der Frau, *Sozialistische Monatshefte* 26, No. 54.

Zur Agitation unter den Frauen n.d. (1922) Referentenmaterial 2, Vorstand der Vereinigte SPD, Berlin Lindenstraße 3. Berlin.

The Battle of Semantics: The West German Christian Democrats' Linguistic Strategies Post-1973

Michael Townson

The language-theoretical starting point for this contribution is that language is not solely a passive or mediating element in the political process — or, to use another image, a vessel into which political substance is poured — but is a significant political factor in itself. Language is a political institution.

As such, one of its functions is to act as a means of identification and demarcation, i.e. a means by which a tribe or community establishes its own identity and at the same time sets itself apart from other tribes or communities.

Language is, however, not only an instrument of politics, but can itself also become an object of political controversy, and thus be both object and subject, as even a superficial glance at countries such as Wales or Belgium can show. In this respect it is important to realise that German is a highly politicised language, and has been since at least the nineteenth century.

Fourthly, it is important to remember that political developments are reflected not only in language itself, but also in perceptions of language and attitudes towards it, as demonstrated, for example, by the development of *Germanistik* as an academic discipline in nineteenth century Germany and by the role played by the discipline and its adherents in the process of political unification and the foundation of the Second Empire (Janota, 1980).

In Germany, the awareness of language as a political factor is closely linked with the 'national question'; the unity of the German language is often regarded as a symbol of the unity of the German nation, and the struggle against foreign political domination is reflected in the many attempts to eradicate 'foreign influences' from the German language. There is a long history of linguistic purism in German culture, and one of the results of this has been the development of a tradition of what is known as *Sprachkritik* — linguistic criticism — as a means of examining the role and use of language, particularly in the political sphere (Cherubim, 1982).

Although linguisticians have often been involved in 'Sprachkritik', it is perhaps useful to make a distinction between linguistic criticism and linguistics, if only because the former often does not meet the demands of scientific rigour which should apply to the latter, and because many of the products of 'Sprachkritik' reveal more about the critic than the object criticised. 'Sprachkritik' does, however, often demonstrate an awareness of language and a sensitivity to its political implications which do not seem present to the same extent in English political culture, where one often feels that the nearest equivalent is to be found in ill-informed — though doubtless well-meaning — readers' letters to the Editor of *The Times* on 'the decline of the English language' and allied topics.

The concerns of political 'Sprachkritik' often mirror dominant political concerns; the linguistic reflections of prevailing issues are seen as part of these issues — indeed there is sometimes even a temptation to look no further than the language, and to criticise linguistic phenomena *per se* without looking beyond or behind them to establish an overall political theory on which the linguistic critique can then be based.

If one views the post-war scene in West Germany, one finds that in the two decades from 1945 to 1965 there were two overriding political concerns which determined the main topics of 'Sprachkritik'. The first was the attempt to process and come to terms with the era of German fascism from 1933-45, and the second was the determination to establish the legitimacy of the new state in the West as the true representative of the German nation and to defend this claim against the opposing claims emanating from the new German state in the East.

Both these endeavours reflect the attempt of the new West German state to establish its own identity and represent instances of what the German social psychologist Peter Brückner calls 'Abgrenzung' — delineation — (Brückner, 1976), the attempt to set the West German state off ideologically against hostile or conflicting ideologies. The one attempt runs along the time dimension, the other is spatial. They are linked in that the fascist era is presented as being — for the West — a temporary aberration, the totalitarian aspects of which are, however, allegedly being continued in the East.

Over the first one and a half decades of the Federal Republic's history, interest was focused on linguistic developments in German beyond West Germany's borders in time and space. Despite a few tentative approaches, there appeared to be little inclination on the part of West German linguisticians and linguistic critics to examine their own ideological presuppositions, or to examine the nature and role of ideology in West German public language. What investigations there were either concerned themselves with the allegedly increasing technocratisation and bureaucratisation of language or, if they did examine persuasive uses of language in the West, tended to concentrate on the language of commercial advertising (Römer, 1972).

That 'Sprachkritik' did not concern itself with linguistic developments within West Germany is itself a reflection of the ideology which regarded the Federal Republic as a 'nivellierte Mittelstandsgesellschaft' (levelled middle-class society) in which social barriers had been removed and social class was no longer regarded as a significant political factor.

It was not until the mid-1960s in West Germany that a body of literature began to develop on language and politics which a) approached the topic from a more systematic and rigorous point of view and b) started looking at ideological manifestations in the public language of the Federal Republic; at least some of the impetus for this second development came from outside the field of linguistics, and was linked to the ideological critique of the Frankfurt School. This second development took place as part of an intellectual reorientation in the West German state against the background of the decline of the CDU as a political force and the radical questioning of 'traditional' values which culminated in the student movement of the late 1960s and found its institutional reflection in the formation of the first SPD-led government in the history of the Federal Republic.

The election of Willy Brandt as Federal Chancellor in 1969 marked the end of an era in a Federal Republic which for the first 16 years of its existence had been dominated by one party, the Christian Democratic Union, and by one man, Konrad Adenauer. The CDU had become institutionalised as the ruling party, and perceived itself as such. Conservative in essence, and anti-communist in orientation, the party embodied those restorative tendencies which determined the political path of the Bonn Republic. The departure of Adenauer, the absence of a strong successor, and the ossification of the party, whose watchword was summed up in the slogan 'Keine Experimente' — 'No experiments' — made it difficult if not impossible for the party to respond to the changing intellectual climate of the mid-1960s and to take the initiatives which were required if it were to remain in power.

The Brandt administration was sustained by a reform ideology which at least potentially extended to most areas of political life. Linguistically, the reform movement manifested itself in a number of different ways, for example, in an interest in sociolinguistics, particularly in the discovery and reception of Bernstein's work on linguistic deprivation (e.g. Bernstein, 1971; Ammon, 1972), and in a rejection of unreflected bourgeois views of language, with their emphasis on the language of literature. Perhaps the best-known manifestations of the 'new' approach to language were to be found in the development of new language curricula for schools in the state of Hesse, as laid down in the *Hessenplan* (1969) and the *Hessische Rahmenrichtlinien* (1973), with their concentration of the communicative needs of advanced industrial society rather than bourgeois humanitarian ideals.

Our concern is not, however, with these developments, but with the politico-linguistic reaction (using the term 'reaction' advisedly) which was set in train at the beginning of the 1970s and which heralded an era of 'semantische Kämpfe' — 'semantic battles'. A typical product was a book published in 1979 by publicist and journalist Wolfgang Bergsdorf, a CDU sympathiser, with the title *Wörter als Waffen. Sprache als Mittel der Politik* — Words as Weapons. Language as a Political Instrument (Bergsdorf, 1979).

Regardless of any inherent merits this work may or may not have, its publication was significant for three reasons:

Firstly, it marked a stage in an intellectual and political development within the CDU initiated by the election of Helmut Kohl as Party Chairman in 1973 and by a keynote speech from the new CDU Secretary-General, Kurt Biedenkopf, at the Party Conference in the same year. This conference was historically significant, as it marked the public beginning of a strategy aimed at regaining power after the traumatic unseating of the CDU as the 'party of government' for the first time in the history of the Federal Republic.

Secondly, the title points to one important aspect of the role language plays in politics, the fact that language mediates policies and politics. Thus the work, or at least its title, possesses a functional significance.

Thirdly, by using the image of 'words as weapons' it demonstrates an antagonistic view of politics and a militarisation of language. Thus the title also has a metaphorical significance.

The reaction initiated by the CDU in the 1970s is interesting for a number of reasons. On one plane it demonstrates how the CDU, having lost the political initiative in the mid-1960s and with it a great deal of intellectual support, tried to regain the initiative on an intellectual level. On a second plane it shows how, for the first time in the Federal Republic, a political party consciously discovers the importance of language in the political process and is forced, as part of the general reflection on strategy and tactics, to reconsider its own linguistic position. On a third plane it illustrates how concrete language planning was approached and provides an insight into the views of language which underlay the planning.

At about the same time that radical students were preaching the strategy of 'the long march through the institutions', the new CDU Secretary-General Kurt Biedenkopf in his keynote speech to the 1973 party conference saw the danger approaching from a different quarter:

> Die gewaltsame Besetzung der Zitadellen staatlicher Macht ist nicht länger Voraussetzung für eine revolutionäre Umwälzung der staatlichen Ordnung. Revolutionen finden heute auf andere Weise statt. Statt der Gebäude der Regierungen werden die Begriffe besetzt, mit denen sie regiert (Biedenkopf, 1973: 61).

For a successful revolution, it is no longer necessary to take the

> citadels of state power by force. Today's revolutions are different. Instead of occupying government buildings, the revolutionaries take possession of the terms the government rules by.

A view echoed by another of the CDU's supporters, Gerd-Klaus Kaltenbrunner in the Preface to his *Sprache und Herrschaft* — Language and Power.

> Die entscheidende Schlacht ist völlig unblutig gewonnen, wenn es gelingt, dem Gegner eine Sprache aufzuzwingen, die ihn daran hindert, seine Interessen und eine eigene geistig-politische Position zu artikulieren (Kaltenbrunner, 1975: 8).

> The decisive battle is won without bloodshed if it is possible to force your opponents to use a language which prevents them from articulating their own interests and an independent intellectual and political position.

The CDU's thesis, as advanced for example by Biedenkopf in his 1973 CDU conference speech, was that the SPD had managed to gain the political initiative through its use of language, and this in two ways: firstly the SPD had launched a number of key terms which were marked as 'its' property, and secondly the SPD had established a claim to certain central terms by 'occupying' them with its 'meanings'.[1]

To combat the SPD's perceived dominance in the mastery of political language, the CDU pursued a dual strategy: on the one hand it developed its own language-critical analysis in an attempt to regain the upper hand intellectually, and on the other it tried to establish the dominance of its own political terms and to gain (or regain) possession of those on which the SPD had staked its claim.

Its efforts on the first level resulted in a spate of publications from the mid-1970s on language and politics which, although addressing themselves to some fundamental issues, were mainly concerned with attacking the way the Left had 'changed the meanings' of key political terms — thus Kaltenbrunner's *Sprache und Herrschaft* bears the subtitle *Die umfunktionierten Wörter* — The Re-functioned Words. Most of these publications, which in the secondary literature are usually classified under the heading 'konservative Sprachkritik', were written not by linguisticians but by journalists, and academics from disciplines such as political science, sociology and philosophy. They range from the scurrilous *The Despotism of Words* (Kuhn, 1975) or Red Semantics (Dietz, 1975) which implicitly equates the 'New Left' with National Socialism to historical accounts of political language *Current Tendencies in Political Language* (Maier, 1979) and philosophical tracts on Being and Naming (Lübbe, 1979).

Many of the products of conservative 'Sprachkritik' remind one of the products of what became known as the 'moralisierende

Sprachkritik' of the 1950s and 1960s, which attempted to establish the moral ascendancy of the German language in the Federal Republic over the 'debased' version peddled in the Democratic Republic, only now the target is not to be found in the past or in another regime, but within the Federal Republic, thus mirroring a significant shift from *Abgrenzung* to *Ausgrenzung*, from the attempt at delineation from the Democratic Republic to the linguistic disqualification of groups or movements within the Federal Republic. In some ways, the standard of argument is lower than that of the earlier epoch, as if the conflict between 'Sprachkritik' and *Sprachwissenschaft* had never taken place. Behrens, Dieckmann and Kehl (Behrens *et al.*, 1982) have undertaken a profound critical analysis of many of the issues involved in the CDU's 'Sprachkritik', but there are three issues which we shall take up again here as significant for the whole field of political uses of language, and these are 1) the functions of language in general and of language in politics in particular, 2) the relationships between linguistic signs and meanings in political language, and 3) the question of the extent to which politics is 'merely' a matter of words.

What is happening in linguistic criticism is that, whereas until the mid-1960s language was used as an instrument of 'Abgrenzung' to consolidate the existence and legitimacy of the Federal Republic, from the turn of the decade there is an indication in West Germany that language is starting to be used as an instrument of 'Ausgrenzung', of internal legitimation and ideological demarcation.

Before proceeding to this, however, let us turn first to the second strand of the CDU's language strategy in the 1970s, to its attempt to establish its terminology within the political agenda.

Organisationally this was done when the party set up an *Arbeitsgruppe Semantik* attached to the Secretary-General's office; the function of the 'Semantik-AG' was to advise on the use of language and to develop a practical language strategy for the party. The objective was a uniform discourse which would encourage feelings of solidarity within the CDU and would be identified with the CDU within the public at large.

In order to achieve this, it was *inter alia* necessary for the CDU to re-establish its claim to positively-charged key terms, and if possible to deny the SPD access to those terms. One such term was *Solidarität* (solidarity), which had traditionally been linked with socialism or social democracy in the sense of working-class solidarity. The CDU attempted to appropriate this term and turn it from a key word of the class struggle to a more general slogan of 'democratic solidarity', i.e. the solidarity of all those who subscribed to the basic constitutional order of the Federal Republic (Greiffenhagen, 1980).

The important point was, however, not just to secure identification with individual terms, e.g. 'Solidarität', 'Freiheit' but to set up terminological networks. As Behrens put it:

> Die betonte Notwendigkeit der 'Koordinierung der Begriffe' hat also zwei verschiedene Aspekte: Ihr Gebrauch muß im Sinne einheitlicher Anwendung in allen Verlautbarungen der Partei koordiniert werden, damit sie sich durch Wiederholung als CDU-Wörter einprägen können; sie müssen aber auch untereinander koordiniert und in einen systematischen Zusammenhang gebracht werden (Behrens, 1982: 226-7).

> Thus there are two sides to the emphasis placed on the need to 'co-ordinate terms': firstly, they must be used in a uniform manner in all party proclamations, so that they can be identified as CDU terms by constant repetition, but secondly they must also be combined with each other and placed in a systematic context.

In the same vein Biedenkopf had stated at the twenty-third party conference:

> Freiheit, Gerechtigkeit und Solidarität, Verantwortung, Sozialpflichtigkeit und Leistung stehen als politische Begriffe beziehungslos nebeneinander, wenn es nicht gelingt, den Zusammenhang zwischen ihnen für die praktische politische Arbeit deutlich zu machen (Quoted in Behrens *et al.*, 1973: 172).

> Liberty, justice and solidarity, responsibility, social duty and achievement stand as isolated political terms unless we can succeed in exploiting the connections between them for our practical political work.

It was not, however, just a question of creating networks of mutually supportive terms; what was also important beyond this was to set up oppositions, so that the CDU could not only establish its own image, but could also set itself off against the SPD; these considerations gave rise to what was probably the most controversial campaign slogan in the history of the Federal Republic: 'Freiheit oder Sozialismus' — Freedom or Socialism.

In this slogan, three basic mechanisms are at work which are of significance for the study of political uses of language. This particular example is an election slogan, the purpose of which is not just to solicit support, but to move people (in this case the electorate) to a particular course of action, namely, firstly to go to the polls and secondly to cast a vote for the CDU/CSU.

The slogan is striking for its simplicity; potentially complex issues are reduced to a simple formula which presents the voter with a straightforward binary choice between two allegedly mutually exclusive alternatives. The voter must of course accept the presuppositions of the discourse (i.e. must accept that s/he only has one choice, and that this choice is correctly reflected); normally this is not too difficult, because in language interaction the initiative participant is usually at an advantage — s/he who asks the questions to a large extent determines the answers. In the case of election slogans, however, there are competing texts, namely the slogans of the other parties.

The slogan 'Freiheit oder Sozialismus' not only appeals through its simplicity and the way it requires the voter to make a clear decision, it also supports a particular view of the political process as an antagonistic one, which reflects a friend/foe, us/them schema.

Of the two terms, 'Freiheit' is without a doubt positively loaded; it is also extremely vague, as indeed are many central political terms (e.g. 'democracy', 'equality', 'justice'). No attempt is made to define what is meant by 'Freiheit' — it is not even clear which preposition it is meant to govern, whether it is freedom 'to' or freedom 'from'; all that the voter needs to know is that the antonym of this positive term is 'Sozialismus', which must then logically be 'unfrei' — socialism as the negation of liberty. Here the authors of the slogan have recourse to a long tradition of anti-socialism in German politics, stretching back to Bismarck's *Sozialistengesetze*. The inference is then clear: 'Sozialismus' is presented as an undefined bundle which can draw on deep-seated antipathies, and it is set up in opposition to the positively associated 'Freiheit'.

The next step is then to associate the negative term with the political opponent, and the positive term with one's own party; this first half is achieved partly by phonetic similarity (*Sozial*ismus: *Sozial*demokratisch) and partly by latent association, the second half by explicit identification on the election posters of the CDU/CSU as author of the slogan.

In discourse terms, the slogan can be regarded as highly successful: it dominated the agenda, and the SPD found little to set against it, in fact the only tactics were either those of ridicule 'Freiheit statt Apfelmus' — Freedom, not stewed apples — or crying 'foul', which involves stepping outside the discursive framework and thus tacitly admitting defeat.[2] In perlocutionary and political terms, however, the slogan did not persuade enough electors to cast their votes for the CDU/CSU, and the SPD/FDP coalition emerged as victors from both the 1975 and 1979 elections.

After this brief excursion, let us now return to the theoretical writings of the pro-CDU circles and to the three topics of particular interest for our present purposes, namely 1) the functions of language, 2) the relationship between *signifiant* and *signifié* in political language, and 3) the extent to which politics is 'merely' a matter of words.

In their writings Maier and Kuhn assume that the primary function of language is to reflect or portray an underlying 'reality'; *Despotie der Wörter* opens with the following thesis:

> Worte sind dazu da, Dinge zu bezeichnen. Sie sollen sagen, was ist; und sofern ihnen das gelingt, sagen sie die Wahrheit (Kuhn,

1975:11).

> Words are there to signify. They should present things as they are,
> and if they do that, then they are telling the truth.

and Maier implies a 'natural relationship' between 'words' and
'things' when he observes that 'zentrale Begriffe unserer politischen
Ordnung . . . aus ihrer Normallage gelöst . . . worden sind' — key
terms in our political order . . . have been unseated (Maier, 1979:
35).

The notion of 'truth', that there is a reality apart from language
which is mediated by language, impinges on the second of our three
interlinked topics, but let us suspend the discussion of this second
question and remain with the first. Even if one assumes that words
exist to denote 'things' — whatever 'things' may be — this still does
not explain to what ends language is used in personal or social
interaction, for the presentation of 'reality' would only be a means to
an end, not an end in itself.

This is not to suggest, however, that the conservative critics
disregard the social and political functions of language; Lübbe, for
example, reveals an understanding of a most important function of
political language when he writes:

> Politik ist nicht zuletzt die Kunst, im Medium der Öffentlichkeit
> Zustimmungsbereitschaften zu erzeugen (Lübbe, 1975: 8).

> Politics is not least the art of generating acceptance in the public mind.

Bergsdorf, in his introduction to *Wörter als Waffen* refers to
Bühler's *Sprachtheorie* when he postulates three basic functions of
political language:

> Für die Politik sind Darstellung, Ausdruck und Appell als Leistungen
> der Sprache in gleicher Weise wichtig und unverzichtbar. Die Sprache
> bietet der Politik das Mittel zu informieren, zu interpretieren,
> anzuweisen, zu überzeugen und zu indoktrinieren (Bergsdorf, 1979:
> 8).

> For the politician, description, expression and appeal are all equally
> important and indispensable functions of language. Language gives
> politicians the means to inform, to interpret, to direct, to convince and
> to indoctrinate.

But even this list is not exhaustive. Bergsdorf sees a link between
'language' and 'action' in politics: 'Die Sprache ist auf Handlung
ausgerichtet' — 'Language is directed towards action' — and this in
fact seems a more promising path to follow. In his popularising
Wörter machen Leute. Magie und Macht der Sprache — People are
the words they use. The magic and power of language — Schneider
(1976) draws up a possible scheme for the relationship between

language and action, in which he distinguishes six possible functions:

1. Language engenders action (commands, appeals)
2. Language controls action (manipulation)
3. Language facilitates action (co-ordinates work)
4. Language accompanies action
5. Language replaces action ('good intentions', 'Utopias')
6. Language is action ('slander', 'insult').

But even this account, which at first sight appears exhaustive, does not present the whole picture, and cannot simply be transferred to the field of language and politics; with the exception of the last point, it presupposes that language and action are two different phenomena, whereas at least in the political field the dichotomy does not always apply. In some points, Schneider's account is not sufficiently subtle in its differentiation to describe political language use adequately: thus, the first category does not account for the difference between actions initiated by administrative acts, e.g. paying taxes, registering a change of address, reporting for military service, and actions initiated by appellative or persuasive uses of language, e.g. voting (for a particular party), making donations, taking part in demonstrations. In the fourth category, language can 'accompany' political action in one of two closely interrelated ways — either as justification, for example, when a court gives its reasons for reaching a particular verdict or as legitimation — which again can be linked to a persuasive function. Language as a substitute for other action is an acknowledged political function, though it is not necessarily viewed in a positive light — e.g. after 1983 in the first Kohl Administration, the West German Minister of the Interior, Zimmermann, was in some circles referred to as the *Ankündigungsminister* — Minister of Announcements — the implication being that he never actually *did* anything.

Although this line of thought could be pursued at greater length, the point has been made, namely, that the conservative language critics operate from a restricted view of the functions which language has in political action. However, the restriction arises perhaps not just from their view of language, but also from a view of politics which is limited to a consideration of *Ordnungspolitik* (the state order) and to the concept of *Staat* rather than being concerned with the whole ramification of economic and social interaction within the body politic, a point which will be taken up again later.

That conservative language critics tend to regard the 'signifiant-signifié' relation in a simple and idealised fashion has already been indicated; there is, however, a danger in postulating a heterogeneous body of 'konservative Sprachkritik' with a uniform approach. Beside Kuhn's idea of 'language as truth' must be set Bergsdorf's awareness that a) certain key terms undergo a process of diachronic change, b) that they are of necessity vague and c) that they contain an emotive element:

> Diese zentralen Begriffe, ohne die Geschichte nicht geschrieben und Politik nicht durchgesetzt werden kann, sind mit Werten befrachtet, sie müssen, um sich ein möglichst breites Verständnispotential zu erschließen, vage sein und sind deshalb anfällig für inhaltliche Veränderungen (Bergsdorf, 1979: 9).

> These central terms, without which history cannot be written or policies implemented, are charged with values; in order to achieve as broad a consensus as possible, they must be vague, and therefore susceptible to changes of meaning.

It is central terms such as 'Demokratie' and 'Freiheit' which show that the extreme form of the position taken up by Kuhn is not tenable with regard to political vocabulary, as otherwise it would deny the processes of historical change and reduce political key words to the unidimensionality of technical terms.

The weaker (i.e. less extreme) position that is actually taken up by conservative critics is to bemoan the fact that languages have changed their meanings, that they are no longer used in their 'traditional' sense, and that confusion is the result. 'Begriffe haben sich aus ihrer Normallage gelöst' ('key terms in our political order. have been unseated'), as Maier puts it (1979); the meanings of terms were established by tradition, by consensus, and now everything is in flux and confusion: 'Im Schaufenster von Worten und Werten läßt man Hüllen und Füllungen der Begriffe durcheinandergeraten.' — 'In the shop window display of words and values, packages and their contents have become all jumbled up' (Dietz, 1975: 21). The fiction is still maintained that the traditional 'meanings' were the correct ones: 'neue Legierungen verfälschen (bewußt oder unbewußt) den Kurs der Begriffe' (new alloys falsify the exchange value of words (either consciously or unconsciously)) — in true conservative style, any change is seen as being necessarily a change for the worse.

It is, however, not sufficient simply to brand the conservative critics as being 'anti-change'; it is also necessary to examine what it is about the change that evokes their censure. The first question that must be asked is about the reference point: if words are no longer used in their 'traditional' sense, to which 'tradition' is it that recourse is had? In the post-1945 discussion of language under German fascism, critics appealed to a mythical state of the German language which they could not actually place in space or time. Their heirs in the 1970s also appeal to a myth, but to a myth from the recent past, a myth which can be located in time and space, and which is extremely powerful in conservative ideology: the myth of social solidarity, of a homogeneous community, the myth of the 'nivellierte Gesellschaft'. The social levelling which is supposed to have taken place after 1945, or 1948, is, it is claimed, also reflected in the language; thus Maier writes:

> Die Sprachentwicklung nach 1945 stand — zumindest in der Bundesrepublik — im Zeichen eines fortschreitenden Abbaus von rollen- und schichtspezifischen Sondersprachen, individuellen und landschaftsgebundenen Idiomen, kurz räumlichen und sozialen Sprachabgrenzungen. Sie spiegelte hierin, wenn auch mit Verzögerungen, die sozialgeschichtliche Entwicklung wider, die einerseits durch soziale Nivellierung, andererseits durch Rangerhöhung bisher sozial zurückstehender Tätigkeiten und Positionen in der Gesellschaft gekennzeichnet war (1979: 30).

> Post-1945, the development of the German language — at least in the Federal Republic — was marked by a progressive dismantling of role-specific and class-specific varieties, of individual and regional idioms, in short, of regional and social language barriers. Thus language reflected, albeit with some delay, developments in society, which were marked by a social levelling on the one hand, and a social revaluing of previously low-status activities and positions on the other.

Thus, as a result of the social and linguistic levelling process, barriers were broken down, with the result, it is claimed, that everybody spoke 'the same language' — or at least knew what everyone else meant. There was, Bergsdorf asserts, a common understanding of key terms:

> . . . in der Gründungs- und Aufbauphase der Bundesrepublik . . . wurde zwar häufig z.B. die Einfachheit und Schlichtheit des Adenauer-Vokabulars kritisiert, aber der Sinn der zentralen Begriffe der Politik war ziemlich scharf umrissen . . .
> Natürlich wurde auch damals um die Inhalte der Politik zwischen den Parteien gerungen. Aber die Bedeutungen der politischen Schlüsselbegriffe waren über einen längeren Zeitraum relativ stabil. Alle an der politischen Auseinandersetzung Beteiligten benutzten die gleichen Wörter und verstanden darunter Vergleichbares (Bergsdorf, 1979: 7).

> . . . in the foundation and development phases of the Federal Republic . . . there was, for example, frequent criticism of the simplicity and naiveté of Adenauer's vocabulary, but the meanings of key political terms were fairly sharply defined . . .
> Of course, then too, the political parties disagreed over policies. But the meanings of key political terms remained relatively stable over a fairly long period of time. All those engaged in political dispute used the same words and understood them in more or less the same way.

The appeal, then, is to the 'democratic consensus' in political discourse, and the charge levelled against the 'New Left' is that it has broken with this consensus, that key political terms are no longer universally recognised tokens of exchange; Dietz (1975) can accuse the Left of 'forgery' — thus he draws on the image of finance, claiming that the metal composition of the coinage has been changed and the currency debased — 'Neue Legierungen verfälschen den

Kurs der Begriffe'.

It is not, however, only the change *per se* that is attacked, but the qualitative nature of the change, which is perceived as a change from reality to irreality. Kuhn, whose writing is a peculiar mixture of the pseudo-philosophical and the defamatory, attacks what he calls 'Neusprache' (shades of Orwell!):

> aber diese neuen Worte bezeichnen nicht eigentlich Dinge, jedenfalls nicht Seiendes, sondern — und das macht ihre Neuartigkeit aus — sie benennen Nichtseiendes, das sein soll (Kuhn, 1975: 12).

> but these new words do not denote things — at least, not things as they are — but they denote that which is not, but which should be — and that is their novelty.

Maier argues in a similar manner, seeing the change as a twofold shift of aspect and modality: from the static to the dynamic, and from the actual to the potential:

> . . . zentrale Begriffe unserer politischen Ordnung (sind) in den letzten Jahren aus ihrer Normallage gelöst, dynamisiert, ja eschatologisch aufgeladen worden: Das gilt für Verfassung, Demokratie, Sozialstaat so gut wie für Rechtsstaat und Grundrecht. Aus Ordnungsbegriffen sind Verheißungen geworden (Maier 1979: 35).

> . . . in recent years, key terms in our political order have been unseated, made dynamic, even charged in an eschatalogical sense. This applies to terms such as constitution, democracy, welfare state as much as for rule of law and basic rights. Terms denoting the present order have been turned into promises of things to come.

This, then, is what the conservative critics cannot accept; they cannot accept the refusal to regard terms describing the body politic as incorporating absolute values; they cannot accept that political language is not only used to describe present or past states, but is also used to articulate ideals and wishes for the future. In the Federal Republic, politics is regarded as the monopoly of the political establishment, it is essentially mediated by the state. In the latter half of the 1960s there was a movement against the tutelage of the political establishment, against a monopolist interpretation of key political terms, there was an attempt to attach different denotations to terms whose main value lay in their connotations and which hitherto had been regarded as absolutes legitimising the *status quo*.

The reaction of the Right was a twofold one: on the metalevel it contested the Left's claim to key terms, partly by accusing the Left of 'ignoring reality', by attacking the discourse of the Left for its *Realitätsverlust*, and by attempting to disqualify the discourse of the Left by putting it 'beyond the pale' through equating it indiscriminately with official discourse in the German Democratic Republic and with the language of German fascism; on the practical level a strategy was developed for regaining control of the central terms and restoring them to their 'rightful owners'.

Having examined the nature of the conservative objection to the 'New Left's' use of certain key terms, let us now conclude by drawing together some of the relevant characteristics of these terms and examining their role in political discourse.

In 'normal' political use, linguistic signs such as *Demokratie*, *Freiheit, Diktatur*, often do not have sharply defined denotations; notwithstanding this, they can also form the subject of theoretical or philosophical treatises and refer to actual political systems or phenomena. Thus they can cover a wide spectrum of possible reference, which makes them extremely difficult to handle in political discussion. As Mario Cattaneo put it:

> Eine der Tatsachen, die bei der politischen Diskussion in besonderem Maße Erstaunen erregen, ist die Verwirrung, die geringe Klarheit der dort gebrauchten Begriffe (Cattaneo, 1967: 330).

> One of the particularly astonishing things about political discussions is the confusion and lack of clarity in the terms used.

Terms such as 'Freiheit, Gerechtigkeit, Demokratie' illustrate in particularly graphic form a statement by Murray Edelmann:

> Language is always an intrinsic part of some particular social situation, it is never an independent instrument or simply a tool for description. (Edelmann, 1977: 58)

The function of these terms is not to *denote* but to *connote*; they appeal not to reason, but to emotion. The passage from Cattaneo quoted above continues as follows:

> Schon die Wörter Freiheit, Gerechtigkeit und Demokratie, die — stark emotional aufgeladen — eine günstige Stimmung erzeugen, werden von Exponenten entgegengesetzter politischer Strömungen zur Bezeichnung ganz verschiedener Dinge benutzt und um auf Werte anzuspielen, mit denen es eine ganz unterschiedliche Bewandtnis hat. Das geschieht, um Sympathien und Treue im Lager dessen zu gewinnen, der sie ausspricht und vertritt. Die Mythen und der Irrationalismus beherrschen unser politisches Leben (Cattaneo, 1967).

> The very words liberty, justice and democracy, all very emotive terms which create a favourable atmosphere, are used by the exponents of diametrically opposed political movements to denote completely different things and to allude to widely differing values. This is done to gain support and loyalty towards those who use the terms. Our political life is dominated by irrationality and myth.

Key words form an important part of a power strategy; they are used to persuade, to gain and maintain support, to control. Although it would probably be wrong to regard them as completely devoid of denotative meaning, this meaning is not of prime importance —

indeed, the 'actual' references are interchangeable, and ultimately it is not possible to state whether a term is used 'correctly' or 'incorrectly' with reference to a given or imagined political construct. For political statements which use such key words and are neither verifiable nor falsifiable, Ernst Topitsch uses the term *Leerformel* — empty formula — (Topitsch, 1960). This reflects a common and current metaphor which regards linguistic signs (or 'words') as cases or containers which have to be 'filled' with meaning; it is to be found when one talks about the 'contents' of a word, or when terms such as *Worthülle* or *Worthülse* — wordcase — are used. A good example for this is contained in the earlier quotation from Dietz. Topitsch's use of the term 'Leerformel' reflects this metaphor, but also gives it an added dimension: the terms, the 'formulae', are not empty, but their denotative core is irrelevant. Their effect is achieved by connotation, which is promoted from a secondary to a primary characteristic.

The terms appeal to hopes, dreams, aspirations, and here there is a clear link with another type of emotive or persuasive language, the language of advertising. As one commentator put it, 'Politik ist Käse — beides sind Markenartikel' — Politics is like cheese. Both rely on brand names — (Schmidt, 1980).[3] Advertising makes its appeal to the irrational; it propagates not a product qua product, but the image of a product, it suggests that the use of a product will result in health, enhanced status, prestige, happiness. To achieve its effect it uses slogans to a persuasive end. What is being sold, in politics and in commercial advertising, is not the product but the effect; to stay with the casing/contents metaphor, not the policy or the product is important, but the packaging. And all the elements of advertising, commercial or political, are but means to an end, the end being power and control. As Mackensen puts it:

> Sprache birgt jedenfalls die Möglichkeit, mit ihrer Hilfe Macht über andere zu gewinnen: das ist eine ihrer Funktionen (Mackensen, 1973: 208).

> Language helps in gaining power over others. That is one of its functions.

In the 1970s, then, much of the discussion on political uses of language in the Federal Republic was dominated by the CDU's 'discovery' of the significance of language in political action, and by their attempts to develop a strategy to counter what they perceived as the 'linguistic dominance' of the SPD.

NOTES

1. The interesting point about this analysis is that, even if it is true, the SPD

was not following a conscious strategy.

2. The linguistic joke here rests on a deliberate confusion of the part-suffix -mus from 'Sozialismus' with the compound element 'Mus' (pulp).

3. Another wordplay. In German, 'Käse' can be used as a derogatory term, meaning 'rubbish'.

REFERENCES

Ammon, U. (1972) *Probleme der Soziolinguistik*, Niemeyer, Tübingen.

Behrens, M., Dieckmann, W. and Kehl, E. (1982) 'Politik als Sprachkampf. Zur konservativen Sprachkritik und Sprachpolitik seit 1972'. In: J.H. Heringer (ed.) *Holzfeuer im hölzernen Ofen. Aufsätze zur politischen Sprachkritik*, Narr, Tübingen.

Bernstein, B. (1971) *Class, Codes and Control*, Routledge & Kegan Paul, London.

Bergsdorf, W. (ed.) (1979) *Wörter als Waffen, Sprache als Mittel der Politik*, Bonn Aktuell, Stuttgart.

Brückner, P. (1976) *Versuch, uns und anderen die Bundesrepublik zu erklären*, Wagenbach, Berlin.

Cattaneo, M.R. (1967) 'Sprachanalyse und Politologie'. In: R.H.Schmidt (ed.) *Methoden der Politologie*, Wissenschaftliche Buchgesellschaft, Darmstadt.

Cherubim, D. (1982) 'Sprachentwicklung und Sprachkritik im 19. Jahrhundert'. In: T. Cramer (ed.) *Literatur und Sprache im historischen Prozeß*, vol. 2, Niemeyer, Tübingen.

Dietz, H. (1975) 'Rote Semantik'. In: G.-K. Kaltenbrunner (ed.) *Sprache und Herrschaft*, Herder, Munich.

Edelmann, M. (1977) *Political Language. Words that Succeed and Politics that Fail*, Academic Press, New York.

Fetscher, I. and Richter, H.E. (eds) (1976) *Worte machen keine Politik — Beiträge zu einem Kampf um politische Begriffe*, Rowohlt, Reinbek.

Greiffenhagen, M. (ed.) (1980) *Kampf um Wörter — Politische Begriffe im Meinungsstreit*, Hanser, Munich, Vienna.

Greiffenhagen, M., Greiffenhagen, S. and Prätorius, R. (eds) (1981) *Handwörterbuch zur politischen Kultur der Bundesrepublik Deutschland. Ein Lehr- und Nachschlagewerk*, Westdeutscher Verlag, Opladen.

Janota, J. (ed.) (1980) *Eine Wissenschaft etabliert sich. Wissenschaftsgeschichte der Germanistik*, vol. III, Niemeyer, Tübingen.

Kaltenbrunner, G.-K. (ed.) (1975) *Sprache und Herrschaft*, Herder, Munich.

Kuhn, H. (1975) 'Despotie der Wörter. Wie man mit der Sprache die Freiheit überwältigen kann'. In: G.-K. Kaltenbrunner (ed.) *Sprache und Herrschaft*, Herder, Munich.

Lübbe, H. (1979) 'Sein und Heißen — Bedeutungsgeschichte als politisches Sprachhandlungsfeld'. In: W. Bergsdorf (ed.) *Wörter als Waffen. Sprache als Mittel der Politik*, Bonn Aktuell, Stuttgart.

Mackensen, L. (1973) *Verführung durch Sprache*, Ullstein, Munich.

Maier, H. (1979) 'Aktuelle Tendenzen der politischen Sprache'. In: W. Bergsdorf (ed.), *Wörter als Waffen. Sprache als Mittel der Politik*, Bonn Aktuell, Stuttgart.

Mueller, C. (1973) *The Politics of Communication*, Oxford University Press, New York.

Römer, R. (1972) *Die Sprache der Anzeigenwerbung*, Schwann, Düsseldorf.

Schmidt, L. (1980) 'Politik ist Käse - beides sind Markenartikel'. Blick durch die Wirtschaft, Supplement to *Frankfurter Allgemeine Zeitung*, 23 June 1980.

Schneider, W. (1976) *Wörter machen Leute. Magie und Macht der Sprache*, Piper, Munich.

Topitsch, E. (1960) 'Über Leerformeln. Zur Pragmatik des Sprachgebrauchs in der Philosophie und politischen Theorie'. In: E. Topitsch (ed.) *Probleme der Wissenschaftstheorie. Festschrift für V. Kraft*, Springer, Vienna, 233-64.

Index

INDEX

For Product Safety Concerns and Information please contact our EU
representative GPSR@taylorandfrancis.com
Taylor & Francis Verlag GmbH, Kaufingerstraße 24, 80331 München, Germany

www.ingramcontent.com/pod-product-compliance
Lightning Source LLC
Chambersburg PA
CBHW061721270326
41928CB00011B/2062